ROME
A Guide to the Eternal City

LORETTA GERSON   SILVIA MAZZOLA   VENETIA MORRISON

© 1999 Napoleoni & Wakefield Ltd

ISBN 0-9537299-0-7

Published by
Napoleoni & Wakefield Ltd
22 Southwood Avenue
Highgate
London N6 5RZ

Graphic design
Alessandro Conti

Fotolito
Gestaff snc - Roma

Photographs by Matthew Jessop, Alfonso Florio, Loretta Gerson,
ENIT, Silvia Mazzola, Alberto Napoleoni
Cover photo by Matthew Jessop
Modern prints by Ornella Napoleoni

Paths to the Past
I. Rome, A Guide to the Eternal City

Forthcoming Publication
II. Assisi, A Guide to the City of Saint Francis

We have provided a visual map of Rome to help you get your bearings but we strongly advise you to obtain a larger-scale map from the tourist office.

All maps and plans have been redrawn from original sources.

PREFACE

Rome, A Guide to the Eternal City *is not a traditional guide but a tale which relates the story of Christianity through the monuments and churches of Rome. The ancient story of the city, carved in its lavish stones of travertine and re-enacted upon its fantastic architectural stages, is both history and myth, a collection of familiar words and symbols hidden in the heart and mind of every Christian.*

As for all stories passed down from generation to generation, this one needs to be narrated once again according to the past, and to the present spirit which is looking forward to the first Jubilee of the third millennium. The story is a film which never ends, projected on the screen of the new century which symbolically starts with the new Jubilee; a film to be shown to pilgrims, rich in old meanings. The tale of the Church, which brings the old and the new together, finds in Rome its ideal stage because it is in this city that the history of the cult began and it is here that we can find the most significant monuments of Christianity.

This guide book tells us a story; the story of Christianity carved in the works of art of Rome, hidden in the city's churches and cathedrals, in the chapels, in the ex votos, in the street shrines and in the alleys bathed in a unique spiritual atmosphere. This is, for Christians the spiritual city par excellence, the one which still preserves the original spirit of the early Christians, and retains the sole authentic spirituality of the ancient religion, the same as that of Mother Teresa of Calcutta and of her followers, who want to embrace the whole world.

Loretta Gerson, Silvia Mazzola and Venetia Morrison have managed to understand and communicate to the reader the true Christian message of Rome, projected in many different ways by the city through the centuries. This book will be very useful to those who are interested in religious art and are willing to dig into the roots of Christianity, down to the birth of the religion and the faith. As a magnifying glass Rome, A Guide to the Eternal City, *enlarges facts and events which took place in this city, giving us the opportunity to observe and study them and ultimately to understand their message. As a telescope it allows us to watch the long story of Christianity and its evolution through twenty centuries of human history.*

Art and architecture in Rome primarily had the task of spreading Christian religion and faith, to give man the wonderful gift of a common faith, to inspire and foster sentiments of brotherhood among man, to help all of us to make our love richer and, finally, to show the great achievements produced by the simple act of loving one another. This book has managed to grasp these messages and to relate them with a passionate style which inflames the reader with the same ardour as that of the characters in its tales. Rome, A Guide to the Eternal City *tells once again the story of Christianity in the present tense, as if the events were part of our everyday life. It is an original contribution, a gift from God.*

*Thank you, love, prayers
and God Bless You,*

Father Sebastian Vazhakala
of the Missionary of Charity in Rome

This book is about Christian Rome, a city with layers and layers of religious history. A tale is told, a story flowing between the divine and the human.

Relax and enjoy the city and its past; put aside the rush and bustle of seeing it all at once. Instead, stop, look and absorb Rome: its works of art, churches and buildings hide stories and legends. Absorb the atmosphere of the places you enter; open your eyes and reawaken your senses and soul.

This is a book that will take you back in time, to retrace the trail of Saint Peter and the papacy, to listen to the voices of martyrs and saints, to be a spectator of the miracles of the Virgin Mary, to lend your ears to the choirs of angels.

The book is divided into five chapters, all easily identified by different symbols printed in the corner of the pages. It follows chronologically the path of Christianity over the last two millennia, from the birth of Christ to the Jubilee of the year 2000.

Each chapter has two sections:

- *an essay, which narrates an episode of the spiritual story of Christianity in Rome;*
- *a thematic walk, which leads to the discovery of those sites relevant to the story told in the essay;*
The inside cover has:
- *at the front, a full map of Rome with an indication of all the churches and places to visit divided by areas. This map serves as a visual geographical index.*
- *at the back, a map of all churches and monuments mentioned.*
The book also includes:
- *a full list of places to visit with addresses, telephone numbers and opening hours*
- *a list of popes*
- *a list of emperors*
- *a chronology of the history of Rome up to nowadays*
- *a glossary*
- *an alphabetical index of places mentioned*
- *a bibliography*

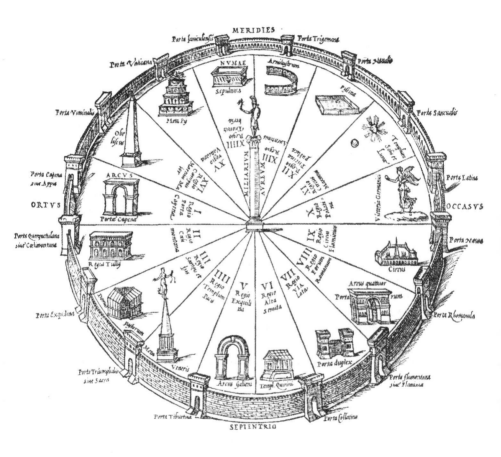

MERIDIES

Porta Ianiculensis   Armilustrum   Porta Trigemina

Porta Vaticana   NVMAE   Porta Naualis

Sepulcrum   Piscina

Porta Numinalis   Porta Sauenalis

Meta Py.   Templum Solis et Lune

Obe liscus   Porta Latina

Porta Capena sine Appia   ARCVS   Vicus Germanici   OCCASVS

ORTVS   IIII Regio Templum Pacis   XV Regio   XVI Regio   XII Regio   XI Regio   X Regio Palatina

Porta Queiquetulana sine Coelimontana   Porta Capena   I Regio   II Regio Coelimontana   IX Regio Circus Flaminius   Porta Naua

Regia Tullij   Circus   Porta Naua

III Regio Suburra   VIII Regio Forum Romanum   Arcus quatuor   Porta Rhomula

Porta Esquilina   IIII Regio Templum Pacis   V Regio Esquilia   VI Regio Alta semita   VII Regio Via Lata   Porta flumentana sine Flamina

Porta Triumphalis sine Sacra   Pasterum Meta   Veneris   Arcus Gallieni   Templ Quirini   Porta duplex   Porta Collatina

Porta Tiburtina   Porta Collatina

SEPTENTRIO

I

ROME, CIVITAS DOMINI

In 753 BC, Romulus and Remus founded a city that was to become the centre of the largest kingdom ever known, a kingdom open to everyone, regardless of race, language or social origin. Built upon the extraordinary heroism and courage of the Romans, the city was *Roma Caput Mundi* (Rome, Centre of the World). Eight hundred years later, Saint Peter and Saint Paul transformed it into the capital of the kingdom of Christ on earth. Thanks to the faith and martyrdom of the Christians, this city became *Roma Civitas Domini* (Rome, City of God).

At the beginning of the first millennium, the Roman Empire stretched thousands of kilometres east and west of Rome and benefited from a main port at Ostia, a fast-growing population and a healthy commercial environment. The Romans who were outstanding soldiers and engineers had built an efficient network of roads that linked the capital to the empire's ever-pounding heart, from which orders, armies and military provisions were dispatched to the provinces and to its far-off frontiers. The network of roads allowed the emperor to keep a tight control over his subjects and at the same time encouraged the latter to make their way to Rome. Soldiers, slaves, artists, merchants - thousands of people used the roads daily to travel to the capital, all laden with their ideas and religious beliefs, all eager to find a place in the great city.

As the core of a multiracial empire, it was inevitable that Rome would be awash with different ethnic groups, each with its own culture and religious practices. The imperial establishment, committed to religious tolerance, encouraged the proliferation of cults. People worshipped Roman, Greek, Middle Eastern and local divinities; in the

The cult of the emperor

Augustus, Vespasian, Claudius and Nero were all considered deities to be venerated. In AD 79, Vespasian himself, moments before dying, foresaw his own death and pronounced these words: 'Pity, I think I am turning into a god'.

The cult of Mithras

Imported from Persia by the Roman troops, this cult was very popular among the nobility and the army because it promised life after death to soldiers and warriors. The religion was open only to men, who formed a militia structured according to a rigid priestly hierarchy. Worshippers of other cults were allowed to join following a harsh and lengthy process of initiation. Mithras was worshipped in caves underground to remind the congregation of the legend in which Mithras had dragged a bull into a grotto, before sacrificing it and eating its flesh in the company of the sun. Worshippers re-enacted the legend by killing an animal and eating its flesh.

Christianity

Unlike the cult of Mithras, Christianity was not a mysterious religion, for it had its roots in Judaism. It had a liturgy and a written text that could be relied upon and followed. In the person of Jesus, the carpenter from Nazareth, God had made himself man, to save humanity. His death upon the cross was the beginning of a new life.

capital, rituals, sacrifices and offerings to thank or placate different gods, considered the main arbiters of the course of people's lives, were performed daily. The Roman emperor himself came to be regarded as a powerful deity on earth. Introduced by Augustus (25 BC - AD 14), the cult of the emperor developed and spread throughout the dominions, assuming different guises, such as that of Apollo, the sun god, who came to be identified with the emperor himself.

During the first century AD, eastern religions gained momentum within the empire and became very popular among the Romans. Imported by legionaries, merchants, freedmen and slaves, the cults of Isis, Seraphis, the Magna Mater and the mysterious cult of Mithras, all captured the people's imagination. Mithraism, the last pagan religion to reach Rome before the arrival of Christianity, established particularly deep roots, both in Rome and in the port of Ostia, largely because it complemented the cult of the emperor, who came to be identified with Mithras himself.

For the Romans, religious cults represented a sort of insurance policy against the odds of life, offering a rational justification for their daily misfortunes: when things went wrong it was because the gods were angry. The cults also served as cohesive forces that shaped the civic sense of their adherents, a fundamental function in a multiracial and overpopulated city such as Rome. A decade after the death of Christ, this tapestry of cults became known as paganism.

When Peter and Paul arrived in Rome they discovered that, among the many religious groups, a Christian community had already begun to take shape. Although new and small, the first Roman congregation enthusiastically welcomed the Apostles and helped them to accomplish their mission: to spread the gospel of Jesus the Saviour.

Following the custom in Palestine, Roman Christians gathered secretly in private houses, or *tituli*, which were regarded as temples of God. Meetings in private dwellings followed the pattern of the first Christian congregation in Jerusalem, which had met in the house of Mary, the mother of Mark, which became known as the first church. Since then, a church has been referred to as a 'house of God' (*domus ecclesiae*). Christian rituals were also often performed in domestic settings: ceremonies re-enacting the Last Supper, the appearance of Jesus to the Apostles after His Resurrection and the coming of the Holy Spirit, all took place in private houses.

As Christianity started to spread in Rome, it became apparent that Christians were fundamentally different from the other religious groups. They provided charitable works to the population, a task traditionally performed by the emperor, and they demanded that followers stop worshipping other gods and participating in other cults. Christians had one God, were part of one Church and regarded pagan cults, including that of the emperor and of Rome itself, as unholy and transient, because they belonged to earthly life. Two thousand years after the birth of Christ life after death, salvation and the reign of God are still of prime importance to the Christian.

For the first time since the birth of the empire, a religious creed had the audacity to question the primacy of the supernatural power of the empire and of the emperor himself. In the face of such a challenge, the initial tolerance that Christians had experienced in Rome could not last long.

In the early hours of 19th June, AD 64, a catastrophe struck Rome. A fire, which had started near some shops in the Circus Maximus, quickly engulfed the streets and spread to the Aventine and Palatine Hills until it was finally brought under control at the Esquiline. While Rome burned, Emperor Nero was in his villa in Anzio on the southern coast of Lazio. When told of the fire, he apparently showed no concern for the victims and continued to play his lyre.

Romans accused Nero of not having intervened soon enough to stop the Great Fire: they suspected that he wanted to clear sites for his ambitious construction projects. Nero retaliated by blaming the

Titulus
Titulus was the inscription outside a Roman house bearing the name of the owner; *Titulus Sabinae*, for example, was the house of Sabina. After the advent of Christianity in Rome, the term *titulus* was also used to denote a private house used by a congregation to worship and carry out Christian rituals

The spoken language of the first Christians
Greek was probably the language spoken by the first Christians. The names of several Christian rituals and religious concepts derive from Greek words.
Although Jews in Palestine spoke Aramaic, many could speak some Greek. By the time Christ was born at the eastern end of the Mediterranean, Greek was considered the language of the educated classes. When Paul wrote his letter to the Church of Rome, he used Greek, even though Latin was the main language spoken on the Italian peninsula. Early documents, later brought together to form the New Testament, were all written in Greek. Three centuries before the birth of Christ, the Jews of Alexandria had translated their scripture from Hebrew into Greek. When Christ was born, the whole of what is now known as the Old Testament was already available in this language. This helped to spread the Christian message.

Christ
According to the Gospel of Saint Matthew, Peter called Jesus '*Mahshiah*', the Hebrew word for Messiah, meaning 'anointed'. *Mahshiah* was translated into Greek as '*Christos*', from which came the name of Christ.

15

The development of Christian culture

Christians absorbed rituals and cults from paganism. The success of Christianity in Rome may have been, in part, due to the presentation of its message using liturgical patterns familiar to pagans. The date of the birth of Christ was set on 25th December, the same day as the celebration of the birth of Mithras. Similarly, the feast day to commemorate Saint Peter and Saint Paul coincides with the ancient Roman feast in honour of Romulus and Remus, namely 29th June.

Years of Christian persecutions

Christians were persecuted under the emperors Domitian (81-96), Trajan (98-117), Hadrian (117-38), Marcus Aurelius (161-80), Septimius Severus (193-211) and Maximinus I (235-38). When attitudes towards the Christians hardened, all citizens were required by edict to make sacrifices to the gods, which had to be certified by the authorities. However, the campaigns against Christianity were not continuous. For example, a period of peace was brought about by the imprisonment of the anti-Christian Emperor Valerian (253-60) by the Persians. In his absence, his son, Gallienus, was able to restore confiscated Christian churches and cemeteries. From 261 to 303, the Church flourished while the imperial powers were distracted by threats from abroad and disquiet at home. However, in 305 the joint emperors, Diocletian and Galerius, launched the worst persecution of all, which lasted for ten years.

Christians for starting the fire. Overnight, the emperors' accusation turned them into enemies of Rome and made its citizens realise that Christians were different from the Jews. From that moment, Christians became the target of imperial persecution. This stemmed largely from their rejection of the cult of the emperor and of the gods, whose favour was believed to be essential for the continuing success of the empire. Furthermore, the Christians' reluctance to serve in the imperial service, and in the army, made them the target of much resentment.

Nero's persecution of the Christians was at first confined to the city and was short-lived; but, before long, the declaration of Christianity became a capital crime, albeit of a special kind. Most capital crimes were automatically punishable by death but the Roman emperors decreed that a Christian could be pardoned through an act of apostasy - the renunciation of faith - which had to be demonstrated by offering a sacrifice to the pagan gods or to the emperor himself. If they refused, Christians were brutally executed.

Peter and Paul were among the first Christians to be martyred in Rome and were soon followed by many others. By shedding their blood in honour of Christ, the martyrs started a spiritual revolution. Inspired by their heroism, and in spite of the persecution, people embraced the Christian message of life after death and flocked to the new religion. Patrician villas were enlarged to house religious meetings and the cult of the martyrs developed in the catacombs, the burial grounds.

Christians, by their deaths, enabled Christianity to become more than just another religion in a land of many rival cults. But Christianity had first to be perceived as an aid to the empire, not a threat. This became a reality 300 years after the birth of Christ: Emperor Constantine, who embraced the faith and transformed Christianity into the state religion, sealed the alliance between the empire and Christianity.

Constantine found himself confronted by Maxentius, an old and long-feared adversary. The pagan gods, whose intercession Constantine had previously sought, had proved unhelpful; he had suffered many defeats and felt more than ever the need for a powerful divine intervention. A vision and a dream came to him and told him to entrust the imperial future of Rome to Christ. In 312, while he and his troops were preparing for the decisive battle against Maxentius, a cross appeared in the sky inscribed with the words: '*In hoc signo vinces*' ('By this sign, you shall conquer'). The emperor did not understand the meaning of the vision until that night when Christ, bearing the same symbol, visited him in a dream and commanded him to use it in the battle. When he woke up, he started to assemble the standard.

The standard, containing the Christian symbol of the Cross, was used to pursue victory over Maxentius and came to be regarded as the most powerful weapon in the hands of Constantine's army. Until then, Roman emperors had been concerned primarily with placating the gods and promoting polytheism. For them, unity of religious belief - except for the cult of the emperor - was unimportant. Under Constantine, the 'just and gentle religion' came to be a cohesive force.

To celebrate his victory and to thank God, Constantine granted, to the Church and the clergy, official recognition and the right to own land and property. Until the Edict of Milan in 313, the Church's only property had been the graves of its members. The emperor also endowed various churches to honour the Christian God. Two shrines in particular added lustre to the new cult: San Giovanni in Laterano and Santa Croce in Gerusalemme, the latter built with a donation from Constantine's mother, Saint Helena. By 315, the cross as a 'sign of salvation' appeared in the hands of a large statue of Constantine in the basilica that his erstwhile enemy, Maxentius, had built in the Forum.

In 382, Emperor Theodosius declared all pagan cults illegal and shut down their temples. In the same year, the Altar of Victory was destroyed by order of the state. In 390, sacrifices were prohibited and, in 394, institutions such as the Vestal Virgins were dissolved. At last, Christianity, the religion of the Roman Empire, had successfully replaced the pagan cults.

The standard
Made of gold and jewels, the standard bore the Greek letters 'CHI-RO' at the top of a cross. These letters were commonly used on sarcophagi and Eucharist vessels and lamps. The inscription contained the Greek letters X (CHI) and P (RO), the first two letters of the word 'Christ' in Greek. X and P are also the alpha and omega, the first and last letters of the Greek alphabet, thus symbolising the role of Christ as the beginning and end of everything as described in the Apocalypse.

Edict of Milan, AD 313
This was a manifesto of tolerance issued by the joint Emperors, Licinius and his Christian colleague, Constantine. By this edict, Christianity became the official state religion.

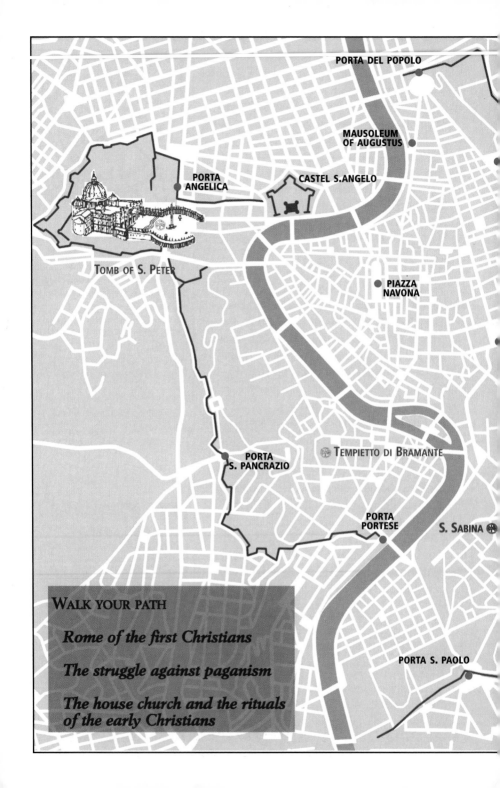

PORTA DEL POPOLO

MAUSOLEUM
OF AUGUSTUS

PORTA
ANGELICA

CASTEL S.ANGELO

PIAZZA
NAVONA

TOMB OF S. PETER

TEMPIETTO DI BRAMANTE

PORTA
S. PANCRAZIO

PORTA
PORTESE

S. SABINA

WALK YOUR PATH

Rome of the first Christians

The struggle against paganism

*The house church and the rituals
of the early Christians*

PORTA S. PAOLO

All humanity is under the dominion of the city of Rome so that the entire world can be under one bond in the name of Christ. Christ gives the Romans a Christian city, a capital that will be Christian like the entire world; Peter and Paul will depose Jupiter.
(Paraphrased from one of the hymns of Prudentius)

Who was Peter?
Peter was a fisherman from Galilee who was chosen by Christ to become the Prince of the Apostles. He was an earthy and simple man. He believed in the words of Christ and abandoned his former life to follow Him, yet he betrayed Him. He was allowed to fall so that he could acknowledge his own weaknesses and the strength of repentance. Peter led the Apostles in spreading the Gospel around the world. With Paul, he was the Apostle of Rome.

Simony
The word 'simony' means the buying or selling of offices from the Church. This meaning derives from Simon Magus' offer of money for the purchase of Peter's God-given power.

WALK YOUR PATH

This chapter's walk will take us to the places that were the scenes of the deeds of Peter and Paul in Rome. Then we shall go on to discover those monuments and shrines that still show evidence of the layers of Roman pagan and Christian history and, thereafter, to the sites where the first Christians performed their rituals.

ROME OF THE FIRST CHRISTIANS

Our journey starts just inside the Roman Wall, a site where paganism challenged Christianity. The chief protagonist is the Apostle Peter, and our story begins with him.

In the middle of the AD 50s, Rome was ruled by the ruthless Emperor Nero; the Apostles Peter and Paul had been preaching the Gospel in the capital for a few years and, since their arrival, the Christian community had begun to thrive.

Church of Santa Francesca Romana
also known as Santa Maria Nuova

In Rome, Peter and Paul were known as the Apostles of Christ. Many converted to Christianity as a result of their testimony, while others thought that they had supernatural powers. A colourful legend tells the tale of Simon Magus, a proud and confident magician from Jerusalem, who had travelled to Rome to show Emperor Nero his magic arts. After gaining the emperor's favour, he attempted to pit his powers against Peter in order to challenge the belief in the abilities of the Apostles. A magic contest was organised, which Simon lost because he was unable to emulate the Apostle's power of resurrection. Impressed and intrigued by the achievement of the fisherman from Galilee, Magus offered to buy the secret of his powers, but Peter refused.

Outraged at Peter's answer, Simon Magus sought another chance to prove the superiority of his magic. He announced that he would throw himself from the top of a high tower and, in front of Nero and a large crowd, he did indeed jump. But he did not plummet to earth at their feet. Instead, he floated, kept aloft by demonic intervention. In the midst of the excited crowd, Peter and Paul knelt and prayed for the demons to release Simon. Their prayers were answered and the magician fell to his death.

This bizarre contest is believed to have taken place in front of Emperor Nero's residence, the *Domus Aurea*, famed for its golden roof. The stone upon which Peter and Paul knelt is today kept nearby, just beyond the Colosseum in the church of Santa Francesca Romana.

☞ **Silices Apostolorum,** in the wall of the transept, behind two small gates

This is the paving stone where the two Apostles knelt. The traces of the knee marks left by Saint Peter and Saint Paul are still visible.

Church of Santi Nereo e Achilleo

In AD 64, after the Great Fire, the Christian community suffered its first persecution. Peter's followers urged him to leave the city to escape Emperor Nero's henchmen. According to a popular legend, while the Apostle was fleeing towards the Appian Way, one of the bandages, or *fasciolae*, protecting his sore and blistered feet came loose. Peter did not pay much attention to it and continued running faster and faster. Near the thermal baths of Caracalla, the bandage came off. Peter sped on, leaving it on the ground.

Church of Domine Quo Vadis?

also known as Santa Maria in Palmis

Leaving the Aurelian Gate behind, Peter headed south on the Appian Way. A few hundred metres outside the city, at the crossroads between the Appian and the Ardeatine Ways, he had a vision of Christ walking in the opposite direction, towards Rome, carrying a cross.

'Where are you going, my Lord?' asked Peter, overwhelmed by emotion.

'I am going to be crucified again,' answered Christ.

Brief history of the Church of Santa Francesca Romana

In AD 135, Emperor Hadrian dedicated, to both Rome and Venus, a colossal temple, of which only the majestic porphyry and granite columns still stand today. They surround Santa Francesca Romana like an enormous fan. On the west side of the temple, Pope Paul I (757-67) erected an oratory in honour of Saints Peter and Paul in memory of the prayers that overcame the demons holding Simon Magus aloft. In the middle of the tenth century, the oratory was incorporated into a larger construction dedicated to the Blessed Virgin Mary. The church was enlarged in the middle of the twelfth century and dedicated to Santa Francesca Romana in the fifteenth century.

Brief history of the Church of Santi Nereo e Achilleo

In the fourth century AD, a church was built among the pine trees, near the baths of Caracalla, on the site where it was believed Peter had lost his bandage. The church, originally known as *Titulus fasciolae* ('the house of the bandage'), was said to have been built to house Peter's relic, which is no longer kept inside. Later, the relics of Saints Nereo and Achilleo, servants of Domitilla, were taken to the church, which, in 595, was renamed *Titulus Sanctorum Nerei et Achillei* in honour of the two saints.

Brief history of the Church of Domine Quo Vadis?

Built in the ninth century, on the site where Peter had his vision of Christ, the church was named after the famous question posed by Peter, '*Domine, quo vadis?*' In 1637, Cardinal Francesco Barberini had the façade remodelled.

The Appian Way
Named after the consul Appio Claudius, who had it built in the fourth century BC, the Appian Way, also known as *regina viarum*, 'the queen of the roads', was considered a sacred road because of the great number of pagan monuments built along it. The road started at Porta Capena, a gate in the Servian Wall (578 BC), and crossed the Aurelian Wall (AD 271) at the Aurelian Gate, renamed, in the Middle Ages, Saint Sebastian's Gate.

Domine, quo vadis?
Eo Romam iterum crucifigi.
('Where are you going, my Lord?' 'I am going to be crucified again.') .

Brief history of the Mamertine Prison
The prison was built on two levels. The upper level, the *tholos*, held prisoners awaiting execution. The lower level, the *Tullianum*, was located in an old cistern that fed into the city's main sewer, the *Cloaca Maxima*, where the bodies of dead prisoners were thrown. The façade was restored in AD 40, as is indicated by the names of the consuls C. Vibius, C.F. Rufinus and M. Cocceius Nerva inscribed on it, and hides another much older façade also built from tufa, the white porous rock of Rome. The original name of the prison was *Tullianum*, from *tullus* ('water spring') and was changed, in the Middle Ages, to Mamertine, probably the name of a *contrada*, the section of the city in which the prison stood. In 1597, the chapel was merged into a bigger construction, the church of San Giuseppe dei Falegnami. In 1726 the Mamertine Prison was consecrated by Pope Benedict XIII. A small chapel, named San Pietro in Carcere ('Saint Peter Incarcerated'), was built above the prison and gives access to it.

Puzzled and speechless, the Apostle stood on the marble paving stone, pondering the meaning of Jesus' answer. 'What should I do?' he asked himself. If he took the Ardeatine Way, he would escape Nero's persecution; if he turned back and walked the short distance to the Aurelian Gate, he would face a certain and agonising death.

☞ **The footprints of Christ,** at the entrance of the church. A copy of the original is kept in the basilica of San Sebastiano
According to a medieval tradition, the stone with Christ's footprints was venerated as an important relic by Romans and pilgrims.

Mamertine Prison

After his vision, Peter decided that as the Vicar of Christ he must return to the city and emulate Jesus' sacrifice. As soon as he passed through the Aurelian Gate, he was arrested and taken to the Mamertine Prison. There he realised that his decision to return to Rome had placed him beyond the fear of prison or death.

While inside the prison, Peter continued to spread the word of Christ and to convert non-believers. When two prisoners, Processium and Martinianum, repented and asked him to baptise them, the Apostle touched the ground and a spring miraculously appeared. He used this water to baptise his two companions.

☞ **The *tholos*, upper room**
Originally this room was accessible only through a hole from above. Today the entrance is through a staircase from the church of San Giuseppe dei Falegnami. It is believed that Peter was imprisoned in this room, chained to the existing column.
☞ **The altar built on the miraculous site of the baptismal spring,** inside the prison, by Jean Bonassieu, 1842
A low relief shows Saint Peter baptising Processium and Martinianum.

Basilica of San Pietro in Vincoli

also known as Eudoxiana

According to an old legend, in 439 Juvenal, Bishop of Jerusalem, gave to Empress Eudoxia, wife of Theodosius II, the chains that had held Saint Peter prisoner in Jerusalem when he was incarcerated by Herodotus, the Roman consul. The empress sent half of the chains to Rome as a present for her younger daughter, Eudoxia, who in turn gave them to Pope Saint Leo Magnum (440-61). When the pope put these next to the chains that once had held Saint Peter in the Mamertine Prison, the two miraculously united.

Many believe that the basilica of San Pietro in Vincoli ('*in vincoli*' means 'in chains') was built to house this very important relic on the site of the Roman tribunal where Peter was sentenced to death. The two rows of the central nave's marble columns are believed to be the original columns of this court, imported from Greece by Emperor Nero himself.

☞ **The Miracle of the Chains,** on the ceiling of the central nave, fresco by Giovanbattista Parodi, 1705

☞ **The Liberation of Saint Peter,** on the second altar of the north nave, painting, copy of original by Domenichino, 17th century

While Peter was imprisoned in Jerusalem he dreamt that an angel unchained him and told him to get up and leave. Peter obeyed and the angel led him out of the prison.

Brief history of the Basilica of San Pietro in Vincoli

The basilica was built at the time of Empress Eudoxia, under the papacy of Sixtus III (432-40), upon an already existing church, most probably a third-century *titulus*. Originally, the basilica was dedicated to the two Apostles and only later, when Peter was identified as the founder of the church, was it renamed San Pietro in Vincoli. The original church was modified by Pope Sixtus IV (1471-84) and Pope Julius II (1503-13), who is buried here.

Basilica

A large public building with colonnades and a semicircular apse used as a law court. The name basilica comes from the Greek word, *basileus*, meaning 'king', or 'royal'. The first Roman basilica was built near the Forum in 184 BC. There were also small basilicas, which were used as commercial or meeting halls. From the fourth century AD, Christian churches were sometimes referred to as basilicas. These consisted of a large hall, similar to those of imperial palaces and aristocratic houses of the period. The interiors had columns, a long central nave and a semicircular apse. The aisles ran down the long sides and did not have upper floors. The central nave was longer than the aisles.

☞ **The Chains of Saint Peter,** underneath the main altar, inside a box with bronze doors, with scenes from Saint Peter's life, by Cristoforo Foppa, also named Il Cardosso, 15th century

One of the scenes from Saint Peter's life shown on the doors represents the angel coming to Saint Peter and leading him out of prison.

☞ **Scenes from the Life of Saint Peter and of the story of the basilica,** main apse, frescoes by Jacopo Coppi, 1577, and Giacomo Carboni, 18th century

☞ **The Dream and the Liberation of Saint Peter,** in the north apse, two engraved wooden candelabras by an unknown artist, perhaps 17th or 18th century

Chapel of the Separation

also known as the Church del Santissimo Crocifisso, demolished in 1910

A popular legend asserts that the Apostle Paul was imprisoned with Peter in the Mamertine Prison and that, after eight months of incarceration, the two Apostles were taken away to be executed. Their journey together ended on the road to the Roman port of Ostia, where they were separated. As a Roman citizen, Paul could not be crucified and was permitted a swift execution; he was beheaded. Peter, on the other hand, faced a particularly cruel death.

Tempietto di Bramante

Peter was taken to the Neronian Circus to be martyred *iuxta obeliscum* ('near the obelisk') in the centre of the circus. He chose to be crucified upside-down because he did not think himself worthy to die in the same way as Christ. Although no historical evidence can confirm the exact location of Peter's crucifixion it was identified , during the Middle Ages, as a site on the Vatican Hill, today called Gianicolo. This was considered the holiest place in Rome and was consequently visited by pilgrims.

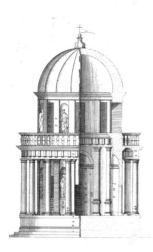

Outside the church:

☞ **Architecture of the** *tempietto*

The tempietto *(a small temple) follows the model of*

the temple of Hercules Victor, excavated under Pope Sixtus IV (1471-84), a classical round temple with Doric columns. It has a circular plan with 16 Doric columns. The Doric frieze features 48 carved reliefs showing papal regalia and various objects linked with the sacrament of the Eucharist. Its circular and domed architectural style echoes that of a martirium, a memorial built over a tomb or above a place where martyrs died.

Inside the church:

☞ **Saint Peter, on the main altar,** statue, by Lombard artist, 16th century

☞ **Martyrdom of Saint Peter,** in the predella, low relief

☞ **The hole in which Saint Peter's cross stood,** in the crypt, below the altar

☞ **Stories of the Life of Saint Peter,** on the walls of the crypt, frescoes by Giovanni Francesco Rossi, 17th century

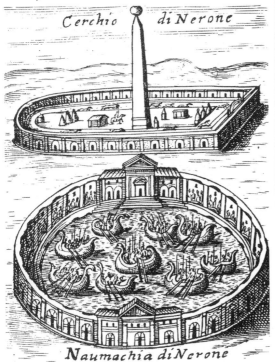

Cerchio di Nerone

Naumachia di Nerone

Inter duas metas
The location of the *tempietto* depends on a curious interpretation of the tradition that Peter had been crucified between two *metas*, the tall posts marking the extremities of the Classical circus. The *metas* were shaped like very elongated pyramids but were the height of an obelisk (the tallest obelisk in Rome is the one in the Lateran square, which is 31 metres high). It was calculated that San Pietro in Montorio, the church adjacent to the *tempietto*, was equidistant from the Meta of Remus, known also as the Pyramid of Cestius, and the Meta of Romulus, which was located near the Vatican.

Vatican Hill
Vatican means 'prophecy', for it was on this hill of Rome that King Numa Pompilius received divination from the sibyls.

25

According to the *Liber Pontificalis*, Pope Saint Anencletus (78-88) built an oratory over the tomb of Saint Peter. Modern researchers, however, have attributed the oratory to Pope Saint Anicetus (155-66) who had it built circa 155. In the fourth century, at the request of Pope Saint Sylvester I (314-35), Emperor Constantine began the construction of a basilica above the necropolis. This was to become the heart of Christian Rome – the great basilica of Saint Peter.

Confessio

A *confessio* is an architectural feature built over a tomb, through which the pilgrim can view the sepulchre.

'Petrus eni'

(I am Peter)

Liber Pontificalis

Sole guide to the biographies of the early popes, this is a catalogue of their life histories from Saint Peter to Pope Stephen VI (885-891). To this list a second was added, which concludes with the papacy of Martin V (1417-31).

Tomb of Saint Peter

After his death, Peter was buried in the nearby necropolis of Nero's Circus. It appears that the pagan tombs overlooking the circus were sited so that the dead could enjoy the games even in the afterlife.

In 1939, during the construction of the tomb of Pope Pius XI inside the basilica of Saint Peter, workers found evidence of an ancient burial place. Throughout World War II, clandestine excavation laid bare the necropolis where the first pope was believed to have been buried. Around Peter's sepulchre, a street of pagan and Christian tombs was found in pristine condition. Despite the crush of tombs, none overlay Peter's, interpreted as a clear indication that his tomb was deeply revered.

Below the high altar, further excavations revealed the red walls of a shrine, or *aedicula*. Inside the shrine is what was believed to be the 'trophy of Gaius', which Constantine enclosed in marble and porphyry and placed under the altar of the original basilica. This *aedicula* may have once contained a bronze casket holding the bones of Saint Peter, but the Saracens raided it and no casket survives. Outside the *aedicula*, the bones of a strongly built elderly man were found; the skull was missing. Around the shrine were graffiti of pilgrims invoking the help of Peter. After years of deliberation, Pope Paul VI (1963-78) confirmed the Papal Bull of Pius XI, which had declared that the bones found under the *confessio* were those of Saint Peter.

☞ **Saint Peter's tomb,** in the Sacred Grottoes

Two angels flank the marble scroll with the inscription, 'Sepulcrum Sancti Petri Apostoli. *The seventeenth-century* confessio, *which includes the Niche of the Pallia (the place where the stoles of newly installed bishops are kept), is a splendid and rich monument, a fitting tomb for the first Vicar of Christ.*

☞ **Saint Peter enthroned,** at the exit from the Grottoes, statue

This statue of the Apostle holding a key is a composite work. The torso comes from the statue of a philosopher of the third century BC; the hands and head come from a fifteenth-century statue.

THE STRUGGLE AGAINST PAGANISM

Our journey continues inside the walls of ancient Rome to the sites where Christians fought their battle against paganism, through the years of persecution, up to the victory of Constantine.

Colosseum

This was a place of gruesome entertainment which, during the persecutions, became an arena of religious oppression. Christians were forced into combat with wild beasts, to be mutilated and eaten alive under the gloating gaze of 50,000 spectators.

The Colosseum was one of the most imposing buildings of the ancient world, a terrifying symbol of pagan cruelty. The huge, triple-arched tiers that remain today are only the skeleton of a body once entirely covered in marble. Majestic columns flanked statues in the centre of each arch, facing outwards like proud sentinels, watching as people entered the amphitheatre.

In the Colosseum, as in modern theatres and sports arenas, seats closest to the action were reserved for the elite, whereas seats at the very top were occupied by the plebeians, the poorest of Rome's inhabitants.

Brief history of the Colosseum

The Colosseum was built on the site of the pond of the *Domus Aurea*. The works began in AD 69, under Emperor Vespasian, continued under Titus and were concluded by Diocletian, who inaugurated the stadium in AD 84. Celebrations to mark its opening lasted 100 days, during which 5,000 wild animals were killed. Originally known as the Amphitheatre Flavium, it was renamed the *Colossum* because a larger than life-size statue, a *colossum*, stood just outside it. The building was 189 metres long, 156 metres wide and 50 metres high. The Colosseum was embellished with 100,000 cubic metres of travertine, marble from the quarries outside Rome.

Vomitoria
From the Latin verb *vomere*, to have out; hence *vomitoria* is a place by which one may come out.

Mithras was born inside a stone at the moment of Creation. With his arrival, darkness gave way to light, which is why a torch was always burning in front of his altar. His mission was to bring not only light to the world, but also fecundity. Hence, in the legend, he captures a bull, the symbol of fertility, drags it into a grotto and kills it.

The slaughter of the bull was graphically portrayed in the *mithraea*. These images showed how Mithras attempted to kill the beast, while other animals joined in to help him: a snake, a dog and a scorpion, each with a different task. The snake writhed around a grail where Mithras spilled the blood of the bull, so that the dog, which was next to it, could attempt to drink from it. The scorpion attacked the bull's genitalia in order to suck the semen from it. The symbolism is clear: nature draws life from the bull, symbol of fertility; Mithras kills it to pass on this gift to men.

The myth continues with the scorpion's betrayal. It spills the semen of the bull, the fertile material from which all things are made, bringing evil into the world.

During the performance, people would go in and out of the large openings, the *vomitoria*, of which there were 80. A huge awning, the *velarium*, was supported on wooden poles to protect the spectators from the hot Mediterranean sun. The best minds of modern engineering have yet to discover how the Romans put up this awning.

☞ **A cross,** placed at the edge of the arena
This cross commemorates the Christians who were killed inside the Colosseum.

Basilica of San Clemente †
Mithraeum

Mithraism was an underground religion. Rituals and worship took place in a cave or grotto, called a *mithraeum*, built to look like the original grotto where Mithras had slaughtered the bull. These grottoes had vaulted ceilings decorated with pieces of crushed pottery. They resembled ancient dining halls, narrow and long, with benches along the sides, where guests could recline for the ritual meal. At the end of the cave, there was always an image of the god slaying the bull. Because of the small size of the grotto, the killing of a bull was impractical, so other animals, such as cocks, pigs and rams, were sacrificed during the rituals.

From the sacristy of the basilica of San Clemente, through the lower basilica, a staircase at the end of the north nave leads to one such underground cave, the *mithraeum* of San Clemente.

Three interconnecting rooms are located exactly below the apses of the basilica. A small room gives access to the second room, the vestibule, reserved for the initiates, which leads to the *mithraeum*, the site where animals were sacrificed and the ritual banquet was celebrated. The room is long and narrow and has a low vault with 11 openings, representing astrological symbols of the cult. Along the walls, the stone seats where the worshippers sat to celebrate the ritual meal are still visible.

☞ *Ara,* in the middle of the *mithraeum*

This is the altar on which animals were sacrificed. It is decorated with a relief showing Mithras slaying the bull surrounded by his animal helpers.

☞ **Caius Arrius Claudianus Pater Posuit,** inscription on the altar

It states that Caius Arrius Claudianus, a member of the Arrian family, the same as that of Pope Antoninus Pius, had reached the status of pater *and donated the altar to the* mithraeum.

☞ **Seven niches decorated with graffiti,** in the second room, the room of initiation

This is where the rituals of initiation took place. The cult of Mithra flourished from the first half of the second century AD. The cult had cosmic connotations. It was divided into seven grades, each of which was denoted by one of seven planetary gods and a figure of the Zodiac. For example, the third level was associated with the planet Mars and the figure of Miles, the soldier. Similarly, the fourth stage was linked to the planet Jupiter and Leo, the lion. Very few reached the upper levels of the cult, which was dominated by the pater, *who fell under the protection of Saturn. As the high priest of the cult, the* pater *wore a pointed Phrygian cap, like Mithras himself.*

The progress of the initiate from one stage to the next required him to participate in elaborate initiation ceremonies, one of which included being plunged into a pool of water in a ritual similar to the Christian baptism. The progress of the Mithraist through the seven grades of the cult was seen as a precursor of the elevation of his soul following his death.

Adjacent to the *mithraeum,* separated from it by a narrow alley, is the world of the first Christians: *Titulus Clementis,* the house of Clement, where Christians met to celebrate their rituals. Originally built around a courtyard, the rooms are now plunged in darkness. In the fourth century, the courtyard was filled with earth and the basilica of San Clemente was built over it.

The eerie sound that can be heard comes from water running through the Cloaca Maxima, the old sewer of Rome.

Brief history of the *mithraeum* and the *Titulus Clementis*

In 1857 and 1870, archaeological research carried out below the basilica by the Irish Dominican monk, Joseph Mullody and the Italian archaeologist, G. de Rossi unveiled several constructions. The lower basilica, considered the first church, was abandoned after the invading Normans had destroyed much of it in 1084. Below the lower basilica there were several Roman buildings, the most ancient being a public building dating from before the Great Fire of AD 64. In the second century, a house was built on this site and, in the third century, a *mithraeum* was constructed inside its courtyard.

The *mithraeum* in San Clemente is one of the best-preserved in Rome. It is likely that the house was *Titulus Clementis,* a place of Christian worship transformed into a church in the fourth century. On the ruins of this church, Pope Pascal II (1099-18) built the present basilica, modernised between 1713 and 1719 by Carlo and Stefano Fontana during the papacy of Clement XI (1700-21). The basilica of San Clemente has been in the hands of Irish Dominican friars since 1367.

Two thousand years of worship

First century: *Mithraeum, Titulus Clementis*

Fourth century: Church of Saint Clement. A church was built over the courtyard of the *titulus*. The building was dedicated to Pope Clement I (90-91), but it was rebuilt under Pope Siricius (384-99).

Eleventh century: In 1084, the church burnt down during the sack of Rome by the Normans. Occupying the same site is another church, two metres higher.

Twelfth century: In 1367, the church was given to Irish Dominicans.

Nineteenth century: In 1861, excavations led to the discovery of Roman ruins.

Arch of Constantine

In AD 312, Constantine's victory against
Maxentius at the Milvian Bridge was a major event
for Romans and Christians alike. The former
triumphed over a long-standing enemy and the latter
proved the unconditional and successful power of
their God. Thus Roman and Christian destinies were
united under a sole God, with Constantine as their
champion.

Considered to be the first monument to the
success of Christianity, the arch also celebrates
Constantine's political and diplomatic skills in
handling the Christian issue. No Christian imagery
appears among the decoration, no sign of the Cross
nor anything else that might suggest the new religion.
Instead, there are roundels depicting Apollo, Diana
and Hercules, recycled from earlier monuments. This
suggests Constantine's ambivalence towards the
transition from paganism to Christianity and his
tolerant approach towards paganism. If Christians
were no longer to be persecuted in his empire, those
who followed other cults were to be accorded the
same freedom of worship. For this reason, there is no
mention of God on the arch, but instead a general
reference to *instinctu divinitatis*.

☞ **The inscription,** at the top of the central arch
*Once shining in gilded bronze, the inscription
commemorated the victory of the pious and fortunate
Emperor Constantine the Great: 'This arch was*

dedicated as a mark of triumph from the Senate and people of Rome to commemorate the divine inspiration and the great spirit of Constantine and his army in defeating both the tyrant and all those of his faction.' Framing the inscription are reliefs.

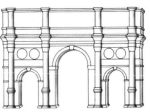

☞ **The eight reliefs framing the inscription,** on the pediment of the arch, in Italian marble

These reliefs, taken from other monuments, are referred to as the panel reliefs of the monument of Marcus Aurelius. They originally depicted Emperor Marcus Aurelius but, to make them fit their new setting and content, the portrait of Marcus Aurelius was modified to look like Constantine. Reliefs on the south side show Emperor Constantine at war; the ones on the north side represent the emperor carrying out his civic duties.

☞ **The roundels,** on the short sides, commissioned for this arch

They represent the moon and sun on chariots that symbolise the everlasting Roman Empire.

☞ **The panel friezes,** all over the arch, commissioned for this arch

They show, on the short, west side: Constantine and his army setting out for Milan; on the south side, in the panel on the left, above the small arch: Constantine's army besieging Verona; in the panel on the right, above the other small arch: the Battle of the Milvian Bridge; on the short, east side: Constantine making his triumphal entry into Rome; on the north side, in the panel on the left, above the small arch: Constantine addressing the Romans from the rostrum in the Forum; in the panel on the right, above the other small arch: Constantine giving out gifts of money.

Basilica of Maxentius

Emperor Maxentius began to build this basilica at the beginning of the fourth century. He wanted an imposing building, larger than all its predecessors. This is why he chose a site next to the great Temple of Rome and Venus, the striking symbol of the Golden Age of Rome. Like all other basilicas, Maxentius' was built as a law court and place of

Brief history of the Basilica of Maxentius

The basilica was started by Maxentius in 306 and finished by Constantine after 313. It was built on the site previously occupied by the vestibule of Nero's *Domus Aurea* and later converted into a warehouse for exotic goods. It was called Basilica Nova, 'the New Basilica'. The central nave was 25 metres wide and was spanned by three cross vaults reaching a height of 35 metres. The columns were 20 metres tall. One column was still in situ until 1614, when it was transferred, with the aid of 60 horses, to Piazza Santa Maria Maggiore by order of Pope Paul V. It is probable that the worst of the damage to the building occurred during the earthquake of 847.

public assembly. However, following the victory at the Milvian Bridge, Constantine converted it into a monument to commemorate the new alliance between himself and the Christian God.

The basilica was splendid. The floor was paved in different-coloured stones, similar to floors found in many Italian cathedrals. The walls were clad in marble and the roof was made of gilded tiles. The main entrance, off the Via Sacra, could be reached via a flight of stairs that led to a portico supported on columns of porphyry.

Today, only the central nave remains, just enough to give us an idea of the original proportions. It should be remembered that Constantine changed Maxentius' original design and dimensions to accommodate a monument that was dear to him: a large statue of himself, seated holding a cross. The statue was made of marble and bronze and was about 12 metres high. When it was inside the basilica, the statue was strategically positioned to be visible from all parts of the building.

Church of Santa Prisca

Priscilla and Aquila were a Christian couple who made curtains for a living. When, in AD 46, Emperor Claudius expelled all the Jews from Rome, they moved to Corinth. There they met the Apostle Paul, whom they invited to stay as a guest in their house, often used as a venue for Christian meetings. In AD 57, having returned to Rome, the couple turned their house into an oratory, as is mentioned by Saint Paul in the Acts of the Apostles (Acts 18:1-4). It is likely that, during Peter's stay in Rome, Priscilla and Aquila offered their hospitality to the Apostle. A legend linked to the founding of the church says that it was in their house that Peter baptised their young daughter Prisca, who later became a victim of persecution under Emperor Claudius.

☞ **Roman capital,** inside the church, in the baptistery

The inscription on the Roman capital probably dates

Brief history of the Church of Santa Prisca
Built in the fourth century on the house of Priscilla and Aquila, the church was enlarged in the fifth century and named *Titulus Priscae*. In 772, it was altered by Pope Adrian I. In 1084, it was raided by the Normans and, during the Middle Ages, it was considered one of the 12 privileged abbeys of Rome. Modernised under Pope Paschal II (1099-1118), it was given, in 1414, to the Franciscan Order and, in 1455, to the Dominicans who held it until 1600, when they were replaced by the Augustinians. Following a fire, Pope Calixtus III (1455-58) modified the interior.

from the thirteenth century. It reads, 'Baptismus Sancti Petri'. According to an old legend, this is the baptistery used by Saint Peter to baptise Prisca when she was 13 years old. The baptistery is still in use today.

☞ **Saint Peter Baptising Saint Prisca,** on the main altar, painting by Domenico Cresti, known as Passignano, 17th century

☞ **Martyrdom of Saint Prisca and Transport of her Relics by Pope Saint Eutychian,** in the apse, frescoes by Fontebuoni, ninth to tenth century

Prisca was sentenced to death in the Colosseum, but, when she was thrown into the arena, the lions would not touch her. Eventually, she was beheaded and her body was buried on the Aventine, where Pope Saint Eutychianus (275-83) found it and had it moved to a burial chamber under the main altar of the church.

☞ **The relics of Saint Prisca,** below the main altar

Pope Leo IV (847-55) had the body of Saint Prisca taken to the church of Santi Quattro Coronati, from where it was soon returned.

☞ **Scenes from the Life of Saint Peter,** in the crypt, by Fontebuoni, ninth to tenth century

Mithraeum

at the beginning of the south nave, via a staircase

Adjacent to the residence of Priscilla and Aquila there was a *mithraeum*, most probably built underneath the house of Licinius Suras. In the fourth century, when Christians gained possession of it, they used the site to build a larger church in honour of Saint Prisca. The apse of the church, for example, was erected directly above the shrine of Mithras.

☞ *Nymphaeum,* the first room

Originally a hall full of water games and fountains, it now houses the museum of the excavations. Fragments of stucco statues of Mithras and Serapis, companion of Isis, the Egyptian goddess venerated by most Roman women, which have miraculously survived centuries of burial, have been pieced together, while the damaged wall paintings have been restored. The nymphaeum was decorated with pieces of glass and pottery over

Archaeological discovery

In 1958, two Dutch archaeologists completed the excavation of the church and found the *mithraeum*. Statues had been smashed and painted walls had been hacked by axes during the laying of the foundations of the church. This testifies to the outrage that the pagan rituals represented for Christian communities and the blasphemy contained in their symbols. At the same time, it underlines the importance among Romans of the cult of Mithras, the most important rival to Christianity. Thus, just as Christ had chased the merchants out of the Temple, so Roman Christians attempted to rid the city of any trace of pagan worship and even built their churches on top of pagan temples.

which towered a statue of Serapis.

From the *nymphaeum*, go through the crypt of the church to reach the *mithraeum*.

☞ **The god Saturn and the god Mithras,** at the end of the room, a large low relief in stucco
It shows the naked god Mithras slaying the bull.

☞ **The stone for the ritual,** below the low relief
This stone has a hole carved in it from which the blood of the sacrificed animal was collected for the use of the worshippers. On the left, inside a niche, there is an inscription: 18 November 202.

☞ **The Seven Stages of the Initiation into the Cult of Mithras,** unique frescoes, on the walls of the *mithraeum*
Mithras and the sun are shown eating a meal after sealing their alliance. On the opposite wall there is a procession of believers with the degree of their initiation written next to each of them. Following the pater, *the Father or high priest, is the Courier, the second highest rank of initiate. The Bridegroom, the Soldier and the Raven follow them.*

Basilica of Santa Prassede

According to an old tradition, during the reign of Emperor Nero, Peter received hospitality from two sisters, Prassede and Pudenziana, daughters of Pudens, a Roman senator, whose house was a well-known haven for Christians. No archaeological evidence has been found to prove that, at this early date, a house stood on the site of the church of Santa Prassede. Today, the two sisters are believed to have existed only in legend.

In 822, 400 years after Constantine's victory at the Milvian Bridge and two decades after Charlemagne was crowned emperor of the Holy Roman Empire in Rome, Pope Paschal I wanted to create a magnificent edifice, a monument to celebrate the triumph of Christianity over paganism, a church to serve as a visible reminder of the terror suffered by Christians during the

Brief history of the Basilica of Santa Prassede
In 822, Pope Paschal I built the church of Santa Prassede over what was believed to be the ancient *Titulus Pudens*, already modernised by Pope Adrian I (772-95). Paschal added a convent for the Greek community and moved the relics of 2,000 martyrs to the church. Pope Eugenius II (824-27) had these transferred to the church of Santa Sabina.

persecutions. He dedicated the church to Saint Prassede, one of the two legendary sisters, who was believed to have witnessed the execution of 23 persecuted Christians who had taken shelter in her home. To promote his message the pope commissioned Byzantine artists, who knew the latest techniques in mosaics and painting, to illustrate the tale of the two sisters.

☞ **A circular disc of porphyry,** on the floor of the church

According to a popular legend this disc sealed the well where the 23 martyrs had been killed.

☞ **Saint Prassede Soaking up the Blood of the Christians,** in the apse, painting by Domenico Maria Muratori, 1735

According to the legend, the bodies of the 23 Christian martyrs were thrown into the well and the zealous Prassede mopped up their spilt blood with a sponge.

This was not the act of an obsessive housekeeper, but a gesture of a believer's devotion and piety at a time when the spilling of Christian blood was a sad and commonplace reality.

A red phoenix

In the mosaic of the apse, above the branch of the palm suspended over Pope Paschal I (who is holding a model of the church), there is a red phoenix. The phoenix is a mythical bird that represents the Resurrection, because it died on a pyre and from its ashes a new phoenix was born.

Rituals

The ceremony of light at the Easter vigil is especially beautiful at Santa Prassede. While the church is plunged into darkness to symbolise Christ's death, the big paschal candle is lit. It symbolises the light of Christ's resurrection and is the only light source in the church. The congregation light their own small candles from this great lighthouse of faith. *Lumen Christi*, the light of Christ, fills the church. When the ritual is over, the lights of the church are suddenly switched back on, symbolising that Christ is resurrected. The darkness of His absence now becomes a glorious triumph of light. The mosaics shed their own golden light on the scene.

What archaeology tells us

The churches of Santa Prassede and Santa Pudenziana stand on the site of a *titulus* erected no earlier than the second century, around 100 years after Saint Peter's death. The name of the *titulus* may derive from somebody called Pudens, who perhaps donated the land and the building for the church. Although archaeology does not confirm the legend of the two sisters, the marvellous mosaics contained in the two churches tell a convincing story of their faith and martyrdom.

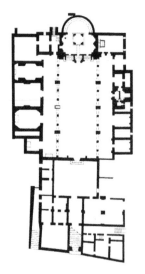

☞ **The relics of Saint Prassede and Saint Pudenziana,** in the crypt of Pope Paschal I, below the floor of the church, inside an early Christian sarcophagus

According to popular belief, the sponge Prassede used to soak up the blood of the martyrs was buried with her.

☞ **Jerusalem in Heaven with Christ, the Virgin, Prassede, Saint John the Baptist and Eleven Apostles,** on the first triumphal arch, mosaics, ninth century

The walls of Jerusalem in Heaven, the city of the Elect, as it is called in the Apocalypse, are inlaid with gold and stones. An impression of receding space is created by means of an illusion which flouts some of the complex rules of perspective. The walls stand on ground embellished with red flowers, under a sky in which little stylised clouds are set out in rows.

☞ **Christ, Saints Peter and Paul and Prassede and Pudenziana are Received into Heaven,** in the apse, mosaics, ninth century

Christ is descending in the middle, wearing a golden robe. Beside Him are Saints Peter and Paul, each with an arm around one of the sisters to be presented to Jesus. The embracing gestures demonstrate the Apostles' affection for these women, which, it was believed, helped Roman Christians bear the tragedy of the persecutions. Next to the two palms are the figures of Saint Zeno, with a tonsure, and Pope Paschal I, with a square halo and holding a model of the church of Santa Prassede.

The magic of Christ's word is palpable in this church: the glorious mosaics, whether lit by candles or sunlight, tell the tale of Christianity like the pages of an ancient book. Behind all this beauty, however, there are terrible years of death and destruction, of Christianity persecuted across the centuries.

Chapel of San Zeno
third chapel on the right of the nave **(1)**

This chapel was referred to in medieval times as 'the garden of paradise' because its golden mosaics shine so brightly.

☞ **Episcopa Theodora with the Virgin and the Two**

Sisters, on the left, over the door towards the apse, mosaic

Episcopa Theodora had a kitchen garden where she grew vegetables for her beloved son, Pope Paschal I. Every day she harvested some of these vegetables which were used to prepare his lunch and dinner. Theodora is represented with the square halo of the living, evidence that the chapel was built during her lifetime. According to tradition Paschal I was also buried in this church to rest near his mother.

☞ **The scourging column,** in a little room to the right of the entrance

The column, which was brought from Jerusalem in 1223 is presumed to be the one upon which Jesus was scourged.

Church of Santa Pudenziana

An old legend says that, after Prassede and Pudenziana died, Pope Pius I (140-55) built a church in their memory in the Vicus Patricius, now the Via Urbana, on the site where it was believed their house once stood. According to an old legend, it was inside this house that the Apostle Paul converted the entire family of Pudens to Christianity.

Brief history of the Chapel of San Zeno

It was built as a mausoleum for the Episcopa Theodora (817-24), the mother of Pope Paschal I. It has a square plan and is decorated throughout with exquisite mosaics.

Brief history of the Church of Santa Pudenziana

It is likely that the church was built on the ruins of a house where the Roman Christian congregation used to meet. Excavations have, in fact, revealed floors and bricks of the time of Emperors Vespasian and Septimius Severus. During the second century, a thermal bath was built adjacent to the church, known, as early as the fifth century, as Novatus Baths. At the end of the fourth century, a section of the house and the baths was converted into a church, which was later modified by Popes Adrian I (772-95) and Gregory VII (1073-85).

Outside the church:

☞ **Agnus Dei with Saints Prassede, Pastore, Pudenziana and Pudens,** on the architrave of the façade, sculpted frieze

Prassede and Pudenziana are depicted as empresses with crowns above their heads. Their father, Pudens, dressed as a Roman senator, accompanies them.

Inside the church:

☞ **Christ Enthroned, Accompanied by the Apostles, Saint Peter and Saint Paul and the Two Sisters,** in the apse, mosaic, late fourth or early fifth century

The two sisters hold crowns of leaves over the heads of Peter and Paul. The sisters crown the two Apostles who represent respectively the Jewish and Roman origins of the Church, the Ecclesia ex circumcisione (Church of the Old Testament) and the Ecclesia ex gentibus (Church of the New Testament).

☞ **Glory of Saint Pudenziana,** main altar, painting by Bernardino Nocchi, 1803

Caetani Chapel
in the north aisle

Built in the area where Christian worship first took place, this chapel was erected on the site of the old oratory of Saint Pastor. Pope Siricius (384-99) dedicated the oratory to Saint Peter after he had successfully ended the schism caused by the antipope Novizianus. Inside, ancient mosaics showed Saint Peter as a pastor among sheep, from which the title of Saint Pastor probably derives.

☞ **A square slab of porphyry,** on the ground, in front of the Caetani Chapel

This slab marks the location of the well where, according to popular legend, Saint Prassede and Saint Pudenziana collected the blood of Christian martyrs.

☞ **Saint Prassede and Saint Pudenziana Collect the Blood of Martyrs,** on the walls, painting by Paolo Rossetti, 1621

☞ **Saint Pudenziana,** inside a niche, statue by Claude Adam, circa 1650

Brief history of the Caetani Chapel

In 1588 Cardinal Enrico Caetani, then in charge of the church of Santa Pudenziana, commissioned the construction of the chapel to Francesco da Volterra. The chapel was later completed by Carlo Maderno.

THE HOUSE CHURCH AND THE RITUALS OF THE EARLY CHRISTIANS

Our journey continues underground, below the churches, in the cellars and inside the foundations of ancient Roman villas, where the remains of early Christian worship are still preserved. It ends in the catacombs, the burial grounds outside the city walls, where the victims of persecution were buried and the cult of the dead developed.

Basilica of San Martino ai Monti
Titulus Equitii

The Suburra, an area that stretched from the Colosseum to the Esquiline, the highest of Rome's seven hills, was densely populated. Inhabited predominantly by the lower classes as early as the first century AD, it was home to a large number of Christians. *Titulus Equitii* was probably the house of Equitius, presbyter of Pope Saint Sylvester I (314-35) and one of the many house churches used for worship by the congregation of Christians of the Suburra. Today, outside the church of San Martino ai Monti, parts of the old stone walls of *Titulus Equitii* are still visible along Via San Equitius.

House church

A house church, or *ecclesia domestica*, was generally a *titulus*, a private house, transformed into a place of worship. As the Christian community grew bigger, walls were taken down to create large meeting rooms. Often an altar was placed on a platform to facilitate the viewing of the services officiated by the priest. Sometimes religious pictures, murals and sculptures, depicting scenes from the Old and New Testaments, were drawn on the walls. A room of smaller size was reserved for the ritual of baptism. It is a sad irony that, when Christian persecution ended, the bulk of the *ecclesiae domesticae* in Rome were destroyed, to be replaced by basilicas and churches built to celebrate Christian power.

Brief history of the Basilica of San Martino ai Monti

Built in the third century, the original *titulus* was rebuilt several times. The first reconstruction was as early as the fourth century. Originally the church was dedicated to Pope Sylvester I and Martin of Tours. It had been Sylvester's wish to have a church erected on the *Titulus Equitii*. Today, the church shows little evidence of this reconstruction. The façade was built in 1650 by Pietro da Cortona.

Martin of Tours

Martin of Tours (circa 315-97), born in Hungary, was made bishop of Tours in 370. He founded the first monastery in France and destroyed many pagan temples and shrines.

Sunday worship in the house churches

Christians behaved differently throughout the empire. We do not know exactly what they did in the house churches in Rome. However, the Greek missionary Justin described Christian practices in order to explain them to non-Christians. His intent was two-fold, to convert pagans and to prove that Christians did not represent a danger to the Roman emperor. 'On the day called Sunday,' writes Justin, 'there is a meeting for all in one place, according to the city or countryside where one lives. The memoirs of the Apostles, i.e. the Gospels, or the writings of the Prophets, are read as long as there is time. When the reader has finished, the President, in a sermon, calls us to imitate these good things. Then we all stand and pray.' Justin also describes the highest moment of Sunday worship, the Eucharist. 'Bread is brought to the President, and wine mixed with water. He says a prayer of thanksgiving, as well as he is able, and the congregation says "Amen", which is Hebrew for "May it be so". The deacons give the bread and wine to all present and take it to those absent. Those who are well off, and who want to do so, give to the collection. This is placed with the President, and he takes care of orphans, widows and those ill or otherwise in need, those in prison and strangers who are staying here. In fact, he becomes the helper of those who are in need.'

The remains of the house church can be reached from the crypt of the basilica. A staircase leads to a labyrinth of small, dark rooms, partly built out of the adjacent thermal baths of Emperor Trajan, which have remained unchanged throughout the centuries. Christians used to gather here to celebrate their faith. In the eerie atmosphere of these underground chambers, one can imagine the excitement and fear of those early meetings, when rituals prohibited by the emperor and punishable by a cruel death were celebrated.

☞ **The relics of various martyrs,** beneath the main altar

☞ **A silver votive lamp and the papal tiara of Pope Sylvester I,** in the sacristy

From the Esquiline our journey takes us to the Aventine, the green hill overlooking the Tiber.

Basilica of Santa Sabina

According to tradition Sabina, a rich and noble *matrona romana*, lived in a beautiful villa on the Rocca Savella, a cliff beside the riverbank. In the peaceful hush of her courtyard, disturbed only by the playful gurgle of a fountain, Sabina listened to the fascinating stories of Seriphia, her Greek slave, about a man from Palestine who promised eternal life. Sabina was mesmerised by the tale of Christianity and converted to the new faith. Her beautiful patrician house overlooking the Tiber soon became a place of worship, a house church where Christians met to perform their rituals.

In 117, under the persecution of Emperor Hadrian, Seriphia was stoned to death. Sabina's life was temporarily spared, but she was arrested and martyred the following year.

In 425, Pietro d'Illiria, a Dalmatian priest, built a church on the foundations of Sabina's house, the original *Titulus Sabinae*.

Outside the church:

☞ Scene of the Crucifixion, on the doors of the church, carved in cypress wood, fifth century

The Crucifixion is an episode in the life of Christ represented again and again throughout the centuries. The ultimate sacrifice of Jesus, who died to redeem humanity, is the core of the Christian faith. This is one of the earliest representations of Christ on the cross.

Brief history of the Basilica of Santa Sabina

Construction was begun in 425 by Pietro d'Illiria, an erudite priest, under the papacy of Celestine I, and was completed in 433 by Pope Sixtus III, who, according to the *Liber Pontificalis*, added a baptismal area. Pope Honorius III fortified the area and moved his residence into the church. In 1222, he donated it to Dominic of Guzman, who later became Saint Dominic. Since then, it has been a Dominican church. In 1586, Pope Sixtus V asked Domenico Fontana to remodel the church. Because, during the Reformation, light was considered a distraction, all but six of the 26 windows were bricked up. Happily, during the restoration works carried out in the 1930s, they were reopened, bringing the church back to the original intentions of the church's founder, Peter d'Illiria. The restored church is a fine example of fifth-century architecture, with the addition of some sixteenth-century frescoes by Taddeo Zuccari in the apse.

During the plague, Pope Saint Gregory the Great (590-604) gathered the faithful inside the church to pray, introducing the famous *Litania Processionale Settiforme*. On the first day of Lent, people rushed to this church to listen to the pope, who spoke to them after collecting offerings.

The door features scenes from the Old and New Testaments. The two are represented together because Old Testament events were traditionally interpreted as precursors of those of the New Testament.

The door was formed by 28 panels, but ten are now missing. The narrative of the large scenes is read from bottom to top, as if in a scroll, while the small ones follow a narrative from left to top right, as in a codex.

Inside the church:

☞ **An epigraph,** above the main door, in a mosaic of gold letters on a blue background

This epigraph mentions Pietro d'Illiria as the church's founder and Pope Celestine I (422-32). It also has references to the Council of Ephesus (431), when the primate of the Church of Rome was sanctioned.

☞ **Two female figures,** over the main door, mosaic

The oldest one represents the Ecclesia ex circumcisione *(Church of the Old Testament) and holds in her hands the book of the Old Testament; the younger one stands for the* Ecclesia ex gentibus *(Church of the New Testament) and holds a copy of the New Testament. Together with the inscription above these are fragments of a larger mosaic, which includes the figures of Saint Peter and Saint Paul and the symbols of the evangelists that once covered the whole wall.*

☞ **The lid of a sarcophagus,** in the apse, in the centre of the *Schola Cantorum,* tenth or eleventh century

In 824, Pope Eugenius II brought the relics of the martyrs Alessandro, Evenzio and Teodolo from the catacombs on the Nomentana to this church and set them in the crypt below the main altar. This is the cover of the sarcophagus where the relics were kept.

☞ **Drawing of a ciborium,** on the wall, on the right-hand side of the nave

A ciborium, or canopied shrine, made out of silver, was built under the papacy of Eugenius II and positioned in the main apse. Unfortunately, it was stolen during the Sack of Rome in 1527. This drawing of it was discovered in the second quarter of the twentieth century.

Catacombs

According to Roman law, burial was prohibited inside the city's sacred walled perimeter, the *Pomerium*. The dead, therefore, were buried outside the wall, mostly along the roads leading into the city. The Jews buried their dead in underground tunnels, called catacombs, built into the porous stone beneath Rome. The Christians did the same, transforming the catacombs into holy places to venerate the dead and the martyred. Previously mistaken as underground churches, the catacombs were in fact large necropolises. They survived the Roman persecution because Roman law prohibited the desecration of burial grounds.

Here we find the language of the first Christians and that of the early cult of the dead. Rituals and ceremonies carried out in the catacombs marked the transition to eternal life. Christians no longer feared death. On the contrary, it was welcomed as the necessary transition to a better life.

The first examples of Christian sculpture were gravestones on which the Christians stressed the message of salvation and eternal life. In the catacombs, early-Christian imagery focuses on the rite of passage from this world to the next.

☞ **Wall paintings, oil lamps, inscriptions,** everywhere in the catacombs

Catacombs

The Latin word *catacombas* comes from the Greek *kata*, 'near', and *kimba*, 'hole'. They were tunnels and caves dug outside the Roman wall in the tufa, the porous white rock that lies underneath Rome.

Death

If any righteous person among us passes away from this world, we rejoice and give thanks to God, and follow his body as if he were moving from one place to another.
(Aristide of Athens, AD140)

43

The visitor can feel the claustrophobic maze of chambers, smell the crumbling volcanic tufa and see the thin shafts of light piercing the darkness.

By the middle of the ninth century, the catacombs were abandoned and completely forgotten. They came back to light in 1578, when a workman digging in a vineyard discovered a tunnel, and soon became a place of pilgrimage. After being the object of much attention and devotion during the years of the Counter-Reformation in the sixteenth century, interest in the catacombs waned until the eighteenth century when, thanks to the enthusiasm of the archaeologist G. de Rossi, they again became a focus of attention.

Catacomb of San Callisto

Pope Zephyrinus (199-217) asked the deacon Callisto, who later became Pope Calixtus I (217-22), to look after the first Christian necropolis in Rome, on the Appian Way, not far from where Saint Peter had had his vision of Christ. Later, the burial ground was renamed after Callisto.

Originally used as a pagan necropolis, the catacombs could be reached by a stepladder leading to the Crypt of Lucina, which was most probably built in the second or third century. In the fourth century, Pope Damasus I embellished the crypt with marbles and a table. To facilitate access for the pilgrims, he also had a staircase

The cult of Pope Sixtus II
The most important cult of the catacomb of San Callisto is that of Pope Sixtus II who, in 258, during the persecution of Emperor Valerian, was martyred with his deacons in the cemetery of San Callisto.

built and several openings made to let in some light.

Faith and history are built into the walls of these chilly underground chambers. This catacomb, which spreads over five levels, was the burial ground of popes until the third century. Pope Cornelius (251-53), who died in exile, was also buried here. In total, 14 popes were buried here, the last being Melchiades (311-14).

☞ Crypt of the Popes

The crypt contains the remains of an altar and a seat and can be found at the end of this rectangular hall. Pope Damasus I provided the inscriptions dedicated to the popes and martyrs buried here.

☞ Crypt of St Cecilia, off the Crypt of the Popes, on the left

This is a copy of the statue of Saint Cecilia by Maderno (the original is now in the church of Santa Cecilia in Trastevere). According to an old legend, Saint Cecilia's remains were found in the catacomb of San Callisto. Pope Paschal I (817-24) had them removed to the church in Trastevere.

☞ Gallery of the Sacraments

It was customary, after a funeral, to celebrate the passage to a better life with a meal, or refrigerium. *The funerary meal centred on the sharing of the Eucharistic bread.*

The Eucharist
The Eucharist is the main sacrament of Christian worship. The name comes from the Greek word for thanksgiving, *eucharistia*. During the mass, the ritual of the Last Supper is repeated: the breaking of the bread and the drinking of the wine. The bread is transformed into the body of Christ and the wine into the blood of Christ. Thus, in the Eucharistic meal, every Christian receives Christ into himself. In the catacombs, early wall paintings of feasts combine the ideas of *agape*, the early Christian communal meal, with the Christian celebration of the Eucharist.

The Eucharist meal included the sacramental fish with wine and a basket of bread. The closely related miracle of this ritual was the Multiplication of Loaves and Fishes. Early Christians identified Christ with the Greek word for fish, *ICHTHUS*, formed from the initials of the words *Iesus Christos Theou Huios Soter* (Jesus Christ of God the Son Saviour). In early Christian imagery the fish, symbolising Christ Himself, is found on lamps and seals in the catacombs.

The Lord is my shepherd.
(Ps. 23: 1)

Catacomb of Via Latina

Discovered in 1956, this catacomb was a private burial chamber for a small number of families who could afford burials in a *cubiculum* or private room, rather than in the *loculi* that were found in the public catacombs. Large wall paintings, in which Christian and Jewish imagery co-exist, decorate the walls. Notable in this regard is the painting of Moses leading the Israelites through the Red Sea and into the Promised Land. For the Christian viewer, Moses was a forerunner of Christ; as Moses saved the Chosen People by freeing them from slavery, so Christ delivered man from evil by promising salvation. As we are in Rome, this parallel can be stretched to include Peter and the bishops of Rome as Christian 'Moseses' leading the faithful through the gate of salvation, fulfilling Christ's promise of the afterlife in Paradise.

Catacomb of Santa Domitilla

Antonio Bosio was the first to enter the catacomb of Santa Domitilla in the seventeenth century. He visited it with friends, using candles to guide them. The tunnels were like a labyrinth, the candles ran out and they got lost. It took them two days to find their way out.

This frightening experience only increased Antonio's fascination with the catacombs; all he needed was a plentiful supply of candles. Thereafter, he continued to explore, reporting his findings in his book *Underground Rome* (1632).

This extensive three-level labyrinth is particularly interesting for its paintings and mosaics.

☞ **Daniel among the Lions,** fresco
☞ **The Good Shepherd,** down the wide stairway from the fresco of David, on the ceiling, fresco

The Good Shepherd is at the centre of the ceiling. He carries a lamb on his shoulders. The Christians saw in this image the representation of the words of salvation as taught in their religion. The lost sheep had been saved.

Welcoming Death

Perpetua, a young woman of Carthage, was about to be martyred in the year AD 202, and described her dream about death as follows: "I saw a huge garden, in the middle of it a tall man with white hair, dressed like a shepherd, and around him many thousands dressed in white. He raised his hand, looked at me and said "it is good that you have come my child" ... He gave me food, which I received on hands laid one upon another and everyone said "Amen". I awoke with the sweet taste still in my mouth.'

Catacomb of Priscilla

Deep down, on two levels, there are three areas to visit within this catacomb: the *Acilii*, the Greek chapel and, the oldest part, the *Arenario*. The catacomb is named after Priscilla, a woman from a noble Roman family who converted to Christianity. Like Sabina, she opened her house to Christian followers.

☞ **The *Acilii***

This was originally the cistern of Priscilla's Roman villa and became the site of a burial ground only later.

☞ **The Greek chapel**

This is formed by three chambers off the main room. It is decorated with frescoes representing biblical scenes. At the entrance, there are images of Moses striking water from a rock, the sacrifice of Isaac, and Noah. At the end of the room is a banquet scene, interpreted as representing the sacred moment of the Eucharist. However, it may also represent the customary funerary banquet, called refrigerium.

☞ **The *Arenario***

Once probably a quarry, it features images from the Old Testament.

☞ **Jonah and the Whale,** fresco

Jonah was sent by God to preach in Nineveh, but he fled and boarded a ship that was sailing for Tarshish from Jaffa (now Tel Aviv-Yafo). God's punishment for Jonah's defection was to send a violent sea storm. Jonah realised what was coming and warned the others on the boat, who, in anger, threw him overboard. In the sea, a big whale swallowed him up. While he was inside the whale, Jonah repented and eventually was disgorged safe and sound after three days. Christians read this story as an allegory for Christ's death and Resurrection.

☞ **Woman with a Child,** fresco

Some have interpreted this as a representation of the Virgin Mary and Child; others as simply a scene of maternity.

'Only believers can receive this food which is called Eucharist'

'Christians have the commandments of Christ written on their hearts. They acknowledge the goodness of God to them.'

Types of Burial

Loculi: Rectangular niches disposed in tiers. This was the most common type of burial. The body was wrapped in a sheet and inserted in the hole, which was then sealed with a marble slab. The slab sometimes carried an inscription with the date and the name of the deceased. Oil lamps, jewels, toys and plates were left next to the tomb.

Arcosoli: Niches topped with an arch. They were situated in *Cubicula*, or small rooms, used generally as burial chambers for a family or by distinguished people of the community.

II

ROME, CITY OF MARTYRS AND SAINTS

For the first three centuries of the Christian era, Rome witnessed the ultimate sacrifice of thousands of early Christian martyrs - men and women who shed their blood on its soil in order to plant the seeds of the new religious faith. The years of persecution were indeed dark years. Christians were hunted like criminals and killed like animals, often savaged by ferocious beasts inside the Coliseum.

It is difficult to imagine how the first congregation of Roman Christians could have jeopardised the power of Rome, how the message of salvation and fraternal love could challenge the strongest military state on earth. The threat that Christianity posed to paganism was not tangible, it was spiritual. The message of life after death was its strength and the martyrs were its army.

Roman emperors were troubled by the strange zeal of the new sect of converted Jews, the Christians, who travelled the world to spread the message of the Gospel. The imperial establishment was alarmed by their religious practices and beliefs: the ritual of baptising people *en masse*, the promise of eternal life after death and the preaching of the existence of only one God. Unlike other cults that had found their way to Rome, Christians sought to make converts to their creed. From their affirmation that their God had fathered all humanity, it followed that all men, including the emperor, were equal. By not recognising the emperor as the ultimate 'Lord', Christianity directly challenged the authority of Roman emperors. This was at the root of Christian persecution.

Roman law, torture and execution were to prove powerless against

Martyr

The word martyr derives from Greek and means 'witness'. Christ was the first martyr, the 'witness of the Christian faith', as he was called in the Apocalypse of John. Originally people prayed to God on behalf of martyrs, often during the celebration of mass near their tomb. Later on, Christians began praying to the martyrs themselves for their intercession with God.

The feast day of Roman martyrs is 30th June.

How Romans saw the Christians

Popular gossip soon began to accuse the Christians of secret vices, such as eating murdered infants (this arose from the secrecy surrounding the Last Supper and the use of the words 'body' and 'blood') and of sexual promiscuity (from the practice among Christians of calling each other 'brother' or 'sister' while living as husband and wife). The governor of Bithynia, in 111, told the Emperor Trajan that, to his surprise, he had discovered the Christians to be guilty of no vice, only of obstinacy and superstition. Nevertheless, he executed without a qualm those who refused to apostatise.
(from an account by Pliny the Younger)

them. In a city in decline, riddled with intrigue and decadence, the fabled heroism of its citizens and soldiers was but a memory. The willingness of Christians to die rather than renounce their faith was a strong and finally insurmountable challenge to the 'supernatural' position of the empire. Ironically, they embraced death with the same heroic courage of the men and women who had contributed to the glory of Rome.

As Christ had endured His martyrdom on the cross to save humanity, so Christians welcomed their destiny, which was to cross the threshold of salvation to the promised afterlife. Persecution intensified as Roman law was unable to curb the spread of Christianity. Thousands of Christians were thrown into the arena of the Colosseum to face a brutal death. A common form of entertainment at the time of the empire, the slaughter of Christians ironically became a powerful 'advertisement' for the new religion. Romans watched defenceless men, women, and children face the beasts while praying to their God. Inside the most magnificent arena in the world, non-Christians became fascinated by the strength of the religion and by the heroism of its followers - martyrs were the spiritual athletes of the powerful Christian God.

With the Edict of Milan of 313, Constantine made Christianity the religion of the empire. However, the fame of the martyrs did not diminish.

Both their physical remains and the instruments of their torture were believed to contain supernatural power. To touch them, hold them and venerate them was to be blessed by divine strength. Tales of martyrdom, known as *passiones*, and life histories of martyrs spread quickly throughout the churches of the empire.

In 366, with the election of Pope Damasus I, the cult of the martyrs blossomed. The catacombs were still the main site for its veneration, so the pope initiated a programme of improvements: he had the staircases built to facilitate access for the pilgrims; he enlarged the openings to let the light penetrate the tunnels and he commissioned paintings, sculptures and decorations to embellish the tombs.

Emerging from the dark period of persecution, the Church honoured its martyrs by building churches to house their relics and images. Bodies were exhumed from the catacombs to be reburied in basilicas; shrines were built and crypts were erected to house their remains. These are often fine examples of art and architecture; as such they can be splendid and dignified altars for the celebration of the ultimate sacrifice of Christian witnesses, as well as sites where their blessing can be invoked.

Inside the dark coolness of Roman churches, chapels or subterranean chambers a variety of memorials can be found: perhaps a crypt, a reliquary in gold and enamel, a coffin or a vivid painted image of martyrdom. When entering these sacred places,

Death in the Colosseum
May I benefit from the wild beasts prepared for me, and I pray that they will be found prompt with me, whom I shall even entice to devour me promptly - not as with some whom they were too timid to touch; and should they not consent voluntarily, I shall force them.
(Ignatius of Antioch, early Christian martyr, in a letter to the Christians in Rome before his death in the Colosseum)

Martyrdom
You keep adding many corpses newly dead to the corpse [Christ] of long ago. You have filled the whole world with tombs and sepulchres.
(Emperor Julian the Apostate to the Christians)

Depositio Martyrum

The *Depositio Martyrum* and the *Depositio Episcoporum* were lists of names containing about 30 martyrs, which were compiled in 354. Both works included the date and the sites, along the consular roads outside the city, where the martyrs had been buried. A revised edition produced in the fifth century added 70 names to the original list.

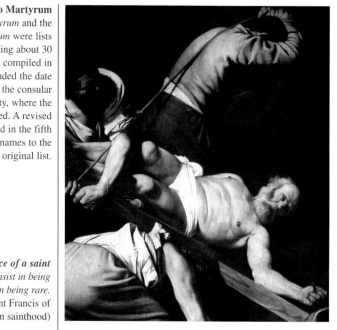

The essence of a saint
Sanctity does not consist in being odd, but it does consist in being rare.
(Reflection of Saint Francis of Sales, a French saint, on sainthood)

one can still sense the power emanating from the martyrs. With the end of the persecutions, Christians were able to reach the perfection of Christian life not only through martyrdom, but also by freely professing their religion. They became saints simply by living their daily lives according to the teachings of Christ.

A saint is someone from whom others can learn patterns of life that no spiritual or moral code can give. Since the late Roman Empire, when the Christian cult of saints took shape, the life of a saint was regarded as an example of the life of Christ. Saints are men and women who manage to live so close to His teaching as to represent, for Christians, His light and force.

It is not easy to be declared a saint by the Church. A Christian has to have a widespread reputation among the people for self-sacrifice, martyrdom, asceticism or confessions. Stories and legends that develop around holy personalities, containing symbols of heroic virtue for the faithful, are highly important. For canonisation a miracle is required, either during a saint's lifetime or through the efficacy of relics. These are the saints recognised by the Church and celebrated officially with a popular cult. Saints are examples of virtue; their life is conducted on a high spiritual and moral plane; they have the strength of faith that makes them invincible. For Christians, they are models, intercessors and protectors to whom people turn for divine intervention in times of difficulty.

Saints and martyrs provide evidence of the ultimate victory of faith over death. They die on earth, but live ever after in the glory of Heaven. Death is not an ending but a rebirth into eternal life. Thus the liturgical calendar, which regulates Christian worship during the year, celebrates saints and martyrs on the day of their death, their birthday of life in Heaven.

As Christianity became the most popular faith professed in Europe, private families, corporations

Intercession

Intercession is a form of prayer, petition or entreaty in favour of another. It is a sort of mediation that the Virgin and the saints offer to the faithful. The only one mediator of God's grace is Christ. When we ask the saints for grace, it is not granted directly by them but is always granted by God. As the saints, during their lifetime, used their holiness to help the faithful, so in Heaven they continue to intercede for us.

Canonisation

The word 'canonisation' describes the system under which an individual can be deemed worthy of inclusion in the 'canon', the approved list of saints. In the early years of the Church there was no official route to sainthood. Instead, the bishops supervised the cults of the martyrs in their communities. When a martyr's body was removed from its initial burial place in order to be reburied in a church, the individual was automatically considered to be a saint. Over time, however, the process became more centralised until ultimately, by the tenth century, it came to be controlled by the pope. Ulrich, Bishop of Strasbourg, was the first to be canonised by Pope John XV during the Lateran Council in 993. In the sixteenth century Pope Sixtus V gave the responsibility for the recognition of saints to the Congregation of Rites, one of the departments of the Roman curia (senate). This office undertook the supervision of canonisation and of the associated process of beatification, which is a form of partial sainthood during which the individual may be venerated in a limited way.

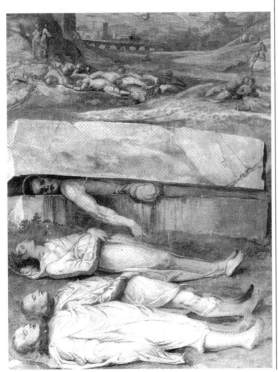

The path to official sainthood

A candidate's background is investigated for proof of a life lived according to God, in which the nominee has demonstrated sanctity and virtue. Miracles believed to have been performed by the individual (both during his life and after his death) are considered, as well as any writings or other surviving evidence. In order that the fullest possible assessment is achieved, an official is appointed to investigate every aspect of the case; he is popularly known as the 'devil's advocate'. If the candidate is deemed qualified, the pope may, at this point, authorise a beatification. This investiture is heralded by a solemn proclamation, followed by a mass. The path towards canonisation goes further than beatification, in that evidence of miracles is required before the case can proceed. A minimum of two reliably authenticated miracles, which have occurred in response to invocation, is a necessary requirement for the process of canonisation to begin. Beatification and canonisation can be of two kinds: ordinary or extraordinary. The extraordinary type does not require the normal procedure of a process of canonisation, but it is issued only by a pope's decree.

of artisans, of craftsmen, guilds and merchants financed the building of churches dedicated to specific saints or martyrs with whom they had some connection. For private individuals, it was a way to obtain prayers and celebrate masses for the salvation of their own souls. For business people, it represented a sort of insurance against the vagaries of business - saints and martyrs were asked to look after their trade. In Rome, foreign communities also built their own churches, often featuring a patron saint from their city of origin (such as the French community, which owns the church of San Luigi, and the Milanese community, which owns the church of Sant'Ambrogio).

Religious orders built churches to celebrate their founders, often around relics of martyrs or saints. These became shrines, where members of the orders found inspiration in the images picturing the life of their spiritual leaders (for example, the church of San Francesco, for the Franciscan Order, and the church of San Domenico, for the Dominicans).

In the sixteenth century, following the spread of Protestantism, the cult of saints and martyrs became the core of a dispute between Rome and Martin Luther, the German theologian who was a monk of the Order of Saint Augustine. Luther condemned the adoration of images of saints and martyrs as a form of superstition. He perceived this almost as a betrayal of Christian monotheism and in his Reformation he abolished the cult of saints and martyrs. God was the sole supernatural entity to whom man could turn. Amid the uproar caused by Luther's denunciation of the Church, the papacy was forcefully criticised for its excessive wealth and its lack of control over these forms of adulation.

Drawn by the preaching of men such as Luther, large numbers of followers flocked to the Protestant doctrine, especially in Germany, Switzerland and Holland. Fuelled by Protestant preaching, remonstrance against the Vatican - more worldly than worthy - poured in from

Luther and Protestantism

Luther was born in Germany, the son of a miner and metalworker. Having studied law, in 1505, against his father's wishes, he suddenly joined the Augustinian Friars. He became a priest in 1507 and was sent to Rome on church business in the winter of 1510-11. Here he found the lavish lifestyle of some members of the papacy and Roman clergy deeply shocking. He began to question many of the ceremonial functions of the Church, such as pilgrimages, the saying of mass for the dead, the role of saints and the selling of indulgences. During the next five years Luther was greatly troubled by his doubts. By 1517 he had arrived at a form of belief that embraced the doctrine of salvation through Christ alone. He considered that the sinner could do nothing to advance the cause of his soul, nor could the clergy assist in bringing about salvation; it could only be granted by God. He reduced the role of a priest from that of an intermediary between the Christian and God, to that of being merely the preacher of the word of God. Similarly, he discounted the importance of saints. He did not view them as exemplary Christians, but rather as individuals who had, through their faith, been granted grace by God. The good works that they performed he understood to be the result of their salvation, not the cause of it. The 95 Theses that he famously nailed to the door of the church at Wittenberg in 1517 led, ultimately, to a period of acute religious turmoil, which in turn resulted in the Protestant Reformation.

The main Protestant religions
The four main Protestant religions (Churches) are: Lutheran, Calvinist, Anabaptist and Anglican. They all reject the authority of the pope and stress the value of the Bible and individual faith.

northern Europe. For the first time since the dark period of persecution, the Church trembled; the unity of the Christian realm of Western Europe had been broken, never to be reunited.

In 1527 Rome, already undermined by the threat of Protestantism from the North, was to suffer another blow: the sack of the city. The imperial troops of Charles V descended into Rome. A mercenary army of German Protestants, the *Landsknechte* (peasant soldiers) marched together with Spanish troops. On the Gianicolo hill, they were posted between Porta Settimiana and Porta San Pancrazio, on the other side of the Tiber. The enemy was a breath away from its bounty: the Vatican City. Denounced by Luther for its love of wealth and luxury, this was no longer seen as the core of Christian values, but rather as the festering sore on the Christian body corporate. The Vatican City was taken first and then Rome was looted. Pope Clement VII and some citizens took refuge in Castel Sant'Angelo, the fortress that had originally been the tomb of Emperor Hadrian. For several months the pope remained inside, a virtual captive, while churches, monasteries, nuns and priests became the targets of fierce attacks.

Protestant worship
Historically the liturgy had combined two types of service, the instructional and the Eucharist. Following Luther's reforms, these were now separated and greater emphasis was given to the scriptures.
Luther was guided by the New Testament in his reform of religious practice. Protestant worship reflects, as a result, some influence of the synagogue. The Protestant Sunday service was based on the word of the Bible, and on the liturgy of the synagogue.

Rome was under siege for nine months: it was occupied, devastated, ruined and stripped of its beauties.

On 17th February 1528, the military scourge finally ended. Only 20-30,000 inhabitants had survived, like ghosts in a city of ashes. The invasion seared the spirit of the Church, which came to regard the Sack of Rome as a punishment for its love of luxury. Humiliated and racked with guilt for flouting Christ's teachings of poverty, the Church now gathered its strength to fight back.

The Council of Trent (1545-63) was Rome's reply to Luther. Cardinals reaffirmed the role of the Roman Church and its dogmas. The Council established rules and guidelines for the process of creating objects of devotion such as paintings, statues and churches. It laid down that images should be edifying in subject matter and should increase the piety of the faithful.

The Council also stressed that the cult of saints and martyrs was crucial for Catholic Christians because it represented a way of reaching God through the intercession of people who had emulated

The baroque language, propaganda for the Christian faith
To convert more people, the reformed Catholic Church attempted to widen its appeal. Missionaries spread the divine word beyond Rome. Subjects that reinforced the Gospel were featured in works of art of the sixteenth and seventeenth centuries. Paintings, sculptures and murals depicted scenes of martyrdom, visions and saints' ecstasies that showed the joy and glory of Christianity. These works were intended to inspire Christians to follow saints and martyrs towards salvation and to embrace the faith fully. A change in the language of art took place in the first quarter of the seventeenth century. The Church, with the scare of Protestantism left behind, adopted images that were richer, larger and more dramatic, with corresponding stories to proclaim and justify its power. The pope was portrayed as the Prince of Christian Rome and the city as his emblem.

the life of Jesus. The lives of saints and martyrs were examples of Christian practice to be followed by others and therefore worthy of devotion and prayer.

In the sixteenth and seventeenth centuries art, with its celebration of sainthood, was employed as an aid and inspiration for Catholics seeking salvation. Whereas the Protestants had opted for whitewashed churches, in which images were shunned because they were considered evil tools of idolatry, Roman Christians not only refused to abandon the custom of embellishing their churches, but used art and architecture to further celebrate and glorify Christianity.

This veneration of saints, coupled with an emphasis on the apostolic role of the Church in spreading the Gospel, gave rise to new orders and saints. The established orders, such as the Benedictines, Augustinians, Carmelites, Franciscans and Dominicans, were joined by many other orders, including the Barnabites, Theatines, Oratorians, Capuchins and Jesuits. They all focused on the value of preaching the Gospel, confession, and assisting and educating the faithful. The female religious Order of Ursulines (Sant'Angela de Merici is their patroness and saint) concentrated, for example, on girls' education.

Saint Ignatius of Loyola, Saint Teresa of Àvila, Saint Bridget of Sweden and Saint Carlo Borromeo were but a few of the new saints. Altars and churches were built to honour them. In addition, Rome took on a new patron alongside the venerable figures of Saint Peter and Saint Paul and the Archangel Michael. He was Saint Filippo Neri, affectionately nicknamed 'Pippo Buono' by the Roman people.

The tradition of elevation to sainthood is preserved in Rome to this day as the pope canonises new saints every year on major feast days.

On sacred images and relics
Twenty- fifth Session, Council of Trent, December 1563:
Furthermore in the invocation of the Saints, the veneration of the relics, and the sacred use of images, all superstition shall be removed, all filthy quest for gain eliminated, and all lasciviousness avoided, so that images shall not be painted and adorned with seductive charm, or the celebration of saints and the visitation of the relics be perverted by the people into boisterous festivities and drunkenness, as if the festivals in honour of the saints are to be celebrated with revelry and with no sense of decency... no one is permitted to erect or cause to be erected in any palace or church, however exempt, any unusual image unless it has been approved by the Bishop: also that no new miracles be accepted and no relics recognised unless they have been investigated and approved by the same bishop... So however that nothing new or anything that has not hitherto been in use in the Church, shall be decided upon without having first consulted the most holy Roman pontiff.
(from H. J. Schroeder, *Canons and Decrees of the Council of Trent*)

The saints have always been the source and origin of renewal in the most difficult moments in the Church's history.
(from *Lumen Gentium*)

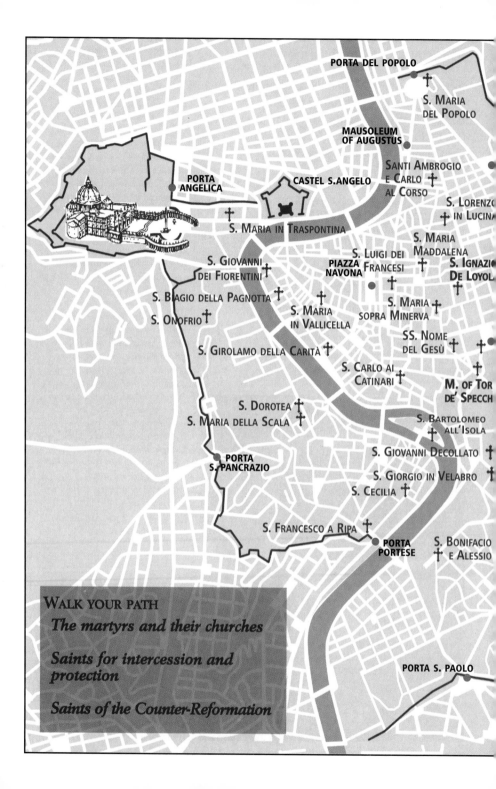

PORTA DEL POPOLO

S. MARIA DEL POPOLO

MAUSOLEUM OF AUGUSTUS

SANTI AMBROGIO E CARLO AL CORSO

S. LORENZO IN LUCINA

PORTA ANGELICA

CASTEL S.ANGELO

S. MARIA IN TRASPONTINA

S. MARIA MADDALENA

S. LUIGI DEI FRANCESI

PIAZZA NAVONA

S. IGNAZIO DE LOYOL

S. GIOVANNI DEI FIORENTINI

S. BIAGIO DELLA PAGNOTTA

S. MARIA IN VALLICELLA

S. MARIA SOPRA MINERVA

S. ONOFRIO

S. GIROLAMO DELLA CARITÀ

SS. NOME DEL GESÙ

S. CARLO AI CATINARI

M. OF TOR DE' SPECCH

S. DOROTEA

S. MARIA DELLA SCALA

S. BARTOLOMEO ALL'ISOLA

S. GIOVANNI DECOLLATO

PORTA S. PANCRAZIO

S. GIORGIO IN VELABRO

S. CECILIA

S. FRANCESCO A RIPA

PORTA PORTESE

S. BONIFACIO E ALESSIO

WALK YOUR PATH

The martyrs and their churches

Saints for intercession and protection

Saints of the Counter-Reformation

PORTA S. PAOLO

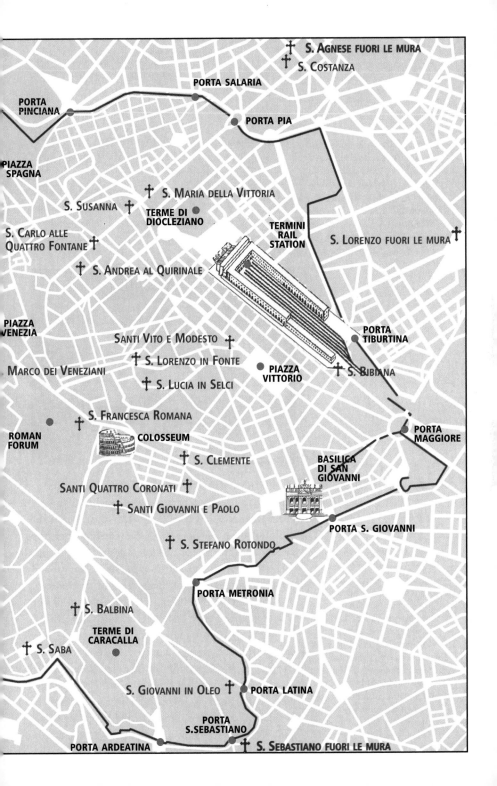

Our friend tells us that when he was a boy it was customary to go and visit the Crucifix in San Paolo that spoke to Saint Bridget...and that one day the Madonna of the church of Saint Cosmus and Damian, in the Forum, scolded Saint Gregory because he passed by her without greeting her... He went on to say that, less than a century ago at San Sylvester, the self-portrait of Jesus sent to him by King Abgar was shown.... And that the ark of the alliance, the rod of Noah and that of Aaron were kept in San Giovanni in Laterano. Furthermore, in the church of Santa Croce in Gerusalemme silver coins that belonged to Judas used to be on show together with his torch and the Cross of the good thief.
(Stendhal)

WALK YOUR PATH

Our journey will take us to places of worship where the voices of early Christian martyrs can be heard - the churches and crypts dedicated to such martyrs. Here we will find the murals, paintings, statues and altarpieces within churches and chapels built to house relics and saintly remains. In the quiet and holy atmosphere of these churches let us listen to the spellbinding tales of martyrdom and sainthood. Rome speaks to us as monuments, buildings and churches narrate the fascinating and unique tale of this city, the *Civitas Domini*.

THE MARTYRS AND THEIR CHURCHES

Our first journey begins with churches that were either dedicated by the faithful to the martyrs or built in their memory by Constantine. After the victory at the Milvian Bridge, these constructions came to be known as *martiria*, the most famous and important being that of Saint Peter in the Vatican. The *martiria* were built either on martyrs' tombs or where they had died, and were intended as places of prayer. They were circular and domed, a style that derived from funerary architecture and was foreign to the Roman basilica tradition. The best examples of *martiria* were churches built by Constantine in the Holy Land, such as the church of the Nativity in Bethlehem, and the churches of the Holy Sepulchre and of the Resurrection in Jerusalem.

Martiria

All *martiria* are circular and domed. One explanation for the choice of this form is linked to the Passion of Christ. On Mount Golgotha, where Christ was crucified, stood a gold cross protected by a sort of ciborium, a dome-shaped baldachin, ornate with gold and mosaic. A pilgrim who saw it in the seventh century described it as a golden dome of Heaven towering over a cross of gold and embellished with precious stones. The cupola had the function of protecting the place of Redemption. For the believer, this was the mystical centre of the world.

Wherever the mystery of the Redemption was to be re-enacted through the Eucharistic liturgy, the dome was to symbolise the sheltering of the faithful. Every cupola suspended over an altar had the same function; each church that it protected was a microcosm of Christianity in which divine grace was to be found.

Basilica of San Lorenzo fuori le Mura

In 258, the year in which Pope Sixtus II nominated Lawrence as deacon, Emperor Valerian decreed that all bishops and priests should be executed. While the pope was on his way to be martyred, Lawrence walked beside him and wept. Touched by his sorrow, Sixtus reassured him. They were parting from each other for only a short time, he said, and would be reunited in three days. The pope then asked him to distribute the Church's treasure to the needy to prevent it from falling into the hands of the Church's persecutors.

When the prefect of Rome uncovered this plan, he ordered Lawrence to bring the Church's wealth to him within three days. On the third day, Lawrence presented the prefect with the true 'treasures of the church', hundreds of faithful Christians. Feeling that he had been mocked, the prefect sentenced him to death.

Lawrence was lashed to an iron grid, which was lowered on to burning coals. While Lawrence was slowly burnt alive, he welcomed his suffering and prayed for the conversion of the entire city.

After his death, his martyred body was secretly transferred to the cemetery of Cyriac, on the Via Tiburtina. This allegedly happened on 10th August, the feast day of Saint Lawrence.

Outside the church:

☞ **Life of Saint Lawrence, Saint Stephen and Count Henry,** in the portico, frescoes, 13th century

Count Henry was a German noble. To repent for his sins, he donated a golden chalice to the church and, on the feast day of Saint Lawrence, he offered a banquet to

Feast day of San Lorenzo: 10th August

Brief history of the Basilica of San Lorenzo fuori le Mura
In 330, Constantine had a great basilica built beside Saint Lawrence's burial place. It was 100 metres long and 75 metres wide and was linked to the main city gate, the Porta Tiburtina, by a street with arcades to shelter pilgrims from bad weather. The cult of Saint Lawrence was so popular that in the sixth century Pope Pelagius II added another church to the original one. This time the basilica was built *ad corpus*, incorporating the saint's tomb. To facilitate pilgrims' access to the sepulchral chamber, big naves and upstairs galleries (called *matronei*) were built. In 1191, Cencius Camerarius, the future Honorius III, had a *confessio* built over the tomb of the martyr. In 1216, he completed the unification of the two churches by cutting off the two apses. At that time the naves, the portico on the façade and much of the decoration were added. Unfortunately, the church was bombed during World War II and parts of it had to be restored.

On his feast day, 10th August, the remains of Saint Lawrence's skull are shown in the Vatican.

In the sixth-century text Notitia Ecclesarium Urbis Romae, *this basilica was considered more beautiful than the basilica of Constantine.*

Brief history of the Basilica of Sant'Agnese fuori le Mura
According to legend, the basilica of Sant'Agnese was built in the fourth century on top of the cemetery in which Saint Agnes was buried. The history of this church begins with Constantine's daughter, Constantia, who had prayed on Saint Agnes's tomb to be cured of leprosy. Once recovered, she built the church to honour Saint Agnes. Although Pope Symmachus (498-514) restored the church, it quickly fell to ruins. Pope Honorius I (625-38) realised that the martyr's tomb could not accommodate the increasing number of pilgrims, so he built a basilica ad corpus, in which Saint Agnes's tomb could be reached by stairs. The altar of the new church was situated directly above her relic. Pilgrims used to lower brandea through the opening of the confessio, to touch the relic. The church still retains on the upper level the Byzantine feature of matronei or logge, areas reserved for women during certain functions and religious services.

all pilgrims and poor people visiting the church. When he died, angels and demons weighed on a scale his good and evil deeds. While they were arguing, Saint Lawrence arrived and tilted the scale in favour of salvation by placing on it the golden chalice.

Inside the church:

☞ **Saint Lawrence with Saints Paul, Peter and Hippolytus and Pope Pelagius Holding a Model of the Church,** on the triumphal arch, mosaic, fifth century

Pope Pelagius II holds a model of the church to remind us that he added another church to the original to incorporate Lawrence's tomb.

☞ **The tomb of Saint Lawrence and Saint Stephen,** in the sixth-century crypt, under the thirteenth-century altar

Saint Stephen and Saint Lawrence were among the first deacons of the Church. Saint Stephen was stoned to death in Jerusalem, but his body was transferred to Rome to be buried next to Saint Lawrence.

Basilica of Sant'Agnese fuori le Mura
patroness of purity

Agnes, a beautiful 13-year-old girl, was sought in marriage by many Roman nobles. She spurned all of them because, as she explained, she had consecrated her virginity to a heavenly spouse who could not be beheld by mortal eyes. One of Agnes's suitors, the son of the prefect of Rome, denounced her as a Christian. She was immediately asked to prove her innocence by making sacrifices to the Roman gods and, because she refused to comply, she was taken to a brothel.

As Agnes was dragged along the streets of Rome, her naked body was covered by her hair, which had miraculously grown to hide her nudity. This episode is said to have taken place in Piazza Navona, in front of the stadium of Domitian, which is today the site of another Roman church dedicated to Agnes, Sant'Agnese in Agone.

In the brothel, an angel appeared and clothed her. The angel was wrapped in a shining light that blinded

Brandea
Brandea are strips of cloth that were lowered through the openings of the *confessio* to touch the sacred relics. The *brandea* were used because direct contact, physical and sometimes visual, with relics was not permitted.

Feast day of Sant'Agnese: 21st January

Ritual
On the 21st January, two lambs are blessed on the church's altar and a cloth, called a *pallium*, is woven from their wool by the Benedictine nuns of Santa Cecilia in Trastevere. The pope presents a *pallium* to each new archbishop.

everyone around her. When her suitor went to see Agnes in the brothel, he was struck dead. Agnes was taken away to be burnt, but the flames did not harm her, instead burning her executioner. Eventually, on the orders of Emperor Diocletian, Agnes was beheaded.

Eight days after her death, another miracle occurred. Agnes appeared covered in jewels that symbolised the hair that had preserved her purity. She was holding a lamb, a further representation of her purity. Since then, she has always been portrayed either wrapped in her own hair or covered with jewels.

Agnes was buried in the catacomb near Via Nomentana, which was later named after her.

☞ **The Miracle of Saint Agnes,** in the apse, mosaic, seventh century

Saint Agnes is in the centre flanked by Pope Honorius I, who is holding a model of the church, and Pope Symmachus. She is dressed in jewels, as she appeared in the second miracle. The instruments of her martyrdom are illustrated: the fire and the sword used

Pallium
A *pallium* is a woollen cloth, decorated with the cross, which symbolises the nomination of archbishops. In the eighth century, when it became compulsory to receive it in Rome, the *pallium* came to symbolise the subordination of Christian clergy to the papacy.

to decapitate her.

☞ **Saint Agnes,** on the main altar, statue, by Nicola Cordier, 1605

The hands and the dress are in gilded bronze, while the torso comes from an ancient sculpture and is made of alabaster.

☞ **Saint Agnes relic,** in the crypt

A small *protiro* links the basilica of Sant'Agnese to the church of Santa Costanza.

Church of Santa Costanza

Inside the *martirium* people could come to commune spiritually with the deceased, particularly with someone who had been dear to them and in whom they hoped to find an intercessor with the Lord, as Constantia did with Saint Agnes.

☞ **Early-Christian mosaics,** on the church's walls

These mosaics are among the oldest in Rome. They portray peacocks, pomegranates and birds perched on goblets (canthari) *that have come to drink from the baptismal water of immortality. The images are from the ancient Roman repertoire of funerary iconography, which later assumed a new significance according to Christian symbols, in this case promising the deceased princess her rebirth in Christ. The vine trees become a decorative motif in the mosaic, but in church tradition the vine represents the blood of Christ; here it is a symbol of the Crucifixion. It is the collecting of the vine's blood that generates new life, as it is blessed and distributed during every mass.*

☞ **Replica of the sarcophagus of Constantia,** in a niche at the far end of the church, in porphyry

The original has been in the Vatican Museum since 1790.

Basilica of San Sebastiano fuori le Mura
protector against the plague

Sebastian was born in Narbonne, in Gaul, but lived most of his life in Milan, where his parents came from. He was a fervent Christian and although he

Brief history of the Church of Santa Costanza

This is a circular construction, a *martirium*, built on the burial place of Constantia, daughter of Constantine. Originally it was meant to be a simple annex to the adjacent basilica of Sant'Agnese, under whose protection Constantia wished to be buried. Until the thirteenth century, when it became independent, this church was used as the baptistery of the church of Sant'Agnese.

Saint Constantia

The historian Marcellino describes Constantia and her husband, Hannibalianus, as violent. Some people think that her canonisation was the result of some confusion with a saintly nun of the same name.

disliked military life, he decided to become a soldier to assist the martyrs in their sufferings. In 283, he went to Rome and joined the army.

Sebastian was instrumental in converting several people, including the governor of Rome and his son. He also performed miracles; for example, he restored to Zoe, the wife of an officer in charge of Christian prisoners, the power of speech after she had been unable to speak for six years.

Emperor Diocletian admired Sebastian's courage in battle and promoted him to captain of the Praetorian Guard. For years, Sebastian managed to conceal his faith but in 286, he was discovered and denounced to the emperor. Enraged by his ingratitude, Diocletian delivered Sebastian to the archers of Mauritania. His body bristling with arrows, Sebastian was left on the ground to die. Irene, the wife of Castulus, a Christian Roman officer martyred by Diocletian, discovered him and, seeing that he was still alive, rescued him.

Miraculously, Sebastian recovered fully. Despite his suffering at the hands of Romans, he refused to flee from Rome. In 304, he publicly reproached the emperor for his cruelty towards Christians. Shocked and angry, Diocletian once again ordered him to be killed. This time, Sebastian was beaten to death with cudgels and his body was thrown into the Cloaca Maxima, Rome's central sewer. A pious lady, admonished by a vision of the martyr, retrieved his body and buried it in a catacomb.

Always depicted in art as the most handsome and dashing of saints, Saint Sebastian clearly had a most potent charm.

Chapel of the Relics
first on the right (1)
Pilgrims used to flock to this chapel to see the relics of Christ.

☞ **The original set of footprints of Christ,** in the chapel
These are the footprints from Christ's meeting with

Brief history of the Basilica of San Sebastiano fuori le Mura
In the fourth century a *Basilica Apostolorum ad catacumbas* was built where Saints Peter and Paul were first buried (the remains of both were eventually transferred, Saint Peter's to the Circus of Nero and Saint Paul's to Via Ostiense). Saint Sebastian's tomb was placed beside that of the Apostles. An altar dedicated to him was installed next to the one dedicated to Peter and Paul, which is in the middle of central nave. Restored by Pope Adrian I (772-95), the church was only then dedicated to Saint Sebastian. In 1612, Cardinal Scipione Caffarelli Borghese had the basilica completely redesigned by Flaminio Ponzio. Cardinal Francesco Barberini commissioned a new altar for Saint Sebastian with a marble statue executed by Giorgetti.

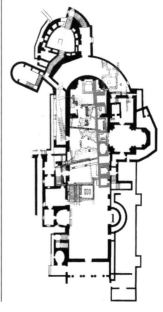

On Saint Sebastian's feast day, 20th January, entry to the catacombs of San Sebastiano, underneath the church, is free of charge.

Brief history of the Church of Santo Stefano Rotondo
The church dates back to around 468 under the papacy of Simplicius. It is reported to be the site of Castra Peregrina, the military headquarters in Rome of the provincial army. Santo Stefano Rotondo is circular, with four radiating chapels forming a cross. The dimensions of the church approximate to those of the Holy Sepulchre in Jerusalem, built by Constantine. The unusual shape of Santo Stefano Rotondo conforms with the circular plan characteristic of *martiria*. In the seventh century a small *confessio* was built on the east side for the remains of two other martyrs, Primus and Felicianus, which were transferred from the catacomb of the Nomentana. Pope Innocent II (1130-43) added a portico at the entrance of the church and embellished the interior with three great transverse arches. The 22 windows that illuminate the church were restored by Pope Nicholas V (1447-55) to the design of Bernardo Rossellino. An oratorium, with a *xenodochium*, a hospice for the poor and pilgrims, once stood near the church, but it was destroyed in the sixteenth century.

Peter on the Appian Way.

☞ **The arrows and the column,** in the chapel
These are the arrows of Sebastian's martyrdom and the column to which he was tied during the fatal beating.

Chapel of San Sebastiano
first chapel on the left

During the papacy of Gregory V (827-44), Saint Sebastian's remains were transferred to the Vatican basilica to keep them within the city walls. In 1218, Pope Honorius III had the saint's remains returned to the church. The altar in the crypt was redecorated and embellished with a precious ciborium with decoration in Cosmati work (a type of mosaic).

☞ **Saint Sebastian,** below the altar, marble statue, by Antonio Giorgetti based on a design by Bernini, 1671-72
The chapel of San Sebastiano, which was modelled on the chapel of the Relics, was built on the burial place of the saint inside the catacombs.

Church of Santo Stefano Rotondo

Saint Stephen was the first Christian to be martyred in Jerusalem, where he died in 35. He was a Greek-speaking Jew (*Stephen* in Greek means 'crown'). He was chosen by the Apostles to look after the needs of Greek-speaking Christian widows living in Jerusalem.

Charged with blasphemy against Moses and God, Stephen was taken to the Jewish Council, where he refused to defend himself. Instead, he addressed the Council, preaching the Word of Christ. While speaking he kept his eyes fixed on the sky, and saw the heavens open. Jesus looked down on him, ready to embrace and crown His servant.

As he described this vision, the members of the Council became more and more irritated. They grabbed him, rushed him out of the city and, in their rage, stoned him to death.

Standing among the crowd who watched the gruesome execution with approval was Saul, a young man from Tarsus, who was later to become Saint Paul.

☞ **Stories from the Life of Saint Stephen,** on the octagonal marble balustrade, at the centre of the church, monochrome frescoes

☞ **Stories from the Life of Martyrs,** along the church walls, frescoes by Pomarancio and Tempesta, 16th century

These frescoes tell the stories of several martyrs. The gruesome representations of martyrdom were intended to evoke powerful emotions in sixteenth-century viewers. The viewer was meant to be horrified by the martyrs' deaths and, in turn, admire the strength of their Christian faith. The function of the frescoes was linked to that of the nearby monastery, in which missionaries were taught before going to spread the word. The didactic value of the frescoes is underlined by the presence of written explanations of each scene.

Chapel of Santi Primo e Feliciano
first chapel to the left of the entrance

☞ **Mosaic of Christ with Saint Primus and Saint Felicianus,** apse, mosaic, seventh century

This work was executed to commemorate the transfer of the bodies of the two saints from the catacombs of Via Nomentana.

Church of Santi Quattro Coronati
patron saints of stonecutters

According to an old legend, the Four Crowned Saints were four stonemasons from Hungary who, after refusing to sculpt the statue of Esculapius, a pagan god, were sentenced to death by Diocletian. *Coronati*, which means crowned, is a reminder of the crown of their martyrdom. The martyrs' bodies were transferred to the cemetery of saints Peter and Marcellinus. The stonemasons' and sculptors' guild chose them as their protectors; the Four Crowned Saints were asked to look after their profession, ensuring that their work was always done according to virtuous practice.

☞ **Story of the Four Crowned Saints and the**

**Saint Stephen
to the Jewish Council**
Behold, I see the heavens opened, and the Son of Man standing at the right hand of God.

**Saint Stephen's invocation
to Jesus**
Lord Jesus, receive my spirit ... Lord, lay not this sin on their charge.

**The healing power
of Saint Stephen**
In 415, the relics of Saint Stephen of Jerusalem were found and distributed to various locations in Christendom, where churches were built to honour him. Soon, a rumour circulated that the relics had the power to heal illness. Reports were written and the saint's reputation for working miracles spread.

**Feast day of Saint Stephen:
26th December**

**Brief history of the Church
of Santi Quattro Coronati**
The church is built where a fourth-century Roman house once stood. The first church was commissioned by Pope Leo IV (847-55). Seriously damaged during the Norman invasion of 1084, Pope Paschal II had the church rebuilt, together with the attached abbey, into a veritable castle with some of the thickest walls in Rome. In medieval times, thanks to this fortified structure, Santi Quattro Coronati was often used as a temporary papal residence whenever the city was deemed unsafe. It was at one time called the Royal Hospice of Rome, because it housed the French King Charles I of Anjou.

Martyrs of Hungary, in the apse, frescoes by Giovanni Menozzi, known as Giovanni da San Giovanni, 1630

The four stories of the Santi Quattro Coronati are in the upper register; in the inferior register are the stories of the martyrs from Pannonia.

☞ **Relics of the four saints,** below the apse, in the crypt

Inside the semicircular crypt there are four arks containing the martyrs' relics which were discovered. during the works in 1200. The crypt dates back to the ninth century and borrows its shape from the confessio of Saint Gregory the Great in Saint Peter.

☞ **Monument to the Four Crowned Saints,** in the cloister

Sculptors and stonemasons carved this monument to honour their patron saints.

Through the cloister, in a second courtyard linking the church to a nunnery, is the entrance to the oratorio of Saint Sylvester.

Chapel of San Silvestro
in the oratory adjacent to the Church
of Santi Quattro Coronati

While Pope Sylvester (314-335) was living as a hermit on Monte Soratte, north of Rome, Constantine contracted leprosy. The emperor was advised to try a remedy as barbaric as it was useless: to bathe in children's blood. Constantine could not bring himself to do it. One night, tossing and turning, he was visited in a dream by Saint Peter and Saint Paul. The Apostles urged him to seek out Sylvester to be cured and, following their advice, he sent three men to bring the pope to him.

Sylvester bathed the emperor three times in a pool of water, baptising him and washing away the leprosy. In gratitude, Constantine donated to Pope Sylvester the emblems of power, namely, the tiara and the *sinichio*, the ritual parasol.

Another legend says that, in Rome, Sylvester performed a second miracle: he saved the citizens from a dragon by capturing it and locking it behind a bronze door.

Feast Day of Santi Quattro Coronati: 8th November

Brief history of the Chapel of San Silvestro
Cardinal Stefano had it built in 1246. In the sixteenth century it was given to the guild of the stonemasons and sculptors and it still belongs to them. This chapel was used for private ceremonies held by the pope and the curia.

☞ **Story of Saint Sylvester and Emperor Constantine**, frescoes, circa 1246

The story of the frescoes follows the iconography of the Acta Silvestri. *The story begins at the bottom register, close to the entrance, and then continues on the left wall. The episodes represented are: Constantine suffering from leprosy; Saint Peter and Saint Paul appear before Constantine and urge him to call on Pope Sylvester; Constantine's messenger leaves to find Pope Sylvester; Pope Sylvester enters Rome and shows Constantine the images of Saint Peter and Saint Paul; Constantine is baptised by Pope Sylvester; Constantine, having recovered from leprosy, sits on his throne and offers gifts to Pope Sylvester; Pope Sylvester brings back to life a bull killed by a Jewish priest: many witnesses of this miracle are converted to Christianity; Helen, Constantine's mother, finds the True Cross; Pope Sylvester frees the Romans from the dragon.*

Frederick II who was emperor when the frescoes were created was excommunicated many times and deposed. The story of the frescoes stresses the miraculous power of Sylvester over Constantine and the Roman citizens. They carry strongly the voice of papal supremacy over imperial power. This chapel was used for private celebrations of the pope and of the curia.

Church of Santi Giovanni e Paolo

According to the *passiones*, the fourth-century biographies of the saints, John and Paul, they were two Christian officers in Emperor Constantine's army. They were designated to Constantine's daughter, Costanza. When she died, she left all her wealth to John and Paul and, with this money, the two officers bought a house on the Coelium. In the first half of the fourth century the two men had already retired, but they were ordered to come to court and serve the new pagan emperor, Julian the Apostate. They refused and, in 361, they were beheaded in their own house under the Emperor Terenzian. Their story was told by this emperor himself, who later converted to Christianity.

Brief history of the Church of Santi Giovanni e Paolo

It is believed that a church was built towards the end of the fourth century where the saints' house once stood. Recent excavations uncovered two Roman houses situated below the church dating back to the second or third century. The houses had been joined together and used as a Christian burial place. Among the many rooms, most of which are still decorated with pagan and Christian frescoes, are a bath, a library and a cellar. The arches to the left of the church were part of the third-century street shops of Rome. The building of the church is attributed to Pomacchio, a noble and learned man, who died in 410. The church was damaged during the Sack of Rome and the Normans' invasion in 1084. Cardinal Thobaldo rebuilt the convent adjacent to the church between 1099 and 1118. In the twelfth century, Nicholas Breakspear, who became Pope Adrian IV, the only English pope, added the apse and bell-tower, the base of which rests on part of the Temple of Claudius. In 1216 Cardinal Savelli, the future Pope Honorius III modernised the church.

☞ **Burial place of the martyrs,** indicated by a slab in the main nave

☞ **Relics of the martyrs' bodies,** under the main altar, inside an urn of porphyry and embellished with bronzes

In 1726 Pope Benedict XIII placed the relics of the saints here.

At the bottom end of the right nave is the entrance into the house of the two martyrs and the remains of the old *titulus*.

☞ **Stories of John and Paul's martyrdom,** in the centre of the old house near the *fenestella confessionis* (confessional window), frescoes, fourth century

Pilgrims glimpsed into this room through the *fenestella confessionis*.

Feast day of San Giovanni in Oleo: 27th December

Church of San Giovanni in Oleo

Saint John the Evangelist was banished to the island of Patmos by Emperor Domitian. There he was blessed by the heavenly visions that he recorded in the book of Revelation (or Apocalypse of John). The text of one of the Gospels is also attributed to him.

In 95, during the persecution of Christians and before he was sent to Patmos, John had been immersed in boiling oil. As the executioner was pouring the liquid over his head, John prayed. To the astonishment of his torturers, he came out of the cauldron not only alive, but feeling refreshed. According to an old legend, John dug his own grave in the shape of a cross and descended into it by himself. A church was built where the Romans had attempted to boil him, to commemorate the miracle that saved his life: *in oleo* means 'in oil'.

Brief history of the Church of San Giovanni in Oleo
The present church was built during the papacy of Julius II (1503-13), but it is believed that an earlier chapel may have existed on the site.

Saint John's symbol is a chalice with a snake coiled around it. This symbol derives from the following legend: the priest of a temple dedicated to Diana, in Ephesus, gave John a cup of poison to drink in order to test his faith; not only did he survive the test, but he also saved two others who had been forced to drink from the same cup.

☞ **Episodes from the Life of Saint John,** inside the church, fresco by Lazzaro Baldi, 17th century

On the altar, the immersion of Saint John in boiling oil is depicted. On the left, the saint is seen being venerated by youths. The section on the right depicts the story of the poisoned cup. Opposite, Saint John is imprisoned in Patmos. Cardinal Paolucci commissioned this fresco cycle.

Church of Santa Balbina
patroness of illnesses of the throat

Balbina, a young Roman woman, and her father, Quirin, were imprisoned in the Mamertine Prison during the reign of Emperor Hadrian. There, Balbina found the chains that had once held Saint Peter prisoner. She used these to cure Pope Alexander I (106-16), himself persecuted and imprisoned. As soon as Balbina put the chains over his throat, the pope recovered from his affliction.

Balbina was martyred at the beginning of the second century, at the time of Emperor Trajan. Since then, people suffering from throat and thyroid problems have asked for her help in their prayers

☞ **Remains of Saint Balbina, of her father, the tribune Quirin, and of other martyrs,** below the main altar, in an urn made of jasper

☞ **Crucifixion of Saint Peter,** in the first lateral chapel on the left, fresco

Still visible at the side of the martyrdom fresco is a female figure making a gesture of offering, with her hands covered in veils. These could be the brandea, *the pieces of cloth used to touch the relics. This was most probably a chapel with relics, dedicated to the cult of a saint, perhaps Saint Peter.*

Basilica of Santa Cecilia
patroness of music

Saint Cecilia came from a wealthy Roman family. Educated in the Christian religion, she vowed to consecrate her virginity to God. Disregarding her wishes, her family compelled her to marry a Roman nobleman, Valerius, who later converted to Christianity. Cecilia was also instrumental in

Brief history of the Church of Santa Balbina

The church of Santa Balbina was built on the ruins of an ancient Roman residence, *Titulus Cilonis*, at the beginning of the third century. During the synod of 499, the church was mentioned as *Titulus Tigrade* and, in the official documents of the Synod of 594, as *Titulus Balbinae*. In the ninth century, the church was modernised by Pope Saint Leo III and embellished by Pope Gregory IV.

Ego me Christo sponsam tradidi. (Santa Cecilia)
(I choose to be the bride of Christ)

Brief history of the Basilica of Santa Cecilia

The church was built in the fourth century on the site of the martyr's house. A legend says that before her death, Saint Cecilia planned for her house to become a place of worship for Christians. Pope Paschal I (817-24) commissioned a basilica with three naves, embellished by a mosaic in the apse. The church maintains many medieval features despite having been redesigned by Cardinal Acquaviva in 1725.

Feast day: 22nd November

Vision of Pope Paschal I

Pope Paschal I was unable to find Saint Cecilia's body during the restoration of her house. He feared that her remains had been taken away by the Lombards. One day, while the pope was assisting morning mass in Saint Peter's, he fell into a slumber in which he was advised by a beautiful girl, Saint Cecilia herself, that the Lombards had not taken her remains and that he would find them. Paschal I searched the catacombs of San Callisto and eventually found her body still wrapped in a robe of gold tissue, with linen clothes at her feet stained by her blood. Buried with her were Valerius, his brother Tiburzius, and other martyrs.

converting her husband's brother, Tiburzius. In 230, during the persecution instigated by Emperor Marcus Aurelius, both Valerius and Tiburzius were beheaded. Cecilia was condemned to a different fate. Roman soldiers first tried to suffocate her with hot vapours. Locked in a *calidarium*, a steam room, she remained alive miraculously for three days. They then decided to behead her but she survived for three more days with her head hanging on one side. During that time God gave her strength to show her persecutors the power of faith. Using her hands she unveiled the message of the Mystery of the Trinity by showing three fingers on one hand and one on the other.

Her body went missing for a long time until it was found by Pope Paschal I (817-24) in the catacomb of San Callisto.

☞ **Saints Paul, Agatha, Peter, Valerius, Cecilia and Pope Paschal,** in the apse, mosaics, ninth century

In this mosaic Pope Paschal I is represented with the square nimbus (halo), the traditional attribute of a living pope. He also holds a model of the church.

☞ **Saint Cecilia,** in front of the main altar, statue by Stefano Maderno, 1600

The artist used her miraculously preserved remains as a model when the saint was disinterred in 1599, during the papacy of Clement VIII. The statue shows her exactly as she was lying when her tomb was uncovered, with the cut on her throat clearly visible.

☞ **Apotheosis of Santa Cecilia,** in the dome, fresco by Sebastiano Conca, 1727

The saint is shown in the process of being crowned in Heaven by Jesus Christ surrounded by a plethora of angels. Cardinal Francesco Acquaviva commissioned this fresco.

☞ **The Marriage of Cecilia and Valerius,** in the right nave, in the corridor leading to the chapel of Calidarium, painting by Guido Reni, 16th century

The couple is shown kneeling while an angel crowns them with floral wreaths. Behind Cecilia is the image of an organ, her traditional attribute.

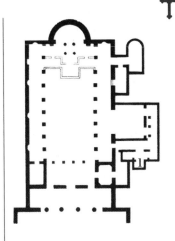

Chapel of the Calidarium

in the right (south) nave, second chapel on the right **(1)**

This is supposed to be the site where Saint Cecilia suffered her first martyrdom.

☞ *Calidarium*

This was the room used in the attempt to suffocate the saint with hot vapours.

☞ **Scenes from the Life of Saint Cecilia,** around the walls in the area of the hot baths, frescoes by Andrea Lilio and Commodi, 16th century

On the front wall, Saint Cecilia is represented disputing with pagans. Above this fresco there is a lunette depicting the martyrdom of Saint Cecilia's spouse, Valerius.

☞ **Decollation of Saint Cecilia,** on the altar, painting by Guido Reni, circa 1603

This painting suffered during World War II when the head of the saint was cut out. The head has now been restored.

☞ **The remains of the house and of a Roman tannery,** beneath the church

☞ **The tomb of Saint Cecilia, her husband, Valerius, her brother-in-law, Tiburzius, Pope Lucius (253-54) and Pope Urban I (222-30),** in the crypt, visible through the *fenestella confessionis*

☞ **Fragments of a 'Last Judgement',** in the adjacent cloister, fresco by Pietro Cavallini, 13th century

Prayer
You died loving your martyrdom, and accepted the sacrifice in order to protect your virginity.

Church of Santa Dorotea
patroness of florists

A church dedicated to Saint Dorothy and Sylvester is mentioned in 1445. The church now retains the eighteenth-century look it acquired after its 1738 restoration under the guidance of the architect Giambattista Nolli, draughtsman of the well-known maps of Rome. He is buried at the base of the main altar. In this church Ettore Vernazza, a notary from Genoa, founded, in 1513, La Compagnia del Divino Amore. This was a lay confraternity that had the aim of promoting communal prayer and encouraged charitable acts towards the poor. The confraternity was responsible for founding the Hospital for the Terminally Ill and the Monastery of the Converted, the latter for courtesans who wanted to repent. The Compagnia del Divino Amore broke up at the time of the Sack of Rome in 1527.

Saint Dorothy was the first female martyr. Dorothy was a virgin and was condemned to death by Fabricius, the Roman governor, because she refused to recant her belief in Christ. On the way to her execution, a young man mocked her by asking if she would send him fruits and flowers from the garden of Paradise. After her death a child appeared before the young man to deliver a basket of roses and apples. He immediately converted to Christianity.

☞ **Body of Saint Dorothy,** under the main altar in an urn

Saint Dorothy's body was transferred to this church on the occasion of the Jubilee in 1500.

*Feast day of Santa Dorotea:
6th February*

Church of San Lorenzo in Lucina

Prayer
San Lorenzo, deacon, teach us to love and serve our church; San Lorenzo, benefactor of the poor, make our life useful to others; San Lorenzo, man of Providence, enrich with hopes our disappointments; San Lorenzo, victorious martyr, makes us achieve, under the guidance of Our Lord, a strong and brave faith.

Saint Lawrence has always been a popular martyr (for his life story see the church of San Lorenzo fuori le Mura), so it is not surprising that he was venerated in more than one church. During the Middle Ages, the church of San Lorenzo in Lucina was an important destination for Christian pilgrims. Many relics were kept here, including the metal grid on which the saint had been burnt.

Chapel of San Lorenzo
first on the right

☞ **Saint Lawrence's grid iron,** under the altar in seventeenth-century reliquary

Two ampullae of the fat and blood of San Lorenzo, a vase full of his burnt skin, a part of the grid iron on which he was roasted, a cloth used by an angel to clean his holy body and many more... (from *Mirabilia Urbis Romae*, sixteenth century).

Church of Santa Susanna

Saint Susanna was a Roman noblewoman who is said to have been the niece of Pope Gaius (283-96), cousin of Emperor Diocletian. Diocletian promised her in marriage to Galerius Massimianus, his adopted son but Susanna, having made a vow of virginity, refused him. Suspecting that she was a Christian, Diocletian ordered her to worship Jupiter, which she refused to do. Her Christianity confirmed, Susanna was beheaded in her own house.

During the Middle Ages, this church was an important place for pilgrims because of the relics it housed, especially the bodies of Saint Susanna and her father, and a locket of hair from the Virgin.

In the church, the tale is told of another Susanna, from the Old Testament. This Susanna was the wife of a wealthy Jew. One day, two elders hid in the garden to watch her bathing. Once her maids had left

**Brief history
of San Lorenzo in Lucina**
San Lorenzo in Lucina is first mentioned in 366, at the time of Pope Damasus's election in Lucinis. The name of the church probably comes from a Christian woman, named Lucina, who offered her house for worship to the Christian community. The church was linked to the catacomb of Saint Valentine, where an inscription relating to a *Titulis Licinae* was found. Pope Paschal II (1099-18) rebuilt the church as a basilica, adding a portico and bell-tower. At that time the church followed the plan of a basilica with three naves. In the fifteenth, seventeenth and nineteenth centuries, the church was altered many times: it has now evolved into a plan with a single dome and chapels.

**Brief history of the Church
of Santa Susanna**
Between the third and fourth centuries a church was built on the site of the home of Saint Gabinus, father of Saint Susanna, next door to the house of his brother, Gaius; hence the topographic denomination *ad duas domos*, 'at the two houses'. In 796 Pope Leo III modernised it. In 1603 the church was rebuilt and given a new façade by Carlo Maderno. In 1587 Pope Sixtus V granted the church of Santa Susanna to the Community of Santa Susanna, a Cistercian order of nuns who followed the rule of Saint Benedict. The Cistercian Order is still based at the church. The church also functions as the church for the American community in Rome.

Susanna
In Hebrew the name means 'lily',
the flower symbolising purity.

her alone, the men came out from their hiding place with the intention of seducing her. They told her that if she did not give herself to them, they would tell everybody that she had been seen committing adultery. Adultery was considered a serious crime and was punishable by death. Susanna refused them and the elders duly denounced her as an adulteress. She was found guilty and sentenced to death. But just before her execution the prophet Daniel, who represents Justice, cross-examined the elders and exposed their lie. Susanna was proclaimed innocent and freed.

Outside the church:
The representation of the head of the saint, over the main portal, in the tympanum, low relief
The head of Saint Susanna is a graphic reminder of her martyrdom.

*A day in the life
of a Cistercian nun*
*The day starts at 5 a.m. and it is
divided into:*
*community and personal prayer,
manual labour,*
lectio divina, *meditation on the
Holy Scripture and on daily life;
the day ends at 9 p.m.*

Inside the church:
☞ **Six scenes from the Lives of Saint Susanna and Susanna of the Old Testament,** in the central nave, frescoes by Baldassare Croce, 1595
Painted to look like tapestries, the frescoes tell the tale of the Susanna of the Old Testament. The two Susannas are often compared because they both succeeded in keeping their virtue. For this reason, they have come to symbolise the Church's triumph over paganism and persecution.
☞ **Saint Susanna Refusing to Worship Jupiter,** on the curve of the apse, right-hand side, fresco by Paris Nogari, 16th century
☞ **Saint Susanna Threatened by Galerius,** on the curve of the apse, left-hand side, fresco by Nebbia, 16th century
☞ **Beheading of Saint Susanna,** on the main altar, painting, by Tommaso Laureti, 16th century
☞ **Relics of Saint Susanna, Saint Gabinus, Saint Felicita and of her son, Silenus,** in the crypt, inside the altar
☞ **The House of Saint Susanna,** in the nun's sacristy, mosaic

Church of Santa Lucia in Selci

patroness of the blind

Lucia came from a wealthy family and was raised by her widowed mother, Euthychia. Lucia offered her virginity to God without telling her mother who arranged for her to marry a young non-Christian man. Lucia refused but her mother insisted. The older, woman, however was suddenly struck by an unknown illness and Lucia urged her mother to pray on the tomb of Saint Agatha. Euthychia's prayers were successful and she recovered. Lucia then revealed her desire to remain a virgin and to donate all her wealth to the poor. Her mother understood and accepted her decision.

When Lucia's suitor saw her distributing all her possessions to the needy his suspicions were aroused. He went to the governor and accused Lucia of being a Christian. She was ordered to work in a brothel, but God rooted her to the spot so that even a team of oxen could not drag her away. She was savagely tortured and eventually, in 304, died from her wounds. Saint Lucia is often represented with her eyeballs on a dish perhaps because during her torture her eyes were plucked out. Her name derives from the Latin *luceo*, meaning "light"; she is often depicted holding a lamp.

Brief history of the Church of Saint Lucia in Selci

The church of San Lucia in Selci was originally referred to as *in orphea*, a name that refers to a fountain dedicated to the poet Orpheus. In the Middle Ages it was renamed *in silice* (meaning 'stones') to commemorate the fact that the street on which this church was built was one of the first in Rome to be paved. The church was founded by Pope Symmachus (498-514) and confirmed as a *diaconia*, probably by Honorius I (625-38). At the end of the eighth century Leo III had it modernised. The monastery was added later. Since 1568 it has been a convent of Augustian nuns. In the seventeenth century the church was once again modernised by Maderno and Borromini. It is now considered an exemplar of Roman baroque art.

☞ **Martyrdom of Saint Lucia,** first altar on the right, by Giovanni Lanfranco, 17th century

☞ **Glory of Saint Lucia,** on the vault, fresco, 19th century

This fresco replaced a sixteenth-century one by Giovanni Antonio Lelli.

☞ **Four golden statues, among them one of Saint Lucia,** in four niches, below the ciborium, golden statues

☞ **Communion of Saint Lucia,** in the nuns' choir, painting, by Baccio Ciarpi, after 1617

This is one of six paintings that depict different saints. Saint Lucia is represented kneeling in the act of receiving the Eucharist. A putto is hovering above holding a crown and the palm of martyrdom.

Brief history of the Church of San Lorenzo in Fonte

In 1543 a Spanish dominican cardinal, Juan Alvarez de Toledo, had the church built over the prison in which Saint Lawrence had been incarcerated. Some historians believe that an oratory dedicated to Saint Hippolytus existed here before, as stated in an epigraph of the fourth century, but that it fell into ruins by 1350. In 1628 Pope Urban VIII Barberini commissioned the architect Domenico Castelli to enlarge the church.

Church of San Lorenzo in Fonte

In 258, at the catacombs of San Callisto, Lawrence was captured and tortured by some of Emperor Valerian's soldiers. He was miraculously unhurt and Hippolytus, a Roman centurion, took him to prison where he met a blind men named Lucillus. Lawrence comforted him and baptised him with water from a spring. As soon as Lucillus was baptised, he regained his eyesight. Upon witnessing this miracle, Hippolytus converted to Christianity and asked Lawrence to baptise him together with his family.

Hippolytus was allegedly martyred with Lawrence. This may explain why the church is dedicated to both of them.

☞ **Representation of Saint Lawrence's grid iron,** next to the entrance, inlaid in the floor

The representation was made in remembrance of the saint's martyrdom. The iron grid itself, on which Lawrence was burnt, is kept in the church of San Lorenzo in Lucina.

☞ **The Baptism of Saint Hippolytus and his Family by Saint Lawrence,** main altar, painting by Andrea Camassei, 17th century

☞ **Martyrdom of Saint Lawrence,** right-hand side of the main altar, painting by Marco Caprinozzi, 18th century

☞ **Saint Lawrence Distributing Bread to the Poor,** left-hand side of the main altar, painting by Marco Caprinozzi, 18th century

Prison of Saint Lawrence

access to the underground prison can be gained via a small staircase

The room is circular with a small well from which Lawrence took water to baptise Lucillus and Hippolytus.

Fonte

It means 'spring' in Italian and probably refers to old thermal springs. According to tradition, this was the spring Lawrence used to baptise Lucillus, Hippolytus and his family.

☞ **Saint Lawrence in the Act of Baptising Hippolytus,** on the well, marble relief, 17th century

The marble relief is on the architrave of the two columns around the well.

Church of Santi Vito e Modesto

Vitus's father used to beat him to punish him for refusing to pray to pagan idols. Vitus was a Christian and, according to an old legend, he performed several miracles in the name of the Lord during his lifetime.

When a demon possessing Emperor Diocletian's son demanded Vitus's intervention to set the boy free, Vitus was taken to the emperor. Diocletian asked him how he could help his child and Vitus answered that he did not have any power himself because only the Lord was powerful. As he spoke, he rested his hands on the boy's head and the demon left.

After this amazing performance, the emperor said to Vitus, 'My child, have pity on yourself and make sacrifices to the gods'. Vitus refused and Diocletian sent him to prison along with his teacher, Modestus. Vitus was then tortured, but nothing seemed to hurt him. Enraged, Diocletian ordered him to be hanged, while Modestus and Vitus's nanny, Crescenzia, were tortured. As this was happening, the earth suddenly started to tremble and some statues of pagan gods fell to the ground, breaking into pieces.

☞ *Pietra scellerata* (the evil stone), on the right-hand wall, behind a grille, Roman stone
According to tradition, this was the stone that was used to kill Modestus and Crescenzia and many more Christians at the time of Diocletian's persecution. The stone is believed to have miraculous powers; it can cure the bites of rabid dogs.
☞ **Virgin and Child with Modesto, Crescenzia, Vitus, Sebastian and Margherita,** beyond the evil stone, on the right-hand wall, on an altar, fresco, by Antonazzo Romano, 1483

Church of Santa Bibiana

During the brief period of persecution when Julian the Apostate (361-63) was emperor, Bibiana was flogged to death along with her mother, Dafrosa, her father, Flavianus, and her sister, Demetria, because they had refused to make sacrifices to idols. She continues to be a popular saint in Rome.

Brief history of the Church of Santi Vito e Modesto
The church was first called San Vito al Macello because of its proximity to the abattoirs. It is first mentioned in the biography of the Pope Leo III (795-816). The church was neglected for many years until Pope Sixtus IV della Rovere restored and rebuilt it in 1477. After this renaissance, the church of San Vito e Modesto again fell into disrepair. This necessitated yet another restoration in 1834, done by Pietro Camporese il Giovane, and a rebuilding in 1901 commissioned by Cardinal Francesco Cassetta. This included a new façade by the architect Attilio Ricci.

Brief history of the Church of Santa Bibiana

According to the *Liber Pontificalis*, the church was founded in 467 by Pope Saint Simplicius on the very site where the martyr lived and died. In the sixth century a cemetery known as the Cemetery of Anastasius was attached to the church. A large number of martyrs were buried there. For the 1625 Jubilee, Pope Urban VIII asked Bernini to redesign and modernise the church.

☞ **Column of the Flagellation,** inside the church, next to the entrance, on the left, a red column

According to tradition, this is the column where the saint was tied and flogged to death with leaded cords.

☞ **Relics of Bibiana, her sister, Demetria, and their mother, Dafrosa,** below the main altar, in an alabaster urn

The container was found below the altar during the modernisation works of 1624. It is believed to come from the baths of the imperial residence of Trajan.

☞ **Saint Bibiana,** in a niche above the altar, statue by Bernini, 1624-26

Bernini's sculpture depicts Saint Bibiana on the verge of death, standing beside a column and holding the cords with which she was flagellated.

☞ **Scenes of the Life of Saint Bibiana,** in the central nave, on the right-hand side, frescoes by Agostino Ciampelli, late 16th, or early 17th, century

The scenes represented are: Saint Bibiana given to the beasts; the burial of the saint; the building of the church.

☞ **Scenes from the Life of Saint Bibiana,** in the central nave, on the left-hand side, frescoes by Pietro da Cortona, 17th century

The scenes are: Saint Bibiana being sentenced to death by Apronianus; Rufina attempts to undermine Saint Bibiana's faith; the flagellation of the saint.

Saints for Intercession and Protection

Our journey now takes us to those churches built to celebrate saints and to honour them as protectors and intercessors between people and God. Our guides are the tales of their miracles, of their faith and of their exemplary Christian lives.

Durita cordis vestri saxa trahere meruist.
'You deserve nothing better than to drag stones'.
(Saint Clement to the blinded soldiers)

Basilica of San Clemente

Pope Clement was a Roman citizen of Jewish descent who had been a disciple of Saint Paul. Saint Peter nominated him bishop and, in 90, Clement became pope. He was responsible for the conversion of Theodora, the wife of the Roman prefect Sisinnus, who allegedly made a vow of chastity.

Sisinnus blamed his wife's decision on Clement's preaching and ordered his soldiers to arrest him. The pope was celebrating mass in a catacomb when Sisinnus and his soldiers made their move. God intervened by blinding them and corrupting their speech. In their confusion, the soldiers mistakenly grabbed a column instead of Clement. As they wrestled with it, under the amused eyes of the Christian congregation, they encouraged each other, uttering distorted, incomprehensible sentences. Pope Clement, watching as they passed in front of him, told them that, indeed, they deserved nothing better than to drag stones. Eventually, Sisinnus recovered his sight and speech with the help of his wife.

In 97 Clement was exiled to Crimea where he was sentenced to hard labour in the marble caves. There he preached the Gospel to 2,000 Christians. Emperor Trajan, outraged by this, demanded in vain that Clement apostatise. As punishment for his disobedience, Clement was thrown into the Black Sea with an anchor tied to his neck. On each anniversary of this event, the waters of the sea were said to part, allowing Christians to build a chapel to house his relics. Later, Christian pilgrims visited the site on the day of the miracle and honoured the martyr in a procession around the chapel.

Anchor

The anchor is Clement's symbol because it played a part in his martyrdom. In Christian symbolism, the anchor usually represents hope.

☞ **Episodes from the Life of Saint Clement,** in the main nave, above the cornice, on the left-hand side, framed frescoes by various artists, 18th century

The scenes represented are: Saint Clement offers the veil to Flavia Domitilla, by Pietro de Pietri; Saint Clement in Crimea, by Antonio Grecolini; the transfer of the body of Saint Clement from the Sea of Azov to the present church in 867-68, by Giovanni Odazzi. The framed frescoes are embellished with stucco decorations. On the opposite side on the right are episodes from the Life of Saint Ignatius of Antioch.

☞ **Saint Clement's tomb,** under the high altar

The tomb is said to contain the remains of Saint Clement and of Saint Ignatius.

☞ **Saint Clement's symbol: the anchor,** on the canopy of the high altar

The canopy may belong to the early fourth-century church.

☞ **The cross,** in the apse, mosaic, 1120

The cross is decorated with twelve doves to symbolise the Apostles. It is flanked by the Virgin Mary, the Apostle Saint John grieving for Christ's death, and small figures. The composition is enriched with foliage scrolls and with small spirits and birds. The Doctors of the Church are also represented, together with people busy in their daily tasks. Above the cross is the Hand of God. The whole composition symbolises the Tree of Life.

☞ **The miracle of Saint Clement**, in the old church below ground, on the wall on the right-hand side, frescoes, 11th century

Beno de Rapiza, his wife Maria Marcellina, and their sons, Clemente and Altilia, went on a pilgrimage to Saint Clement's chapel. One of the boys became lost when the waters closed over the chapel. A year later, Maria Marcellina went back to the Crimea to look for him. When the Black Sea parted she saw her son alive and well. The story of this miracle is depicted in the Rapiza chapel along with the story of the apocryphal 'Acts of Saint Clement'. The frescoes were donated by the family of Beno and Maria Marcellina to thank Saint Clement for saving their son. All four are depicted; the sons carry votive candles as a sign of thanks for the miracle received.

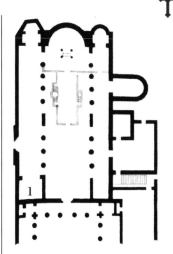

Chapel of Caterina d'Alessandria
first chapel on the left-hand side of the aisle **(1)**

Inside the church of San Clemente is a chapel dedicated to another martyr, Catherine of Alexandria. It is said that she was a princess of great erudition who, after being baptised, saw in a vision that she was to become the mystic bride of Christ. According to one legend, Emperor Maxentius desired her and tried to convince her to break her vow of chastity. Unable to succeed, he called in a group of philosophers to persuade her with logic. Catherine convinced them, as well as Maxentius' wife, that her decision was right. Furious, Maxentius put the philosophers to death. For Catherine he reserved a special instrument of torture, a wooden wheel studded with spikes, to which she was tied.

While she was being tortured lightning struck and burnt the wheel. Catherine was saved but soon afterwards she was beheaded. After her death, angels came down to collect her body and they carried her all the way to Mount Sinai where a sanctuary was built in her memory.

☞ **Life of Saint Catherine of Alexandria and Saint Ambrose,** fresco by Masolino da Panicale, 15th century

On the left wall, the fresco portrays the highlights of Saint Catherine's life: refusing to adore pagan idols, defending Christianity among philosophers in Alexandria, converting the emperor's wife, and martyrdom. On the right, the fresco tells the story of Saint Ambrose, a learned Doctor of the Church.

Church of Santi Bonifacio e Alessio

Alexis was born into a Roman patrician family. His father, Eufemiano, was a Roman senator. On his wedding day, Alexis decided to leave his bride and dedicate his life to helping the sick and poor in Edessa, in northern Mesopotamia. After a while, he returned secretly to Rome and took employment as a servant in his father's house. He lived there in a hole under a ladder, for 17 years, until he died.

Brief history of the Chapel of Santa Caterina
In 1427 the titular cardinal of the basilica, Branda Castiglioni, wanted to designate a chapel to honour Saint Catherine of Alexandria. He had founded a *collegium* for studies and it seemed appropriate, given her interest in learning and rational discourse, to dedicate a chapel to honour her.

The legend of Sant'Alessio and the Opera
The story of the saint's life is detailed in a fresco in the lower basilica of San Clemente, in the middle nave. In the seventeenth century Stefano Landi wrote a short opera about it using a libretto written by Cardinal Rospigliosi. This opera was first performed, on 8th February 1634, in the theatre of Palazzo Barberini. In the eleventh century the legend of Sant'Alessio inspired a French poem, 'La vie de Saint Alexis'.

Brief history of the Church of Santi Bonifacio e Alessio

The original church was built between the third and fourth centuries to house the remains of a patrician named Boniface who was martyred in Tarsus. In the sixth century the church was enlarged and embellished and the relics of Saint Alexis were deposited next to Saint Boniface's house. A community settled in the church in the tenth century under the auspices of Archbishop Sergius of Damascus, who had fled here from the Saracens. The community was divided into two groups: Greek members, who followed the Rule of Saint Basil, and Latin ones, who followed the Rule of Saint Benedict. Also in the tenth century, Pope Benedict VII gave the church the title of basilica. In 1426 the Gerolamini monks took possession of the church and, in 1582, they restored it. Another restoration took place in the eighteenth century, during which the façade was renewed. In 1846 the Gerolamini monks were replaced by the Somaschi fathers who continued the work of Saint Jerome. The bell-tower, dates back to the twelfth or thirteenth century.

According to legend, the moment Alexis died all the bells in Rome started ringing and Saint Peter's voice resounded: 'Look for the man of God to make him pray for Rome'. Alexis' dead body was then discovered under the ladder. In his hands was a scroll telling the story of his life.

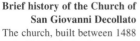 **Saint Alexis' relics**, under the main altar

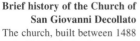 **Saint Alexis' ladder,** first chapel on the left from the entrance

This is the ladder under which Alexis lived and died. Under the ladder is a statue of Alexis dressed as a pilgrim and lying on a rough mat.

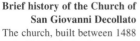 **The well of Saint Alexis' house,** on the left-hand side of the church

This is the well that belonged to the house of Alexis' father. The rims of the well are worn away by the rope of the bucket. Here Alexis, as a humble servant, washed his family's clothes for years and years.

Church of San Giovanni Decollato

Brief history of the Church of San Giovanni Decollato

The church, built between 1488 and 1504, is the headquarters of the Florentine Archconfraternity of Mercy.

John the Baptist was the forerunner of Christ. He was the son of Elizabeth, the Virgin's cousin, and her husband, Zacharias. As well as preaching he baptised people, including Christ, in the river Jordan. He performed the ritual of baptism under the guidance of the Holy Spirit.

During a banquet, Herod asked Salome to dance for him and promised her whatever she wanted in exchange. After the dance Herod's wife persuaded Salome to ask for John the Baptist's head because John had rebuked Herod for marrying his brother's wife. John was decapitated and his head delivered to Salome on a platter.

John represents the link between the Old and the New Testaments. He is the last of the prophets in the style of the Old Testament and the first of the saints in the New Testament.

☞ **Beheading of Saint John,** on the main altar, painting by Vasari, 1553

☞ **Seven manholes,** in the cloister

Bodies of the condemned were taken through these holes. One hole was designated especially for women. Above these there is the inscription: 'Domine cum veneris iudicare noli nos condemnare`. (God, judge us with mercy and do not condemn us). The cloister was built between 1535 and 1555 and in 1600 it was rebuilt by Pope Clement VIII.

☞ **Historic room,** through a steep entrance, at the bottom of the cloister

In this room there are mementoes of Roman justice: the basket where the head of Beatrice Cenci was placed, the hood of Giordano Bruno and many wooden tablets, featuring sacred images, that used to be kissed by those condemned to death. Capital executions were held in the nearby Piazza dei Cerchi up to 1870.

Oratory of San Giovanni Decollato
on the left of the main entrance of the church

☞ **Scenes from the Life of John the Baptist,** frescoes by Jacopino del Conte and Francesco Salviati, 1535-53

To the right of the entrance: John the Baptist preaching, by del Conte; the birth of Saint John and the

Ritual

On the 29th August, Pope Paul III (1534-49) used to give freedom to one of the condemned. The lucky person was then walked in a procession along the streets. The members of the confraternity used to collect the hoods of those who had been hanged and these were burnt in a pyre on the 24th June, the traditional day of Saint John's Bonfire.

Feast day: 24th June
In old times Saint John's feast day used to be on the 29th August, date of the finding of the saint's cranium in Syria. Up to 1870 the cranium was in the church of San Giovanni Capite, today the cranium is in the private chapel of the pope

Arciconfraternita della Misericordia

The church of San Giovanni Decollato has been linked since 1490 with a Florentine confraternity who covered their faces with a black hood. It was considered an act of humility to conceal their identities while performing pious or charitable acts. They tried to make condemned prisoners repent before execution and gave them a decent burial. This is the Roman branch of the Florentine confraternity and it was instituted by Pope Innocent VIII (1484-92). Their headquarters consist of a church, an oratory, and a convent with a cloister. Today this is still the headquarters of the Arciconfraternita of the Misericordia.

According to the *Liber Pontificalis*, the church was built by Pope Leo II (682-83), in honour of Saint Sebastian, in an area called the Velabro. Originally a marsh, it was considered to be the site where the twins Romulus and Remus were raised by a she-wolf. The dedication to Saint George was added later by Pope Zacharias (741-52), a Greek, who had Saint George's head brought back from Cappadocia. At that time the Velabro area was inhabited by a wealthy Greek community, which included a Byzantine colony in the Palatine. Saint George was also the patron of the Byzantine army located near by.

Code of Saint George

The Code of Saint George describes the lives of two saints: Saint George and Saint Peter Celestine. It was written by Jacopo Stefaneschi at the beginning of the fourth century and was kept in the church. The book is illustrated with beautiful miniatures by the artist Simone Martini, known as 'Master of the Code of Saint George'. The illuminated book is now kept in the Vatican Library.

Feast day: 23rd April

Rituals

The church used to house the ancient banner called the *Gonfalone di San Giorgio* ('the standard of Saint George'). In 1966 Pope Paul VI donated it to the City Hall of Rome where it is kept, in the Palazzo Senatorio, in the hall of the flags. On the feast day of Saint George it used to be customary to carry the second-century banner in a procession of the municipal authorities of the church, who went to San Giorgio to listen to a mass in honour of the saint. After the service they donated a silver chalice. This ritual is no longer performed.

Visitation, by Salviati; *the announcement of the birth of John the Baptist*, by del Conte. On the opposite wall: *the beheading of John the Baptist and the dance of Salome*, by Pirro Ligorio; *John the Baptist made prisoner*, by Battista Franco. To the left of the entrance: *the baptism of Christ*, by del Conte. In the fresco of the Visitation the bearded character allegedly represents Michelangelo Buonarroti, who was a member of the Arciconfraternita Misericordia.

☞ **Deposition flanked by Saints Bartholomew and Andrew,** altarpiece, by del Conte and Salviati, 16th century

The Deposition scene is by Jacopino del Conte and the saints are by Salviati.

Church of San Giorgio in Velabro
patron saint of England

According to an old legend, George, a knight from Cappadocia in Asia Minor, rescued a maiden from a dragon by killing it with a spear. Since then Saint George has come to personify victory over evil. The dragon symbolised the threat of paganism and Saint George, the defence of Christianity.

George had to survive many trials at the hands of his enemies, such as being forced to drink poison and being stretched on a wheel. Only his faith kept him alive. Finally he was beheaded in 303, during Diocletian's reign.

☞ **Saint George's head, his sword and part of the banner,** in the *confessio*, under the altar

These relics were brought here by Pope Zacharias (741-52).

☞ **Christ, the Madonna, Saint George, Saint Peter and Saint Sebastian,** in the apse, fresco attributed to Cavallini, 13th century

Church of San Saba
Chapel of San Nicola di Bari
in the truncated fourth aisle

A father of three daughters, anxious that he would not be able to afford their dowries and not knowing what else to do, encouraged them into a life of vice. Nicholas intervened: one night he threw a bag of gold through their window, thus saving the three girls from a life of prostitution.

For his generosity and because he appeared at night, Saint Nicholas came to be associated with Father Christmas. In Rome children can meet Father Christmas at the Christmas fair in Piazza Navona.

☞ Tale of Saint Nicholas and the Three Spinsters, on the walls, frescoes, Maestro di San Saba, 13th century

The other frescoes show: Pope Gregory the Great (590-604) on a throne flanked by two saints, the Virgin enthroned with Saint Andrew and Saint Sabas.

Brief history of the Church of San Saba
According to legend, the church was built where the house of Saint Silvia, mother of Pope Saint Gregory the Great (590-604), once stood. Silvia grew vegetables and sent a selection of them to her son, who would eat nothing else. In the seventh century, after the Arabs invaded Syria and Jordan, oriental monks who had fled from the Arabs built a monastery on the site. They dedicated the monastery to Sabas, the founder of their religious order. In 768 the antipope Constantine was imprisoned here.

Church of Santa Francesca Romana
also known as Santa Maria Nova
patroness of motorists

Feast day of Santa Francesca Romana: 9th March

In 1396 Francesca married Lorenzo Ponziani. She had three children, two of whom died very young. After this personal tragedy, Francesca dedicated her life to helping the poor and sick.

On 15th August 1425, in the church of Santa Maria Nova, she founded a society of women dedicated to pious tasks, under the rule of Saint Benedict of the Monte Oliveto. It was called the Order of Oblates.

In 1608 she was canonised and the church of Santa Maria Nova was renamed the church of Santa Francesca Romana.

Ritual
On 9th March car-owners make a pilgrimage to the church to have their vehicles blessed.

Founded in 1433 by Saint
Francesca of Rome, the monastery
was originally in one of the houses
of the Clarelli family. It was
subsequently extended to the Tower
of the Mirrors (*Torre degli
Specchi*), named for the shape of its
windows which resemble mirrors.

☞ **Saint Francesca's body,** under the main altar

Monastery of Tor de' Specchi
via del Teatro Marcello 40

On 25th March 1433, the day of the
Annunciation, the house of the Oblates was
inaugurated in the monastery of Tor de' Specchi. In
1436 Francesca moved there, having looked after her
sick husband. Francesca's room and monastery can be
visited on her feast day, 9th March.

☞ **Saint Francesca, Saint Benedict and the
Madonna,** over the entrance door of the monastery,
1600

☞ **Holy stairs,** beyond the entrance

*Originally outside the monastery, this is a steep
staircase decorated with frescoes.*

☞ **Twenty-five episodes of the Life of Saint
Francesca,** on the first floor in the oratory, by an
anonymous Roman painter, 1468

*Each episode comes with a caption in vulgaris that
explains the scene. The scenes are: the oblation of the
saint and her sisters in Santa Maria Nova; the Virgin
greets Saint Francesca in Heaven and Saint Peter gives
Francesca communion; the Virgin protects Saint
Francesca and her sisters; the saint receives Baby Jesus
in her arms; the apparition of the Redeemer to the
saint; the apparition of her son, Evangelista,
accompanied by the angel; the miracle on the bridge;
Francesca restores the woodcutter to health; she
restores Jacovello to health; she restores life to a
drowned child; she heals Stephen's head wounds; she
brings a battered man back to life; she gives speech
back to Camilla; the miracle of the wine; the miracle of
the wheat; Francesca cures the hunchback; she cures
Paul, who is fatally wounded; Francesca's ecstasy in
the vineyard; the saint cures Janni; Francesca receives
communion in Santa Maria in Trastevere; she
multiplies the bread for her sisters, the Oblates; she
restores life to the drowned Paul; Francesca in the
vineyard; the death of Saint Francesca; the funeral of
Saint Francesca in Santa Maria Nova.*

*Cubiculum in quo quatuor annis,
Francisca vitam duxit.*
(The cell in which Francesca lived
for four years)

☞ **Saint Francesca against the demons and other miracles,** in the refectory, frescoes, 1485

☞ **The chapel,** at the end of the corridor, on the left

This chapel was the room in which Saint Francesca lived from 1436 until her death four years later. Some of her belongings are stored inside a cupboard, on the left of the chapel.

Basilica of San Marco dei Veneziani
patron saint of Venice

The Christian community in Rome purportedly asked Mark to record Peter's teachings because the Apostle did not speak Greek. While living in a house on the Roman Capitol, he wrote the Gospel that Saint Peter revised and approved.

☞ **Saint Mark the Evangelist,** in the atrium, above the door, low relief, attributed to Isaia da Pisa, 1464

☞ **Rampant lion, symbol of Saint Mark the Evangelist,** on the ceiling, in the coat of arms of Pope Paul II (1464-71)

Paul II was the titular cardinal of the church from 1451. He was responsible for a programme of refurbishment that included the reconstruction of the new roof, the restoration and embellishment of the ceiling, the walls of the central nave and the main apse, and the construction of the external portico with a loggia.

☞ **Scenes from the life of Pope Saint Mark,** along the walls of the central nave, left-hand side, by various artists, 17th and 18th century

Starting from the entrance the scenes are: the crowning of Pope Saint Mark, by Gu.Courtois; Saint James the Less, by C. Monaldi; another scene from Pope Saint Mark's life, Saint Mark approves the project of the basilica; Saint Bartholomew, by Jean B. Le Doux; Pope Saint Mark consecrates an altar of the basilica, by F. Allegrini; Saint James the Great, by Jean B. Le Doux; transfer of the body of Saint Mark to Rome, by Fabrizio Chiari.

☞ **Pope Saint Mark's body,** under the main altar, in a porphyry urn

☞ **Saint Mark the Evangelist and Pope Saint Mark**

Feast day : 25th April

Brief history of the Basilica of San Marco dei Veneziani

Pope Mark founded the church in 336 and dedicated it to his namesake, Saint Mark the Evangelist. It was built over a *titulus,* one of the 25 Roman churches of early Christianity. By the ninth century it required rebuilding, which was commissioned by Gregory IV. Cardinal Pietro Bardo, a Venetian patrician, became cardinal of this church. When he became Pope Paul II (1464-71), Bardo designated it the church of Rome's Venetian community. St Mark the Evangelist's remains are kept in Venice, in the basilica of San Marco.

ALTARE SS APOSTOLORVM

As Papias considered Saint Mark the Evangelist the interpreter of Saint Peter

Brief history of the Church of Santa Maria Sopra Minerva
This church was built to honour the Madonna on the site where three ancient temples stood: the *Minervium*, built by Pompey the Great in honour of the goddess Minerva Calcida; the *Iseum*, dedicated to Isis; and the *Serapeum*, dedicated to Serapis. The name *sopra Minerva*, or 'above Minerva', refers to the first of these temples. A small church is known to have existed on this site since the eighth century. At the request of Pope Zacharias (741-52), the church was looked after by a community of Basilian nuns, refugees in Rome from the East. By 1255, both the church and the nearby convent belonged to the Benedictine nuns of Campus Martius; a year later the nuns were transferred elsewhere and the nunnery was given to the Dominican preachers who later obtained the church as well. The magnificent Gothic church that occupies the site today was begun in 1280, probably at the request of the Dominican Order. Over the centuries it has been added to many times, most radically in 1848-55 when the restorers attempted to enrich the interior by adding fake marble and inappropriate pictorial decoration to the walls and vaults. While the church is renowned for its sepulchre of Saint Catherine, it is also rich in images devoted to the Virgin Mary.

and Pope Gregory IV with other saints, in the apse, mosaics, tenth century
☞ **Saint Mark the Evangelist,** in the sacristy, fresco, by Melozzo da Forlì, 15th century

Chapel of the Sacrament
at the end of the right-hand nave
☞ **Pope Saint Mark,** on the altar, by Melozzo da Forlì, 15th century

Church of Santa Maria sopra Minerva
Saint Catherine, patroness of Siena

Catherine, who came from Siena, joined the Dominican Order in 1365. During her three years of silence she contemplated God and spoke only to her confessor. Prayers and meditation filled her life. In 1375, while she was praying in front of a crucifix in a chapel in Pisa, rays of light beamed from Christ's wounds and she was blessed with the stigmata, the marks corresponding to the wounds inflicted on Christ by the nails of the Crucifixion. When pestilence reached Tuscany, Catherine devoted herself to curing the sick.

In 1376 she went to Avignon to plead with Pope Gregory XI to come back to Rome. Catherine and the pope communicated with each other through an interpreter who translated the Sienese language spoken by Catherine into Latin and she eventually managed to persuade him to return.

During Urban VI's papacy Catherine moved to Rome, where she led an exemplary life and wrote an essay on the Annunciation, as well as six treatises and many letters. She is a Doctor of the Church.

☞ **Saint Catherine's relics,** main altar, in a sarcophagus, by Isaia da Pisa, 15th century
The sarcophagus contains the saint's headless remains. The head was donated to the city of Siena in 1385.

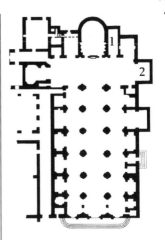

Chapel of the Madonna del Rosario or Capranica
right transept, next to the altar (1)

☞ **Madonna and Child with Saints Dominic and Catherine,** over the main altar, painting, 16th century

☞ **Scenes from the Life of Saint Catherine,** along the walls, frescoes by Giovanni de Vecchi, 16th century

The relics of the saint were kept in this chapel for more than four centuries until they were moved to the main altar.

Carafa Chapel
also known as Chapel of the Virgin and Saint Thomas Aquinas, eighth chapel in the right (south) transept (2)
patron saint of students

Saint Thomas Aquinas was a Dominican friar and theologian who lived in the thirteenth century. He attempted to combine Aristotelian philosophy and Catholic thought. His life was devoted to writing and teaching to prevent heresy. He taught in Cologne and Paris, among other places. In 1261 Pope Urban IV asked him to come to Rome to teach theology. He wrote a treatise called *Summa Theology.*

Feast day of Saint Thomas Aquinas: 28th January

For my mouth shall speak truth; and wickedness is an abomination to my lips. (Prov. 8:7)

Brief history of the Carafa Chapel

Cardinal Oliviero Carafa commissioned the decoration of the chapel from Filippino Lippi. It was to be dedicated to Saint Thomas Aquinas, who would function as the cardinal's intercessor with the Virgin, as shown in the image above the altar, where the saint is represented in the act of introducing the cardinal to the Virgin Mary.

The chapel was built between 1489 and 1493 on the site of the chapel of the Rustici.

☞ **Cardinal Carafa is Introduced by Saint Thomas to the Virgin of the Annunciation,** above the altar, frescoes by Filippino Lippi, 1489

Oliviero Carafa was made cardinal in 1472 and, in 1481, became cardinal protector of the Dominican Order. Carafa, shown in profile, is wrapped in his red cardinal's robe and is kneeling as if he were himself present at the moment of the Annunciation. The Virgin, so beautifully and elegantly depicted, has her hands raised as though to bless the cardinal, although her eyes are looking to the side towards the angelic messenger.

☞ **Scenes from the Life of Saint Thomas Aquinas,** right-hand wall, frescoes by Filippino Lippi, 1489-93

The fresco above represents Saint Thomas in prayer, with the Crucifix congratulating the saint on his ability to relate the story of Jesus' death correctly. The fresco below depicts the triumph of Saint Thomas over error. The saint is here represented on his throne holding a book in his left hand and pointing with the right one to the error that has now been corrected. The four female figures are: Grammar, Rhetoric, Dialectic and Philosophy. In the foreground we see Thomas's disciples and the statue of Marcus Aurelius.

Feast day of Saint Catherine: 29ᵗʰ April

Saint Catherine's Room
through the sacristy

In 1637 the room where Saint Catherine died, on 29th April 1380, was transported from Via Santa Chiara 14 (the vault is still in situ) to the church of Santa Maria sopra Minerva by order of Cardinal Antonio Barberini.

☞ **Saint Catherine,** outside the room, marble relief by Paolo, 1380

The relief was commissioned by Beato Raimondo da Capua.

☞ **Crucifixion,** main altar, fresco by Antoniazzo Romano, 15th century

This fresco and the others along the walls were taken from Catherine's room. They show: Saints Onophrius, Augustine and Jerome; Saints Lucia and Apollonia; Saint John the Baptist; the Pietà; Saint Jerome.

Prayer
Saint Catherine, you, who had the privilege of being similar to Christ in your sufferings to save our souls, you, who are consumed by the love of peace, pray for us all with the strength of your faith and love so that we can follow His will to give us peace. Saint Catherine, intercede for us, pilgrims of our time

Church of San Luigi dei Francesi
patron saint of the city of Paris

In the thirteenth century Saint Louis IX was king of France. He is remembered for having fought in the Crusades in Egypt and Palestine. He brought back several relics from the Holy Land, including Christ's crown of thorns and part of the true Cross, now housed in Sainte Chapelle in Paris. He was canonised in 1217.

Brief history of the Church of San Luigi dei Francesi

This is the church of the French community and was founded in 1518 at the time when France was fighting against Spain for power over Italy. Its construction was completed in 1589. Many Frenchmen are buried in this church.

Outside the church:

☞ **Shield linking symbols of Rome and France,** on the façade

☞ **St Louis,** on the façade, statue, 18th century

Chapel of Santa Cecilia
second chapel on the righ (1)

When Cecilia was about to get married she entered the house of Valerius, her groom. Music - *'cantantibus organis'* - filled the air and she prayed to God that she might keep her soul and body pure.

Saint Cecilia is the patroness of musicians and is invoked before concerts and important performances.

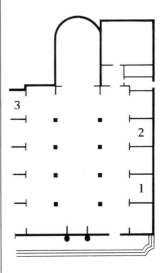

☞ **Scenes from the Life of Saint Cecilia,** fresco by Domenichino, 17th century

In 1614 the priest of the diocese of Noyon asked Domenichino (1581-1641) to decorate the chapel with fresco scenes from the life of the martyr Saint Cecilia, whose remains had been discovered at the end of the sixteenth century. The story is told on the walls and the vault.

On the right wall, the saint is shown distributing her clothes and wealth to the needy. On the left wall is a representation of her martyrdom, with the image of an angel carrying the crown and the palm, both symbols of her martyrdom. On the vault there are three other episodes depicted: Cecilia and Valerius receiving a crown of flowers, Cecilia's refusal to worship pagan idols; and the saint in glory.

☞ **Saint Cecilia,** altarpiece, painting, copy by Guido Reni, 1599

Ritual

To request her protection during a concert performance, or for a music examination, the petitioner must write the name of the saint on a white ribbon and his or her name on a yellow ribbon. The two ribbons must then be tied to a green candle in which the petitioner must hold two laurel leaves. When the musician succeeds in his or her task, the ribbons and the candle must be buried in a big plant pot filled with pink flowers, or in a garden. Ashes from the burnt laurels are to be kept in a small wooden box. If the aid of Saint Cecilia is requested several times, it is advisable to collect all the ashes from the burnt leaves in the same box.

Organum
Organum in Latin means any musical instrument, but in the sixteenth century artists identified it with the contemporary organ, especially the portable one.

Set your mind on God's kingdom before everything else. (Matt. 6:33)

Cardinal Paolo Emilio Sfondrato commissioned Guido Reni to copy Raphael's painting of Saint Cecilia, now in the Pinacoteca Nazionale in Bologna. The saint is represented with a portable organ to symbolise her role as patron saint of music.

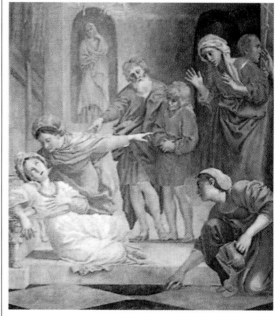

Chapel of San Remigio
fourth chapel on the right (2)

Clovis, king of the Franks, married a Christian princess named Clotilda. She desperately wanted her husband to embrace the Christian God, and to stop sacrificing to pagan idols, but nothing could make him change his faith. In 496 Clovis had to fight a great battle against the king of the Germans at Tolbiac (now Zülpich). Before the war he vowed that, if he returned victorious, he would convert to Christianity. He won the battle and kept his promise. Clovis called for Remigius, a Frenchman who had become archbishop of Reims at the age of 20, and in front of Remigius, his subjects and his wife, he underwent baptism.

☞ **Clovis shows the broken idols to an image of**

Jesus Crucified, altarpiece, Jacopino del Conte, 16th century

☞ **Scenes from the Life of Clovis,** frescoes on the left wall, right wall, and vault, by P. Tibaldi and G. Siciolante Sermoneta, 16th century

On the left wall, by G. Siciolante Sermoneta: Saint Remigius in the act of taking the sacred container of oil used to anoint the French king, Clovis. On the right wall, by Pellegrino Tibaldi: Clovis preparing for battle at Tolbiac. On the vault, by Tibaldi: episodes relating to the battle.

Chapel of San Matteo
fifth chapel on the left (3)

Matthew was a tax collector who became a follower of Jesus. He was one of the Apostles and is believed to have written the first Gospel, with the help of an angel. Having been beheaded for his beliefs, he became a martyr.

☞ **Scenes from the Life of Saint Matthew,** paintings by Caravaggio, 1597-1600

On the altar: Saint Matthew and the angel who is helping him write the Gospel. On the right: the saint's martyrdom. On the left: the calling of Matthew.

Raphael Sanzio (1483-1520)
Born in Urbino, Raphael was taught by Perugino whose style is strongly reflected in his early works.
Between 1504 and 1508 he worked in Florence where he learnt much from the drawings and paintings of Leonardo and Michelangelo.
In 1508 Raphael went to Rome and by 1509 he was working on the *Stanze della Segnatura*, for Pope Julius II, in the Vatican.
The frescoes that he painted for these small rooms represent, in its purest form, the High Renaissance style. After the death of Julius II in 1513 Raphael became the chief artist to his successor, Leo X, who commissioned further *Stanze* from him. Leo also appointed Raphael as Bramante's successor as architect of Saint Peter's and also made him Superintendent of Antiquities. One of his last great commissions was for the cartoons of the tapestries to be hung in the Sistine Chapel, beneath Michelangelo's recently completed ceiling.
His early death in 1520, aged only 37, left the Transfiguration, now in the Vatican, unfinished. Raphael's mastery is difficult to exaggerate; amongst the many aspects of his art that were influential was his revolutionary approach to the art of the portrait. His ability to convey psychological insight is demonstrated in his Julius II of 1512 a portrait that, like the *Stanze*, marks a pinnacle of the High Renaissance style.

Follow me! And Matthew rose and followed him. (Matt. 9:9)

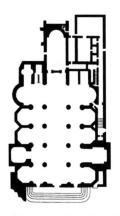

Church of Santa Maria del Popolo

The site where the church was built is believed to be the place where Emperor Nero was buried. His tomb was in fact at the foot of the Pincio, the hill that overlooks Piazza del Popolo. Accounts from the Roman historian Suetonius suggest that his ashes were kept in the square, inside the sepulchre of the Domitian family. During the Middle Ages a popular Roman legend claimed that a tree had grown, out of the bones of Nero, which was infested with demons disguised as black crows. The ghost of the emperor, tormented by his destiny in the afterlife, wandered in the vicinity. Superstitious Romans avoided the area. In 1099, the ghost of Nero finally disappeared after Pope Paschal II had a chapel built on the site. Pope Sixtus IV (1471-84) transformed the chapel into the church of Santa Maria del Popolo.

☞ **The medieval legend of the ghost of Nero,** above the main altar, five decorations in gold stucco, by order of Cardinal Antonio Sauli

Key scenes from the legend are depicted: the tomb of Nero with the chestnut tree infested by demons; the dream of Pope Paschal II, who orders the cutting down of the tree; the placing of the first stone of the chapel dedicated to the Virgin; the consecration of the altar, which took place in 1099 on the very spot where Nero was buried.

Brief history of the Church of Santa Maria del Popolo
The church was financed with money raised among the people of Rome; it is linked to one of the most important events of that time, the end of the first Crusade on 15th July 1099 and the freeing of the Holy Sepulchre. To thank God for the victory, the church was consecrated to the Virgin. The analogy between the two sepulchres - that of Nero freed from the demons and that of Christ freed from the Moors - is evident. During the Crusades, the church was very important as a site of devotion and thanksgiving after the battles to free the Holy Land. In the fifteenth century, under the papacy of Sixtus IV, the church was renamed *Sancta Maria Populi Romani*. In 1510, Martin Luther celebrated mass here with the Augustinian monks.

Feast day: 29th June

Brief history of the Cerasi Chapel
The chapel became identified with the Cerasi family in 1601 when Tiberio Cerasi endowed the site for a family tomb. The altarpiece representing the Assumption, to which the chapel is also dedicated, is by Annibale Caracci, 1601.

Cerasi Chapel

at the end on the left (north) aisle,
dedicated to Saint Peter and Saint Paul, patrons
of Rome, and to the Assumption of the Virgin **(1)**

Saint Paul was born in Tarsus, in Asia Minor. He was raised as a Jew but inherited Roman citizenship from his father. One day he was on his way to Damascus, to obtain the authorisation for the arrest of some Christians, when a light suddenly came from Heaven. Blinded by the light, Paul heard God say, 'Saul, Saul, why do you persecute me?'

In Damascus, Paul's blindness was cured by Ananias, a disciple of Christ, who also baptised him. Paul became one of the Apostles and spent the rest of his life preaching the Gospel to Gentiles. In 60 he arrived in Rome where he preached among the Roman congregation. His letters to the Romans were instrumental in spreading the Gospel.

He was kept in custody in the Mamertine Prison. He was not crucified but beheaded, a privilege reserved for Roman citizens.

☞ **Conversion of Saint Paul and Crucifixion of Saint Peter,** respectively on the right and left hand-side walls, paintings, by Caravaggio, 1601-1602

Caravaggio

Caravaggio arrived in Rome around 1592 when he was in his twenties. After having worked with Cavalier D'Arpino on various still-lifes he found, in Cardinal Francesco Maria del Monte, a patron who introduced him to the best Roman families. Commissions flocked to him from the Giustiniani, Barberini, Borghese, Mattei and Patrizi families. His style combined drama, daring composition and brilliant handling of paint, which created smoothly finished and realistic works. In the first decade of the seventeenth century, his pleasing style and his valuable connections brought him commissions for the Contarelli Chapel in San Luigi dei Francesi and the Cerasi Chapel in Santa Maria del Popolo.

Although a genius, he was also a troublemaker often at odds with the law. In 1606 he killed a man in a brawl and had to flee Rome. There followed years on the run. First he escaped to Naples; after a year, he went to Malta where, either because his reputation had followed him or because of new misdeeds, he was imprisoned. He escaped and moved to Sicily where he stayed for another year before returning to Naples in October 1609. Here he was assaulted and wounded by hired killers in retaliation for a fight in Malta. When the news came that the pope had pardoned him for the murder committed in Rome, Caravaggio sailed to Port'Ercole, a Spanish possession near Grosseto, in order to convalesce. Here he was arrested again, this time by mistake. On his release he learnt that the boat that was to take him to Rome was about to sail, taking his belongings. In sight of the departing ship he collapsed on the beach, exhausted, disappointed and delirious with fever. He died alone, a few days later, on 16th July 1610.

Commissioned by Pope Leo X, construction began in the sixteenth century by Jacopo Sansovino and was continued by Sangallo and Giacomo della Porta. It was completed in the following century by Carlo Maderno. The main altar is by Francesco Borromini. The architects Maderno and Borromini are buried inside the church.

John looked towards Jesus and said: 'This is the lamb of God'. (John 1: 36) Saint John is often represented holding a lamb.

Ritual

At Easter the blessing of the lamb takes place here. In this church animals are allowed to stay inside during mass.

Brief history of the Church of San Biagio della Pagnotta

The church was rebuilt in 1072. In 1730, the façade was remade by G. A. Perfetti. Pope Gregory XVI donated the church in 1832 to the Hospice of the Armenians of Santa Maria Egiziaca. They still look after the church.

Feast day of San Biagio: 3ʳᵈ February

Ritual

On 3ʳᵈ February, Saint Biagio's feast day, *pagnotte* (loaves of bread) are blessed and distributed among the faithful. It is also customary to anoint participants' throats with blessed oil. This religious ceremony is conducted in Armenian.

Church of San Giovanni dei Fiorentini
church of the Florentines

The Florentine community of merchants, bankers and artists was prominent in fifteenth-century Rome. When Giovanni de' Medici became Pope Leo X in 1513, he wanted a church dedicated to the patron saint of Florence, Saint John the Baptist. Florentines invoked him for protection and guidance when they were away from home.

☞ **John the Baptist as a boy,** in a niche above the entrance to the sacristy, statue, 15th century
☞ **Baptism of Christ,** on the high altar, marble group by Antonio Raggi, 1669

Church of San Biagio della Pagnotta
patron saint of woolcombers and of sufferers from diseases of the throat

Saint Biagio, Bishop of Sebaste, in Asia Minor, was a Christian martyr who died in the fourth century under the persecution of Emperor Licinius. His flesh was torn with iron combs before his execution. During his life he miraculously saved a boy who had swallowed a fishbone.

Church of San Bartolomeo all'Isola
patron saint of plasterers

Bartholomew was one of those chosen by Christ as His Apostle. He was there at the sepulchre when Christ was resurrected and he went to the Indies to preach, baptise and exorcise demons. He was gruesomely executed in Armenia by being flayed alive. He is often represented in art with his flayed skin over his arm (as in the fresco of the Last Judgement by Michelangelo in the Sistine Chapel). His relics were taken to Rome in 983. One of his arms, however, reached England. Saint Edward the Confessor received it as a gift and donated it to Canterbury Cathedral.

☞ Saint Bartholomew's body, under the altar, in an urn

Church of San Francesco a Ripa

patron saint of Italy, animals and birds

Francis came from a wealthy family, his father, Pietro Bernardone, was a rich merchant, however, he decided, in spite of his father's anger, to rid himself of all his wealth. In front of bishop Guido, he threw away his clothes and the bishop covered him with a cloak. Having shed his earthly goods, Francis started on the path of Jesus.

One day, when he was praying in Assisi, a crucifix spoke to him and urged him to repair the Church. Francis thus became the founder of the Franciscan order. He observed and preached three rules: poverty, chastity and obedience, symbolically represented by the three knots in the girdle that the Franciscan friars wear with their brown habit.

The humble Saint Francis of Assisi came to Rome in 1219 to ask the pope to sanction his order and grant its members authority to preach. Saint Bonaventure tells us that this request was granted after the pope had a dream in which the Lateran church collapsed and Francis put it back in place.

☞ **Saint Francis**, above the main altar, statue, attributed to Frà Diego da Careri, 1746

Feast day of Saint Bartholomew: 24th August

Brief history of the Church of San Bartolomeo all'Isola
The church was built on the ruins of the temple dedicated to Asclepius, in honour of the Bishop of Prague, Adalbert, who was martyred in 998. The church became dedicated to Saint Bartholomew only when the remains of the saint reached Rome. It was restored under Paschal II (1099-1118) and subsequently underwent many modifications through the centuries.

The Isola Tiberina
In pagan times this island in the Tiber was the centre for the cult of the god Asclepius. A story tells that in 293 BC Epidaurus brought to Rome the attribute of Asclepius, the snake of healing, in order to save the city from the plague. As they were approaching Rome the snake escaped in order to show where it wanted the temple of Asclepius to be built. Since then a hospital has always existed on the island.

Feast day: 4th October

Chapel of San Francesco
entrance past the sacristy

☞ **Saint Francis' crucifix and pillow of stone**

Saint Francis used these items when he was staying in Rome.

☞ **The reliquary chest**

This chest, dated 1696, features, in the centre, a copy of a panel painting attributed to Margheritone d'Arezzo. It is thought to be a true likeness of the saint. The original is kept in the Vatican picture gallery.

Church of Sant'Onofrio

Onophrius was, according to legend, a hermit who had renounced earthly possessions and who prayed in the solitude of the Egyptian desert. He managed to survive thanks to a raven that brought him a loaf of bread every day. At the time of his death animals came to help: it is said that lions dug his grave.

Brief history of the Church of San Francesco a Ripa
The church was built on the site of the Hospice of San Biagio and of a tenth-century Benedictine monastery in which Saint Francis stayed during his visits to Rome.

Only the scorpions and wild beasts for company.

Brief history of the Church of Sant'Onofrio
In 1439 a church was built on the site of the oratory dedicated to Saint Onophrius (founded by the Beatus Nicola da Forca Palena in 1419). In 1517 Pope Leo X consecrated it *diacona cardinalizia* and in 1588 pope Sixtus V elevated it to *titolo presbiteriale*. On 15th April 1595 the poet Torquato Tasso died in the nearby convent. He is buried under a tree in the garden.

☞ **Life and Legend of Saint Onophrius**, in the cloister, on the right-hand side, frescoes by Cavalier D'Arpino, 16th century

The four frescoes were commissioned for the Jubilee of 1600. The cloister dates from the mid-fifteenth century.

This little church, tucked away from the hustle and bustle of Rome's busy streets, also celebrates another hermit, Saint Jerome. Jerome went into the Syrian desert for four years where he prayed and battered himself with stones to expiate his sins. Jerome is known for befriending a lion by pulling a splinter from the animal's paw. In 386 he went to Bethlehem where he translated the Old and New Testaments into Latin. In the sixteenth century the Council of Trent declared his translation the official Latin text.

☞ **Scenes from the Life of Saint Jerome**, in the portico at the entrance to the church, frescoes by Domenichino, 1605

The scenes represented are: the Baptism, the Vision of Saint Jerome, and the temptation of Saint Jerome. All the scenes carry a double inscription in Latin and Italian.

Church of Santa Maria in Traspontina

Chapel of Santa Barbara (1)
patron saint of the Italian navy

Barbara, a young and attractive woman of oriental origin, was locked in a tower by her father, Dioscorus of Nicomedia, to discourage suitors. Once, when he went away, she asked a workman to build a third window in the tower through which a priest, disguised as a doctor, came to baptise her. When her father discovered this deceit she admitted to him that she had

Feast day of Saint Barbara:
4th December

converted to Christianity, and the three windows represented the mystery of the Holy Trinity. Her father was furious but Barbara managed to run away. She was eventually caught by the Roman authorities, brought before a magistrate and sentenced to death. Her own father beheaded her and was immediately struck dead by lightning.

Ritual
Since 1928, the Italian army and navy have sent their representatives to the church for the celebrations in honour of Saint Barbara on her feast day.

Saint Barbara is the patron saint of artillerymen, bomb-disposal experts, miners, firemen and all those who risk a sudden death, a reference to the manner of her father's death. She is also the patron saint of the Confraternity of Bombardieri di Castel Sant'Angelo, who commissioned the construction of this chapel.

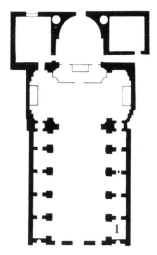

Brief history of the Church of Santa Maria in Traspontina

Originally the church was on the bridge of Castel Sant'Angelo. Demolished in 1564, to leave space for the pentagonal fortifications of the Vatican fortress, it was rebuilt in 1566 on the site of another church destroyed during the Sack of Rome. In 1594 Cardinal Pietro Aldobrandini and his lieutenant, Amerigo Capponi, commissioned the construction of the chapel of Santa Barbara on behalf of the Confraternity of Bombardieri di Castel Sant'Angelo. The decoration of the chapel was carried out by Cavalier D'Arpino. The chapel was restored in 1740.

Confraternity of Bombardieri di Castel Sant'Angelo

In 1592 Pope Clement VIII founded a school of artillery to create a permanent militia to obviate the need to use mercenaries. On 16th February 1594, under the supervision of the prefect of Florence, Amerigo Capponi, and encouraged by the pope's nephew, Cardinal Pietro Aldobrandini who was the commander of Castel Sant'Angelo, the Confraternity of the Bombardieri di Castel Sant'Angelo was founded. This religious confraternity was devoted to Saint Barbara. In 1798 the confraternity was dissolved and the care of the cult of the saint was passed on to the Corpo di Artiglieria Pontificia (the Vatican artillery) and subsequently in 1870 to the Italian army.

☞ **Saint Barbara,** above the altar, painting by Cavalier D'Arpino, 1597

The painting was shown to the people for the first time on 1st October 1597, the feast day of Saint Michael, in the nearby church of San Michele Arcangelo where a relic of the saint was kept.

☞ **Scenes from the Life of Saint Barbara,** along the walls, frescoes by Cesare Rossetti, 1610-20

Cavalier D'Arpino produced the images from drawings. In the vault they are: the pastor shows Saint Barbara to her father, who is chasing her; on the right wall: the saint refuses to venerate idols; on the left wall: the flagellation; on the left pillar: the Saviour appears to the saint in prison and comforts her; on the right pillar: the martyrdom of Saint Barbara.

SAINTS OF THE COUNTER-REFORMATION

The fight against Protestantism sparked renewed religious fervour. The Church searched for the means to gain in strength and influence and to spread the Gospel.

The saints of the sixteenth and seventeenth centuries were charged with the task of replenishing the ranks of believers. They became examples of dedication to God, not only for their private devotion and spiritual insight, but also for their creation of movements focused on educating Christians and helping those in need.

Our journey along the path of the Counter-Reformation saints starts with the church dedicated to Saint Filippo Neri who, along with the Apostles Peter and Paul and the Archangel Michael, shares the guardianship of Rome.

Church of Santa Maria in Vallicella

also known as Chiesa Nuova
dedicated to Saint Filippo Neri

Filippo Neri was the son of a Florentine lawyer who, at the age of 18, came to Rome after the city had been sacked in the sixteenth century, to find it in ruins and ravaged by the plague.

Nicknamed 'Pippo Buono' ('Good Philip') he succeeded in persuading Roman aristocrats to do voluntary church work. Filippo explained that true wealth belonged to those disposed to do good and charitable acts, to people who had dedicated their lives to God and Christ the Saviour.

In 1575 Filippo founded the Oratorian

Brief history of the Church of Santa Maria in Vallicella
The church was rebuilt in the sixteenth century with the help of Pope Gregory XIII on the site of an earlier church dedicated to Santa Maria in Vallicella. Work began in 1575 and the church was completed in 1599 apart from the façade which was finished in 1606. The interior, lavishly decorated with colourful marble, was completed after Saint Filippo's death. It was the headquarters of the Order of Filippini.

Saint Filippo's words at the apparition of the Virgin
When You appeared You enlarged my heart. (Ps.118; 32)

Brief history of the Chapel of San Filippo Neri
The chapel was planned by Onorio Longhi and finished by Marucelli at the beginning of the seventeenth century. It is a multicoloured feast of material: red marble, mother-of-pearl and semi-precious stones richly decorate the two rooms of the chapel.

Feast day: 26th May

Order, a brotherhood of laymen mainly from aristocratic families, who together worshipped Christ and helped needy people.

He introduced into devotional practice the oratorio, a sacred text and story, sung and accompanied by music.

On one occasion, he experienced a vision of the Virgin Mary and fell into a state of ecstasy.

Chapel of Filippo Neri
on the left of the altar

☞ **Saint Filippo's body,** under the altar of the chapel

The body of the saint is preserved in a bronze sarcophagus.

☞ **Saint Filippo and the Virgin,** on the altar, mosaic, 1774

This is a copy of the original painting by Guido Reni kept in the rooms of the saint. It was replaced with a mosaic in the eighteenth century in order to protect the original from damage by humidity.

Saint Filippo's Rooms
reached through the sacristy

Saint Filippo's room is called the 'red room' because it is lined with red fabric. There are various relics and objects here that belonged to the saint. The chapel contains a section of the wall of the saint's original room, which was destroyed in 1620 by an exploding firework thrown from the Castel Sant'Angelo.

There are two rooms with a connecting spiral staircase built by Francesco Borromini.

First room:
☞ **Scenes from the Life of Saint Filippo,** on the vault, frescoes by Niccolò Tornioli, 1643

The scene in the centre represents the Apparition of the Virgin to the sick Saint Filippo.

☞ **A cypress coffin with a bust of the saint,** silver bust, by Algardi, 17th century

At one time this contained the saint's remains, which

are now under the altar in the main church in the chapel of Filippo Neri.

☞ **Vision of Saint Filippo,** in the chapel of the red room, on the altar, painting by Guercino, 1643

☞ **Letters to the saint, his clothes,** in the first room

The letters are by Saint Carlo Borromeo and by Pope Clement VIII (1592-1605).

☞ **A banner with the saint's image,** in the first room

This banner was carried during the street procession that celebrated the day of his canonisation in 1622.

Up the stairs:

Here we enter the private chapel of Saint Filippo, which is preceded by an antechamber.

☞ **Filippo's Ecstasy,** in the antechamber, on the ceiling, painting by Pietro da Cortona, 1636

The saint is depicted during one of the many ecstasies he experienced. This ecstasy took place in this very chapel and, indeed, the door of the room is faithfully represented in the painting.

☞ **Filippo Contemplating the Virgin,** in the antechamber, on the altar, painting by Guido Reni, 1615

This is the original that once stood in the chapel of Saint Filippo Neri.

☞ **Miracle of Saint Filippo Appearing before the Cardinal Vincenzo Maria Orsini,** in the antechamber, painting by Pier Leone Ghezzi

The cardinal, later Pope Benedict XIII (1724-30), was the victim of an earthquake in Benevento, but he was saved by invoking Saint Filippo in his prayers. This is an ex voto that the cardinal dedicated to the saint as a form of thanks.

☞ **Filippo's rosary, spectacles, death mask, a bell, a Byzantine triptych and a chalice,** along the walls and on the altar of the private chapel

The bell is the one he used in the service of the mass and the triptych is the one in front of which he prayed. The chalice has the marks of the teeth of Saint Filippo; he is said to have bitten the chalice in the passion of his devotion of the Sacred Blood.

☞ **The saint's bed and his confessional stall,** on the side walls of the private chapel

Ritual

A very popular event in Rome occurs on the 26th of May, the feast day commemorating Saint Filippo. Since 1609, it has been customary for the City Hall to offer a votive chalice to the church of Saint Filippo Neri on this day.

Brief history of the Church of the Santissimo Nome del Gesù
This was the first Jesuit church to be built in Rome. Work started in 1568, under the sponsorship of Cardinal Alessandro Farnese, nephew of Pope Paul III (1534-49), and was completed in 1584. Most of the work was carried out by Jacopo Barozzi, also known as Giacomo da Vignola. The church of the Santissimo Nome del Gesù is a great example of a Counter-Reformation church, in both its architecture and its functions. To accommodate more people, the nave was made much larger than in previous churches. The façade, which was the work of Giacomo della Porta, was added in 1575.

Feast day of San Francesco: 3rd December

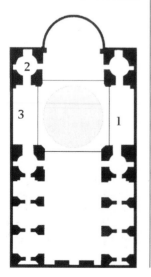

Church of the Santissimo Nome del Gesù

In 1521 Ignatius of Loyola, then a Spanish soldier, left the army after being wounded in battle. In 1537, during the time of the Protestant Reformation, he came to Rome where, in 1540, he founded the Order of the Society of Jesus, known as the Jesuits. Ignatius installed the new order just a few steps away from San Marco dei Veneziani, a papal residence.

Through their missionary work, the Jesuits strove - and continue striving to this day - to win converts to Catholicism all over the world.

☞ **The Triumph of the Name of Jesus,** on the nave ceiling, fresco, by Giovan Battista Gauli, known as Baciccia, 1672-85

The dome of the church seems to open up to Heaven as a golden light streams down into the church itself. The illusionist effect of the painted images by Baciccia is increased by the stucco figures executed by Antonio Raggi at the edges, which seem to break into the painting. Some figures are tumbling down and others are sucked up into Paradise, in a vortex of divine energy.

☞ **Bust of Saint Robert Bellarmine,** in the apse, on the left, statue, by Bernini, 1621-24

Saint Robert Bellarmine (1542-1621) was a theologian who fought against Protestantism. Saints such as Luigi Gonzaga, Robert Bellarmine and Filippo Neri came to pray and meditate at Chiesa del Gesù.

☞ **Scenes from the history of the Society of Jesus,** in the sacristy, on the wall, paintings by unknown artists

The themes of the paintings are: Pope Paul III approving the Society of Jesus; Cardinals Alessandro and Odoardo Farnese (respectively founder of the church of the Santissimo Nome di Gesù and of the Casa Professa); canonisation of Saints Ignatius and Francis Xavier; canonisation of Saint Francis Borgia.

Chapel of Saint Francis Xavier
in the right transept (1)
patron of missions

Francis Xavier (1506-52), originally from Navarre, is also referred to as the 'Apostle of the Indies' because of his missionary work. He spent his life preaching the Gospel, baptising and looking after the needy and sick. He travelled extensively, including trips to Japan, India and Ceylon. He also travelled to China but became ill and died on Sancian (now Shangzhuang Dao) Island off the coast, while awaiting permission to enter.

☞ **Death of Saint Francis Xavier on Sancian Island,** altarpiece, painting by Carlo Maratta, 17th century

The painting replaced a previous one of the Resurrection, by Giovanni Baglione, painted in 1603.

☞ **Saint Francis Xavier's arm,** on the altar of the chapel

A reliquary contains the arm of the missionary saint who baptised many converts to Christianity. It was brought to Rome in the seventeenth century.

☞ **Saint Francis Xavier Finds the Cross,** on the vault, painting by Giovanni Andrea Carlone, 17th century

The other paintings show the missionary baptising an Indian princess and the Glory of Saint Francis Xavier.

Chapel of the Madonna della Strada
left of the tribune (2)

On the day dedicated to the Annunciation of Mary, during a ceremony that took place inside this chapel, the members of the Society of Jesus used to pronounce their oath of poverty, chastity and obedience and their commitment to missionary work.

☞ **Madonna della Strada,** fresco, 15th century

This fresco comes from the church of the same name. Saint Ignatius of Loyola was particularly fond of the image of the Madonna della Strada and used to celebrate mass and teach the Christian doctrine in front of it.

Brief history of the Chapel of Saint Francis Xavier

Built in the seventeenth century by Pietro da Cortona, this chapel was originally dedicated to the Resurrection of Christ.

IL SOMMO P. PIO IX.
CONCEDE INDVLGENZA QVOTIDIANA
DI 300.GIORNI
APPLICABILE ANCHE AI DEFVNTI
A CHI VISITA CON CVOR CONTRITO
QVESTA VEN.IMAGINE
DI MARIA SS.DELLA STRADA
IN BREV 23 SEPT 1608

The Society of Jesus

Probably the most important work of Ignatius of Loyola's later years was the foundation of the Society of Jesus. His members abandoned some of the traditional forms of the religious life, for example, the chanting of the divine office and physical punishments, in favour of a more authoritative regime. The Society of Jesus was to be, above all, an order of apostles 'ready to live in any part of the world where there was hope of God's greater glory and the good of souls'. Loyola insisted on long and thorough training of his followers and encouraged them to become missionaries. Loyola called the special vow of obedience to the pope 'the cause and principal foundation' of his society. The Society of Jesus was granted official recognition by Pope Paul III in 1540.

Brief history of the Chapel of Sant'Ignazio

Known as the Chapel of the Cross, it was built by Giacomo della Porta and commissioned by Cardinal Giacomo Savelli. It was redecorated by Pietro da Cortona and remodelled, towards the end of the seventeenth century, by Andrea Pozzo. It is a dazzling example of baroque decoration, in which the variety of materials employed - gold, silver, green marble and lapis lazuli - increases the sense of wonder in the spectator.

Brief history of the Collegio of Piazza del Gesù, the Casa Professa

Built on the site where, from 1599 to 1623, the first Society of Jesus resided, the building was commissioned to Girolamo Rinaldi by Cardinal Odoardo Farnese.

Chapel of Sant'Ignazio
in the left transept **(3)**

Saint Ignatius practised a form of prayer that was later published in the *Spiritual Exercises*, which appears to have rivalled that of the greatest mystics. Ignatius of Loyola was beatified by Pope Paul V in 1609 and canonised by Pope Gregory XV in 1622. In 1922, he was declared patron of all spiritual retreats by Pope Pius XI.

☞ **Saint Ignatius,** main altar, statue in stucco covered in silver, by Tadolini, Canova school, 19th century

The statue of the saint is adorned with stones of lapis lazuli. Originally, the statue was cast from silver by Pierre II Legros in 1698, but Pope Pius VI (1775-99) had it melted down to pay for the reparations imposed by Napoleon after the Peace of Tolentino. To the right of the statue is the marble group of Triumph of Faith over Heresy, by the artist Theudon.

☞ **Saint Ignatius's body,** under the altar of the chapel

Collegio of Piazza del Gesù, The Casa Professa

The final period of Loyola's life was spent in Rome, where he resided in the Casa Professa, an institute adjacent to the church of the Santissimo Nome del Gesù. In 1539 the members of the Society of Jesus decided to form a permanent union. In 1540, Pope Paul III approved the plan of the new order. Loyola was the choice of his companions for the office of general.

At first, Loyola had been somewhat opposed to placing his companions in colleges as educators. In time, however, he came to recognise the value of the educational apostolate and in his last years was busily engaged in laying the foundations of the system of schools that was to stamp his organisation as a teaching order, in addition to its original missionary aims.

☞ **Saint Ignatius's rooms,** in the Casa Professa

These are the rooms where the saint and his colleagues lived. On the walls of the corridor leading to them are frescoes representing scenes from the Life of Saint Ignatius. The rooms are modest, with low ceilings. The first room, used as a hall, still contains the desk, tunic and shoes of the saint. On the ceiling, the saint is represented ascending into Heaven. The next room is the saint's chapel, where he slept and studied and where he wrote the constitution of the Society of Jesus. A portrait of the saint by the Jesuit, Gian Paolo, his loyal companion, hangs in here. The third room is the chapel of the Madonna, the sitting room of Saint Ignatius. This is the room in which, on 31st July 1556, the saint died. The fourth room was the residence of the Jesuit, Gian Paolo; today it is used as a sacristy.

Loyola left his mark on Rome. He founded the Roman College, embryo of the Gregorian University, and the Germanicum, a seminary for German candidates for the priesthood. He also established a home for fallen women and one for converted Jews.

Church of Sant'Ignazio de Loyola

The Society of Jesus developed rapidly under the guidance of Saint Ignatius. When he died there were about 1,000 Jesuits divided into 12 administrative units, called provinces. Three of these were in Italy, a like number in Spain, two in Germany, one in France, one in Portugal and one each in India and Brazil. Loyola was, in his last years, much occupied with Germany and India, to which he sent his famous followers Peter Canisius and Francis Xavier. He also dispatched missionaries to the Congo and to Ethiopia. In 1546, Loyola secretly received into the society Francis Borgia, duke of Gandia and viceroy of Catalonia. When knowledge of this became public four years later, it created a sensation. Borgia organised the Spanish provinces of the order and became third general.

☞ **Saint Ignatius in Glory and the Jesuits**, main ceiling, fresco by Andrea Pozzo, 1685

The saint is lifted up to Heaven, bathed in a divine light. Through him the light refracts on to the four different parts of the world. This is the Jesuits' message: faith is what brings us true glory and closeness to the divine.

☞ **Relic of Saint Luigi Gonzaga,** under the altar, in a lapis lazuli urn

Brief history of the Church of Sant'Ignazio de Loyola
Built in 1626, under the patronage of Cardinal Alessandro Ludovisi, the church has a Latin cross plan and faces a little square. It celebrates the ardour and fidelity of the Jesuits' movement. It also houses the venerable memory of other Jesuit saints, notably Luigi Gonzaga and Giovanni Berchmans.

Feast day of Sant'Ignazio: 31st July

Ritual
On the feast day, 21st June, Rome's City Hall offers a votive chalice to the church of Sant'Ignazio de Loyola, as has been the custom since the seventeenth century. A mass is celebrated at 7 a.m., attended by children dressed as Saint Aloysius's pages. Flowers and requests for grace are deposited in front of the saint's body. The following Sunday these requests are burnt in the church of San Saba.

Luigi Gonzaga was the son of Ferdinand Gonzaga, Marquis of Castiglione. After reading a booklet about the Society of Jesus, he renounced his prestigious family title and embraced a life of piety and prayer. He entered the Order of Jesuits in 1585, starting his noviciate in Rome. In 1587 he took his vows. Luigi worked in a hospital, where he helped people stricken with distemper, an epidemic of which spread through Rome in 1591. Unfortunately, he contracted the disease himself and died.

☞ **Glory of Saint Luigi Gonzaga,** in the nave, on the side, over the altar, low relief by Pierre Legros, 1697-99

☞ **The body of Saint Giovanni Berchmans,** at the top of the nave, on the right.

Church of Santa Maria Maddalena

Camillus of Lellis (1550-1614) was an orphan who spent his early years living a life of vice. He lost all his wealth through gambling and went to work as a manual labourer. In 1575 he realised that he had to answer a calling to look after the sick. He died in a nearby convent in 1614.

He founded the Order of Camillians: its members met to worship and help the sick. The members of this order were active in hospitals.

Chapel of San Camillo
third chapel on the right

☞ **Saint Camillus in Glory, in Adoration of the Cross,** on the ceiling, frescoes by Sebastiano Conca, 18th century

☞ **Relics of Saint Camillus,** under the altar
The relics are contained in an eighteenth-century urn made by Francesco Giardoni and Valentino Consalvi.

☞ **Vision of Saint Camillus,** over the main altar, painting by Placido Costanzi, 1749

☞ **Saint Camillus and Saint Filippo Neri Have a Vision of Angels Giving Help to a Group of Poor People of the Congregation of the Camillians,** on the right-hand side of the main altar, by Giovanni Panozza

Brief history of the Church of Santa Maria Maddalena
The church was originally built to honour Santa Maria Maddalena and belonged, together with the hospital, to the congregation of the *Disciplinati o Battuti*. In 1586 it was given to Saint Camillus to use as a headquarters for the Ministri degli Infermi, his charitable organisation for the sick. The church is still managed by the Order of Camillians. The dome and the vault are by Carlo Fontana, 1673; the rococo façade is by Giuseppe Sardi, 1735.

Take courage, faint hearted one, continue the work you have begun.
(Words pronounced by Christ to Saint Camillus)

Feast day of Saint Camillus: 16th July

Brief history of the Chapel of San Camillo
The chapel was originally dedicated to the Assumption, but the dedication changed to Saint Camillus after his canonisation in 1746. Work on the chapel ended in 1749.

Chapel of the Crucifix
at the right of the main altar

☞ **The Crucifix,** 16th century

The Christ on this crucifix is believed to have miraculously detached his arms and spoken to Saint Camillus. Since then it has become an object of veneration and a focus for prayers.

☞ **Saint Camillus is Welcomed in Heaven by the Virgin Mary and Saint Filippo Neri,** in the sacristy, on the ceiling, by Girolamo Pesci, 18th century

☞ **Saint Camillus's relics and rooms**

Reliquaries house the heart of the saint, one of his feet and two of his fingers.

Inscription underneath the cross of the Camillians, on the façade of the church
O Crux ave, spes unica,
piis adauge gratiam.
(I salute you, O Cross, only hope, grant grace to the most pious)

Church of Sant'Ambrogio e Carlo al Corso

Carlo Borromeo (1538-84) came from an aristocratic Milanese family. Nominated cardinal at the early age of 22 by his uncle Angelo de' Medici, Pope Pius IV, he became archbishop of Milan. He spent his life giving away what he had to the poor and caring for the sick. He was particularly active during the 1576 plague in Milan.

When he moved to Rome, he lived near the church of Sant'Ambrogio where, together with Saint Filippo Neri, he looked after those in need. He made every possible effort to have the rules of the Council of Trent observed. He even participated at the Council in 1562. He died at the age of 46 and was canonised in 1610.

Built in honour of Saint Charles, the church houses an important relic, the heart of the saint.

Brief history of the Chapel of the Crucifix
The building of the chapel was directed and executed by the architect Francesco Nicoletti, 1762-64.

Brief history of the Church of Sant'Ambrogio e Carlo al Corso
In 1471, Pope Sixtus IV gave the church to Rome's Lombard community. At that time, it was dedicated to Saint Ambrose, bishop of Milan, who died in 397, and was called San Nicola de Tofu. In 1610, after the Milanese bishop, Carlo Borromeo, was canonised, the church was rebuilt in his honour. Pope Paul V officially conferred the name 'Sant' Ambrogio e Carlo' on the church in 1612.

Ritual
On the feast day, 4th November, Saint Charles's heart is displayed inside the church.

Built for the Order of Barnabites by Rosato Rosati (1612-20) to honour Saint Charles Borromeo soon after his canonisation, the church is called *ai Catinari* ('bowlmakers') because it was built where a concentration of bowlmakers worked. A church dedicated to Saint Biagio in Anello was built just behind San Carlo ai Catinari. When this church fell into ruins its parish was included in that of the church of San Carlo. The church has also been dedicated to Saint Biagio since the eighteenth century.

Feast day of Saint Charles: 4th November

Rituals

On 3rd February, Saint Biagio's feast day, his relics are displayed. The painting by Cerrini is hung on the first pillar on the right and, directly below it among flowers, a ring with a fragment of the saint's vertebra is shown to the faithful. The ring is kissed and the saint is invoked for intercession in the protection from illnesses of the throat.

On Saint Charles's feast day, the cardinal's hat and the rope used for his penance are displayed.

114

☞ **Saints Ambrose and Charles in Glory,** on the tribune, painting by Carlo Maratta, 1685-90

☞ **Saint Charles Frees the City of Milan from Plague and Saint Charles in Glory,** ceiling of the apse, frescoes by Brandi, 17th century

☞ **Saint Charles's heart,** behind the main altar

In 1613 the relic was donated to the confraternity by Charles's nephew, Cardinal Federico.

Church of Biagio e Carlo ai Catinari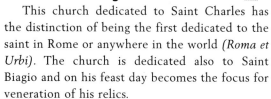

This church dedicated to Saint Charles has the distinction of being the first dedicated to the saint in Rome or anywhere in the world *(Roma et Urbi)*. The church is dedicated also to Saint Biagio and on his feast day becomes the focus for veneration of his relics.

☞ **Saint Charles Giving Alms to the People Afflicted by the Plague in Milan, Saint Charles Ordering Domenico Boerio to Fight Heresy in Graubünden,** inside, beside the lateral entrance doors, frescoes by Mattia and Gregorio Preti, 1642

☞ **Apotheosis of Saint Charles,** in the apse, fresco by Giovanni Lanfranco, 1647

☞ **Saint Charles Carries the Holy Nail in Procession during the Plague in Milan,** fourth chapel on the right, main altar, altarpiece by Pietro da Cortona, 1667

☞ **Saint Charles at Prayer,** in the choir, fresco by Guido Reni, 16th to 17th century

☞ **Saint Charles at Prayer during the Plague in Milan,** in the choir, fresco by Andrea Commodi, 16th to 17th century

☞ **Saint Biagio Saving the Boy who had a Fishbone Stuck in his Throat,** in the sacristy, painting by Cerrini, 17th century

This painting is taken out into the body of the church on Saint Biagio's feast day.

Church of San Girolamo della Carità

While Saint Filippo Neri lived in the adjacent convent, between 1551 and 1583, he founded the Order of Filippini on the site where the church of San Girolamo della Carità now stands. It still houses the sanctuary of the Order of Filippini.

Some claim that the site was once the home of Saint Jerome, one of the fathers of the Church.

☞ **Crucifix of Saint Filippo Neri,** second chapel on the right, 15th century

It is believed that this crucifix spoke to Saint Filippo Neri

☞ **Saint Filippo Neri,** on the left-hand side of the apse, statue by Pierre Legros, 17th century

Church of Santa Maria della Scala

Saint Teresa of Jesus or of Àvila - her real name was Teresa de Cepeda y Ahumada - was a Spanish Carmelite nun, born in Àvila, who wrote extensively about her visionary experiences. She was one of the great mystics and religious women of the Roman Catholic Church, and the author of spiritual classics. The most famous account of her spiritual experiences tells of an angel implanting the spear of *Amor Dei* into her heart. Teresa founded the Order of Discalced (barefoot) Carmelites. She was canonised in 1622. In 1970, Pope Paul VI elevated her to Doctor of the Church, the first woman to be so honoured.

☞ **The foot of Saint Teresa,** in the chapel on the left of the main altar

On 19th February 1905, one of Saint Teresa's feet was moved from the choir. To celebrate this occasion, the chapel was renovated: six paintings by Luca de la Haye, representing scenes from Saint Teresa's life, adorn the walls.

Church of San Francesco a Ripa ✝
Chapel of Ludovica Albertoni
fourth chapel on the left

Ludovica Albertoni (1473-1533) married the noble, Giacomo della Cetera. She did considerable charitable works in Trastevere, especially at the time of the Sack of Rome, and had mystical experiences. She died of fever and her body immediately became

Brief history of the Church of San Girolamo della Carità
A church was built adjacent to the convent in which Saint Filippo Neri lived. In 1654 the church was modernised by Domenico Castelli. The façade is baroque and was built in 1660 by Carlo Rainaldi.

Feast day of Santa Teresa:
15th October

Brief history of the Church of Santa Maria della Scala
Works started in 1592, under the supervision of the architect Francesco Cipriani da Volterra, after Pope Clement VIII had placed the project under the jurisdiction of the Order of Carmelites. With the death of Volterra, the construction came to halt. The church was completed in 1610, thanks to the financial intervention of Monsignor Marco Gallio. During the Roman Republic, the church was used as a hospital. Luciano Manara and Andrea Aguyar, nicknamed the Moor of Garibaldi, died here on 30th June 1849.

Discalced Carmelites
In 1562, after nearly 30 years in a Carmelite convent, Saint Teresa founded, in Avila, a small convent where the sisters observed a stricter way of life. It became the Order of Discalced or Barefoot Carmelite Nuns because they wore sandals instead of shoes and stockings. The aim of the reform was to restore and emphasise the austerity and contemplative character of the original Carmelite life. In 1580 the reformed monasteries were made a separate province and, in 1593, this province became, by papal act, an independent order. With the cooperation of Juan de Yepes y Alvarez, later known as Saint John of the Cross, Saint Teresa established a number of friaries of this stricter observance.

Brief history of the Church
of San Francesco a Ripa
The church was originally erected
in the thirteenth century and rebuilt
in the 1680s under the patronage of
Cardinal Pallavicini.

an object of devotion. She was buried in the fifteenth-century chapel of the della Cetera family, which was rebuilt by Giacomo Nola between 1622 and 1625. Her cult was sanctioned in 1671.

Ecstasy

Ecstasy is a mystical experience arising out of a heightening of the senses. The experience manifests itself physically as wounds, which are accompanied by visions. At this level of intensity, prayer reaches the highest level of union with God.

☞ **Beata Ludovica Albertoni's Ecstasy,** marble statue by Bernini, 1674

Bernini's work depicts Ludovica prostrate, with eyes half open and body twisted in the sweet pain of her mystical encounter.

Church of Sant'Andrea al Quirinale

This small aristocratic building is full of family symbols of the wealthy Roman clerics who paid for its construction. The Jesuits' symbol, the initials JHS (which stand for *Jesus Hominum Salvator* – 'Jesus Saviour of mankind'), appear all over the church. Maritime motifs remind us of Saint Andrew, the fisherman Apostle from Galilee, who was Peter's brother.

Saint Stanislas Kostka, a Jesuit from Poland, is celebrated in this church. He was a novice who died, in 1568, at the early age of 19. He came to Rome to see Saint Francis Borgia, the general of the Jesuit Order, following the recommendation of Saint Peter Canisius. He lived with the Jesuits at Sant'Andrea.

☞ **Saint Stanislas Kostka,** behind the sacristy of the church, statue by Pierre Legros, 1703

This statue of Saint Stanislas, clad in a black tunic made of dark basalt, lies on his yellow alabaster deathbed, with his head on a laced pillow of Carrara marble. Behind him is a painting of the Virgin with the Saints Barbara, Cecilia and Agnes, ready to embrace

Brief history of the Church
of Sant'Andrea al Quirinale
Designed by Bernini and
constructed by his assistants
between 1658 and 1670, this
church was consecrated by the
future Pope Innocent XI (1676-89).

him in Heaven. The painting is by Minardi and dates from the eighteenth century. There are two other rooms. One is hung with 12 watercolours by Andrea Pozzo representing episodes of Saint Stanislas's life. The other contains many relics, including the letter in which Saint Peter Canisius urges Saint Stanislas to seek out Saint Francis Borgia.

Church of San Carlo alle Quattro Fontane

This church is nicknamed Carlino, or 'little Charles', because it is so small. The church occupies about the same space as one of the pillars of Saint Peter's cupola.

☞ **Saint Charles Borromeo and the Angels,** on the façade, statue, by Antonio Raggi, 1675-80
☞ **Portrait of Saint Charles in Adoration of the Trinity,** sacristy, painting by Borgianni, 1612

Church of Santa Maria della Vittoria
Cornaro Chapel
last chapel on the left of the main altar

The Cornaro were a Venetian family. When one of their members, Federigo, was made cardinal he asked Bernini, the great Roman sculptor, to decorate their sepulchral chapel. Portraits of members of the family, including the Doge Giovanni and other Cornaro cardinals of the previous century, can be seen on the side walls of the chapel, like spectators in a theatre. They asked to have their chapel dedicated to Saint Teresa, because they had close ties with her Order of Barefoot Carmelites.

☞ **Ecstasy of Saint Teresa,** on the altar, statue by Bernini, 1644-48

An ensemble of different materials coloured marbles, gilded wood, stucco and yellow tinted glass capture the vision of the angel represented in the act of transfixing the saint's heart. She swoons, weakened by the pleasure of her mystical experience, under a divine light. Her bare foot projects as a reminder of her order, the Barefoot Carmelites.

Brief history of the Church of San Carlo alle Quattro Fontane
The church of San Carlo alle Quattro Fontane was commissioned by the Trinitarians in 1634. The façade was finished in 1667 and it was Borromini's last work before he committed suicide later that year. Borromini was a Trinitarian himself and there is a chapel for him in the crypt left empty after his sad and desperate death.

Brief history of the Church of Santa Maria della Vittoria
Originally, this church was built in honour of Saint Paul by Carlo Maderno between 1608 and 1620. The church was rebuilt, in 1620, under the patronage of Cardinal Scipione Borghese. On 8th May 1622, the image of the Madonna della Vittoria, was brought to this church, which was renamed after it.

117

III

ROME, THE CULT OF THE VIRGIN

From her conception Mary was predestined to become the mother of Jesus, the Saviour of mankind. A legend, related by an Apocryphal Gospel, says that her parents, Joachim and Anne, had been married for 20 years and were still childless. One day, an angel appeared to both of them separately, foretelling that Anne would bear a daughter who would become the mother of Jesus. Thus, Mary was born at God's behest. At the age of three she was taken to the temple to be presented to the high priest, Zacharias. She is said to have spent several days there, in holy observance, with other girls.

Mary was the vessel chosen to carry the Saviour. Therefore she needed protection in the form of a husband able to care for her and her son. The man whom God chose for this task was Joseph, a carpenter from Nazareth. Mary married Joseph at the age of 15. There is another apocryphal legend, not accepted by the Church, which relates the first meeting between Mary and Joseph. Zacharias, acting under the instructions of an angel, invited some widowers to come to the temple carrying rods with them. Many arrived with sticks and branches, but Joseph's rod was the only one that blossomed into a flower. With great humility, he agreed to take responsibility for Mary.

The account of the most important event in the life of Mary, the Annunciation, is to be found not in the Apocrypha but in Saint Luke's Gospel. He describes how the Archangel Gabriel revealed to Mary that she would conceive and bear the Son of God and that she should call him Jesus (Luke 1:26-38). Catholics believe that the Annunciation was a momentous event for humankind: in the instant in which Mary accepted the celestial announcement, the Incarnation

21st November

The consecration of Mary to the service of God in the Temple of Jerusalem is celebrated on 21st November, but this feast has no relation to the Gospel preached by the Church. It is an ancient, popular tradition rooted in apocryphal tales. The Church does not accept as canonical these tales of Mary's presentation in the temple, but it does accept the essence of the celebration; that is, that during her childhood Mary completely consecrated herself to God.

The Feast of the Annunciation

When the date of Christmas was fixed at 25th December, in 336, it was logical that the feast of the Annunciation should be set nine months earlier, on 25th March. It is one of the principal feasts of the Christian Church. Its significance is much more than narrative, for it underlines the role of the divine will of God in the birth of Christ. Hence the particular importance of the theme of the Annunciation in ecclesiastical art.

Mary to Gabriel
Ecce ancilla Domini.
('I am the Lord's servant';
Luke 1:58)

Jesus and Mary
During the wedding feast at Cana, Mary came to Jesus to tell him that the guests had run out of wine. His reply was cryptic, 'Woman, what have I to do with thee? Mine hour is not yet come.' But then He did what His mother asked.
(John 2:1-10)

of Christ took place and with that the Redemption of the world from original sin began.

Mary was a loving mother to Jesus but she knew that Jesus was not only her son, but also the gift of God to the world and that He had to fulfil His mission on earth, the saving of mankind.

When the holy family went to Jerusalem, Jesus was 12 years old. As they were leaving to return home, Mary and Joseph lost Him in the crowd. It took them three days to find Him; He was sitting in the temple discussing philosophical matters with learned men. Mary, like any other mother, chastised Him for causing His parents to worry about Him. But Jesus only replied, 'How is it that you sought me? Did you not know that I must be about my Father's business?' Mary was God's *ancilla*, His servant, and she had to submit to His will.

On another occasion He was teaching a large crowd when He was told by His disciples, 'Behold, thy mother and thy brethren without seek for thee'. He replied, 'Who is my mother, or my brethren?'. Then He looked at all those listening to

Him and said, 'Behold my mother and my brethren! For whosoever shall do the will of God, the same is my brother and my sister and mother.' (Mark 3:31)

Mary's submission does not signify that there was no love between her and her son, but merely that she knew and accepted Christ's true role on earth.

The last meeting between the two took place when Jesus was dying on the cross, in order to free mankind from its sins. In the midst of His suffering, Jesus demonstrated His true humanity. He expressed His tender love for His mother; moments before His death, He placed her in the care of His disciple John.

Since the earliest days of Christianity, Mary has been venerated as the mother of Christ and, indeed, of all people. As Jesus was dying on the cross, He entrusted Mary to John, and He placed His disciple in the care of His mother. Jesus' words 'Ecce mater tua' were addressed not only to John, but to every Christian, placed from then on in the motherly care of Mary. As a mother, gentle and merciful, her role is to protect Christians, to help them and to remind them to live life according to the principle of faith.

Rome, the centre of Christianity, is loud in its praise of the mother of God. A quick glance at a list of the churches in central Rome reveals the importance of the Virgin to this city. While most saints have a single church dedicated to them, there are an impressive 49 devoted to Mary. Her nearest rival is Saint John, who has 11 to his name. Saints Peter and Paul can muster only eight between them.

Historically, the cult of the Virgin assumed a new significance in 431 when, during the Council of Ephesus, Mary was confirmed as *Theotokos*.

The confirmation of Mary as *Theotokos* helped to raise her status from a humble mother to a regal figure. From the fifth century, the Christian establishment in Rome decided to harness the cult

The Council of Ephesus

In about 428, the patriarch Nestorius of Constantinople raised his objections to the application of the title *Theotokos* to Mary since, for him, it was a blasphemy that a woman could give birth to God. He argued that the Virgin could not be the Mother of God because God had always existed. She should be described as *Anthropotokos*, the 'mother of man', or perhaps *Christotokos*, 'the mother of Christ'. Nestorius's position was opposed by the patriarch Cyril of Alexandria and the resulting argument embroiled the pope in Rome. At the Council of Ephesus in 431 Nestorius was overruled and excommunicated by Cyril, and Mary was reinstated as *Theotokos*. The people of Ephesus held jubilant processions, cheering for Mary, Mother of God.

Theotokos
The word comes from the Greek words *theos*, which denotes God, and *tokos*, meaning 'having given birth to'. Together the two words mean 'mother of God'.

of the mother of God to the authority of the papacy. Suddenly, she was presented as the Queen of Heaven, dressed in lavish, jewel-encrusted robes, a crown on her head and surrounded by a court of angels and saints.

Thus, the Virgin came to stand for the authority of the Church, serving to reinforce papal ascendancy in the city. During the struggles between the popes and the Byzantine emperors, her image in majesty became a key weapon in the papal armoury.

In the eighth century, the veneration of the Virgin was to reach new heights during the vicious struggles of the Iconoclast controversy, when the strained relationship between the emperors in Constantinople and the popes in Rome finally broke down completely.

During the Iconoclast period the image of Mary served, in Rome, to assert the righteousness of Christian images. A boom in the patronage of churches and church decoration followed. At this time, many pagan buildings were converted to

The Four Dogmas

The cult of the Virgin is built upon four principles in which the faithful must believe:

• Her divine motherhood. Her role as mother of Jesus takes precedence over any other position assigned to her.

• Her virginity. Although Mary remained a virgin, she conceived Jesus in her womb.

• The Immaculate Conception. Mary was the only person never to have been stained by original sin.

• Her Assumption into Heaven. In 1950 Pope Pius XII made this dogma official, declaring that, at the end of her life, Mary was 'assumed body and soul' into Heaven.

Mary versus Eve

For Adam had necessarily to be restored in Christ, that mortality be absorbed in immortality, and Eve in Mary, that a virgin, become the advocate of a virgin, should undo and destroy virginal disobedience by virginal obedience.

(the Church father Irenaeus, in the second century)

Christian use and were frequently decorated with rich mosaics, colourful frescoes and lavish icons, in defiance of the imperial ruling.

Another characterisation of Mary, which became a theme of Christian reflection, is her portrayal as the new Eve. The New Testament draws parallels between Jesus Christ and Adam: 'As in Adam all die, so also in Christ shall all be made alive.' (I Cor.15:22) The comparison is drawn between the disobedience of Adam, which allowed sin to enter the world, and the obedience of Christ, by which salvation from sin was achieved (Rom. 5:12-19).

A similar correspondence between Eve and Mary can be found in the first chapter of Luke's gospel with the story of the Annunciation. Eve tainted mankind with original sin and was the agent of the devil. Mary was the inverse of Eve; virginal and innocent, she spoke only to express her obedience to God. She did not listen to the serpent,

The Magnificat

My soul magnifies the Lord, and my spirit rejoices in God my Saviour, for he has regarded the low estate of his handmaiden. For behold, henceforth all generations will call me blessed;

(Luke 1:46)

Marian feast days

2nd February: Purification of the Virgin, known in the West as Candlemas, later merged with the Presentation of Christ to the Temple, the first time He was recognised as the Messiah by Simeon and Anna

25th March: The Annunciation

15th August: The Dormition, which, in the West, became the Assumption and Coronation of the Virgin

8th September: The Nativity of the Virgin, established in the West about 695 and in the East in the middle of the twelfth century

21st November: The Presentation of the Virgin in the Temple, established in the East as early as 730 and in the West by the late fourteenth century

8th December: The Immaculate Conception

The Immaculate Conception
We must except the Holy Virgin Mary. Out of respect for the Lord, I do not intend to raise a single question on the subject of sin. After all, how do we know what abundance of grace was granted to her who had the merit to conceive and bring forth Him who was unquestionably without sin?
(Saint Augustine)

but to Gabriel, the archangel of God. The parallel ascribes to Mary and her obedience an active role in the redemption of the human race. All men had died in Adam, but Eve had been instrumental in the sin that brought this fate; all men were saved in Christ, but Mary had participated in the life that made this possible.

Mary, the Virgin, the mother of Christ, the Queen of Heaven, the new Eve. She can encompass all these identities because she is set apart from other women: she is a being free from original sin, which stains the human soul.

Throughout the centuries, Mary's virginity has been one of the most common themes of Marian imagery. On the basis of the New Testament, the fathers of the Church taught that Mary conceived Jesus with her virginity intact, a doctrine enshrined in the early Christian creeds. The sixteenth-century reformers, both Catholic and Protestant upheld it.

The perpetual virginity of Mary was taken to imply an integral purity of body and soul. Thus, in the opinion of many theologians, she was also free of other sins, including original sin, the sin with which all human beings are born. The doctrine of the Immaculate Conception, defined as Roman Catholic dogma by Pope Pius IX, in 1854, states that Mary was not only pure in her life and at birth, but that at the first instant of her conception she was preserved immaculate from all stain of original sin, by the singular grace and privilege granted her by Almighty God, through the merits of Christ Jesus, Saviour of mankind.

The attributes of the Virgin Mary are so numerous that, in the 1950s, Pope Pius XII formally defined a number of the traditional ones, including the Immaculate Conception and the Assumption of Mary to Heaven. The characterisation of Queen of Heaven was particularly relevant to relaunch the image of the papacy during the difficult post-war years.

However, the cult of Mary in modern times has focused mainly on her power of intercession: her role as intermediary between the faithful and Christ. Mary exists as a bridge between this world and the next.

Mary's power of intercession can be of succour to the living, but she has an even more important role to play in the salvation of the souls of sinners. She is able to plead to God, to show mercy towards the truly repentant soul on the Day of Judgement. The terrors of Hell await only the unrepentant sinner; all those who confess their sins in a spirit of contrition will be spared the flames of damnation. Between Heaven and Hell lies Purgatory, a sort of waiting room where the soul can be prepared for acceptance into Heaven. It is here that the Virgin has a particular importance, for her pleas are more likely to be heeded than those of any other saint. The tradition of the Eastern Church accepts that Mary went herself to visit the damned in Hell. Horrified by what she witnessed, she begged Christ for mercy. The Western tradition does not include the account of Mary's descent into Hell, but the belief in her ability to banish evil and darkness is widespread.

Among all her numerous roles - as mother of God, mother of the Church, Queen of Heaven and all the other characterisations - it is her intercession on behalf of the souls of the living and the dead that places Mary in this unique and supremely important position

Mary's Intercession
We can receive absolutely nothing ... nothing, unless, God willing, it is bestowed on us through Mary.
(Pope Leo XIII, Encyclical, 1891)

Representation of the Virgin in art
In Eastern art the representation of the Virgin remained static from about the fourth century, since innovation was discouraged. Artists from the East were permitted little freedom to depart from earlier models because they were constrained by the belief that the copy of an image was as venerable as the original icon. Nor did clients want any departure from the original, for fear of losing the work's sacred quality. However, Western artists were not restricted in terms of stylistic or technical development, even if they had to adhere to doctrinal rules.

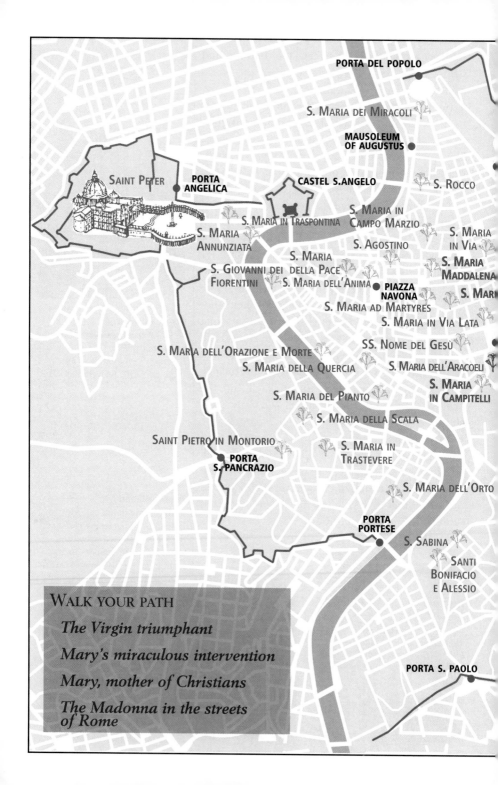

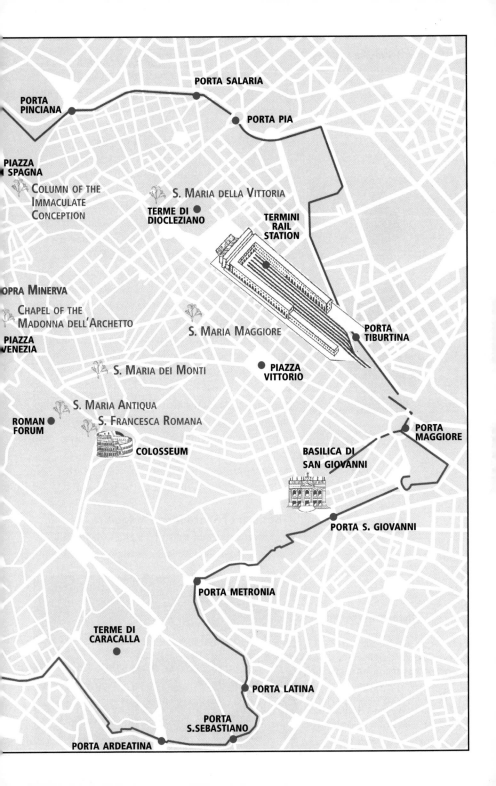

Prayer, Ave Regina Caelorum
Hail, Queen of Heaven,
beyond compare,
To whom the angels homage pay,
Hail, Root of Jesse, Gate of Light
that opened for the world's new
day.

Feast day of the Immaculate
Conception: 8ᵗʰ December

Dormition of the Virgin
It is believed that the Virgin cannot die, but can only fall asleep, hence the term Dormition, or sleep.
When the moment arrived for the Virgin to leave this world, an angel called all the Apostles and brought them to Mary in a cloud. At the moment of her death, or sleep, they surrounded her.

WALK YOUR PATH

Our journey will take us from the early examples of churches dedicated to the Virgin to those founded in celebration of Our Lady's miracles. It will continue with a visit to the shrines and chapels erected in honour of Mary, protector and intercessor.

THE VIRGIN TRIUMPHANT

As the mother of Christ, the Christian community in Rome venerated Mary. As early as the first century, stories of her life reached the city. The cult of the Virgin rested mainly on tales of the Annunciation, the Nativity and the Crucifixion.

During the struggle against paganism, as the primary female figure of Christianity, Mary was regarded as a mediator and defender of the Christian community and her cult blossomed in parallel with that of the martyrs. In the fourth century, when the Christian persecution ended, churches began to be built and dedicated to the Virgin. Many were erected on the sites of pagan temples and embellished with columns and materials taken from the earlier buildings. Others were built where miracles and prophecies relating to the advent of Christ took place.

Our journey starts with a visit to the first churches in Rome dedicated to the Virgin.

Basilica of Santa Maria Maggiore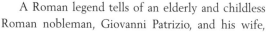

A Roman legend tells of an elderly and childless Roman nobleman, Giovanni Patrizio, and his wife,

who wished to use their wealth to honour the Mother of Christ. They prayed to God for guidance and, following their prayers, Mary appeared to the couple in a dream, telling them to build a church on the Esquiline, one of Rome's seven hills. In the vision, the Virgin explained that the next morning the site would be marked by snow, an event that would require some divine intervention, since it took place in August of 352, the hottest month of the Roman summer! The following morning Patrizio visited Pope Liberius and told him of his dream, only to hear, to his astonishment, that Liberius had had the same vision. They visited the Esquiline together and found, on the spot where the pagan temple of Junonis Lucina once stood, that the ground was indeed covered in snow, in the shape of the plan of a church.

A basilica was financed by the Patrizio couple and built according to the wishes of Mary, following the miraculous plan. Unfortunately, there is no archaeological proof that this was the basilica of Santa Maria Maggiore.

☞ **The Annunciation and other scenes from the Life of Mary**, in the triumphal arch, top left-hand corner, mosaic, third or fourth century

These mosaics stress Mary's role as Theotokos or mother of God. At the moment of the Annunciation, the beginning of her motherhood, she is presented in a grand manner. She is dressed like a Byzantine empress, covered in jewels, with doves over her head and angels around her. She is seated on a throne but she is spinning, with a basket of wool beside her. As a servant of the temple Mary is preparing wool for the veil of the Holy of Holies and, just at that moment, the angel brings her the good news. The other themes of the mosaics are clearly shown following the Apocryphal Gospel, which may signify that they were produced before the time of Pope Sixtus III (432-40). It is possible that they were brought here from an older basilica that, according to legend, Pope Liberius built on the Esquiline. They are: Presentation in the Temple; Adoration of the Three Wise Men; Aphrodisius Welcomes the Holy Family during the Flight to Egypt;

Assumption of the Virgin
Having slept for three days, Mary ascended to Heaven. It is noteworthy that the Virgin went up to Heaven borne by angels, whilst Christ ascended unassisted. In 1950, Pope Pius XII officially declared that the Virgin Mary had been taken up to Heaven, body and soul.

Brief history of the Basilica of Santa Maria Maggiore
This is the largest of the Roman churches dedicated to Mary and the only one in which mass has been celebrated every day without fail since its foundation. It is the fourth of the patriarchal basilicas of Rome and is one of the seven churches designated as landmarks of the city's pilgrimage. Whilst the legend of the miracle of the snow suggests that it was built by Pope Liberius, it actually dates from the papacy of Sixtus III (432-40). It is possible that Liberius' church was another, also built on the Esquiline, now lost. Pope Sixtus III picked the site because it was the location of a pagan temple where women venerated the mother goddess, Juno Lucina. Sixtus III dedicated the church to Mary soon after the Council of Ephesus (431) had confirmed her as *Theotokos*. Mary was not only the Mother of Christ, she was the Mother of God and therefore had supernatural connotations herself. Inside the church, this concept is celebrated with magnificent mosaics. In 1295, the church was enlarged and Jacopo Torriti designed the mosaics in the apse to celebrate the coronation of the Virgin. The exterior of Santa Maria Maggiore is of the eighteenth century, whilst the interior maintains the spiritual atmosphere of the early patriarchal basilicas.

On Christmas Day 1538, Saint Ignatius of Loyola said his first mass in this church.

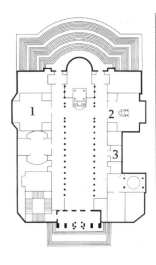

Veni Electa Mea Et Ponam In Te
Thronum Meum
Come, my chosen one, and sit
beside my throne
(Inscription in the book
held by Christ in the mosaic
of the Coronation)

the Slaughter of the Innocents; the Three Wise Men in front of Herod.

☞ **The Coronation of the Virgin flanked by Cardinal Giacomo Colonna (right) and Pope Nicholas IV (left) with angels, Saint John the Baptist, Iacopo and Antonio Colonna and Saints Peter, Paul and Francis,** in the semicircular dome of the apse, mosaics by Iacopo Torriti, 1295

Her position on the throne next to Christ is significant; she is on the same level and of the same height as the Saviour and is thus presented as of equal rank to her Son. She is shown in all her glory to emphasise the Virgin's role as mother of God. The other figures are: on the left, Pope Nicholas IV (1288-92), who commissioned this mosaic, and his two brothers, Cardinal Giacomo and Cardinal Pietro Colonna, who shared with him the cost of the work.

☞ **The Dormition of the Virgin,** in the apse, below the semi-dome, between the two central windows, directly below the Coronation of the Virgin, mosaics, by Iacopo Torriti, 13th century

A scene from the Life of the Virgin, the large central Dormition is memorable for the splendid throng of gilded saints and angels that surround her at the moment of her death. Christ is taking her, in the form of a baby, up to Heaven.

☞ **The Life of Mary,** in the main nave, frescoes by various late Mannerist artists

In 1593, Cardinal Pinelli commissioned the frescoes; in order to accommodate them, half of the windows had to be blocked up. From the altar, towards the entrance, on the right wall, facing the altar: Gloria of Angels, Saints Anna and Joachim with the Immaculate Conception, the Birth of Mary (this is the only fresco dating from the eighteenth century), Presentation in the Temple, the Wedding of Mary, the Annunciation, the Visitation, the Dream of Joseph, the Adoration of the Shepherds, the Adoration of the Wise Men, the Circumcision. On the entrance wall: Flight to Egypt and Rest in Egypt; on the other wall: Jesus, Mary and Joseph Come back to the Temple, Marriage at Cana, the Calvarium, the Crucifixion, the Deposition, the

Resurrection, the Ascension, the Pentecost, the Death of Mary, the Assumption and the Coronation of Mary.

☞ **Assumption of the Virgin,** in the baptistery, to the right of the main entrance of the basilica, high relief by Pietro Bernini, 1608-10

This work is in the old chapel of the Coro Invernale, the 'Winter Choir', converted in 1605 into the baptistery by Flaminio Ponzio and remodelled in 1815 by Giuseppe Valadier.

Borghese Chapel
known also as Paolina Chapel
to the left of the baldachin (1)

During the Middle Ages, pilgrims flocked to this basilica to venerate an ancient image of the Virgin, the *Maria Salus Populi Romani*, traditionally thought to have been painted by Saint Luke with the help of angels. In the seventeenth

century, the icon was placed in this chapel, which is of primary interest to the Marian pilgrim.

☞ **The Legend of the Miracle of the Snow,** above the altar, a gilded relief by Stefano Maderno, 1613

The sculpture celebrates the miracle of the snow and shows Pope Liberius marking the perimeter of the basilica of Santa Maria Maggiore.

☞ ***Maria Salus Populi Romani***, above the altar, painting by Byzantine artists, 12th or 13th century

Set in an incongruously elaborate frame, the painting was moved here on 27th January 1613. Pope Paul V celebrated mass in front of it for the first time on 8th September of the same year.

☞ **The Immaculate Conception among Saints and Apostles,** in the dome, painting, by Ludovico Cardi, nicknamed 'Il Cigoli', 1610

The Virgin stands on a crescent moon. This moon was introduced to images of Mary following the discoveries of Galileo Galilei, the great astronomer and scientist. The moon image is taken from his book, published in Venice in 1610, also the year in which the painting was executed. Correspondence between Galileo and Il Cigoli mentioning this work survives.

Ritual

On 5th August, the miracle of the fall of snow is commemorated by a solemn mass in the Borghese Chapel. White petals fall from above to symbolise the summer snowfall.

Basilica of Santa Maria in Trastevere

According to an old legend, in 38 BC on the day of Christ's birthday, an extraordinary event took place inside the *taberna meritoria*, a tavern where retired Roman soldiers used to meet. A spring of oil erupted from the floor and ran for an entire day. The miraculous episode was interpreted by the Jewish community, who lived in the area at the time, as an omen of the advent of the Messiah. Christians considered the event a premonition of Christ's birth.

During the third century AD, it is believed that Pope Saint Calixtus attended to the local Christian community of Trastevere using a local house church, a *domus ecclesiae*, upon which, a century later, Pope Julius I built the basilica of Santa Maria in Trastevere.

Outside the church:

☞ **Madonna and Child Enthroned,** façade, below the portico, mosaics, 13th and 14th century

The Madonna is surrounded by ten virgins bearing lamps. Some of the virgins bow their heads over unlit lamps, others carry their heads high and carry lit lamps. The lamp is the symbol of virginity, from the parable in the Gospel of Matthew 25: 1-13.

☞ **Annunciation,** in the atrium of the portico, on the left wall, fresco, 15th century

☞ **Madonna and Child with Saint Wenceslas of Bohemia,** in the atrium of the portico, between the main and the left door, fresco, 15th century

These frescoes are included in the small museum of pagan and Christian epigraphs, marbles and sculptures gathered together, during the eighteenth century, by the canon, Marcantonio Boldetti.

☞ **Virgin and Child,** high up on the Romanesque campanile, small golden mosaic

Inside the church:

☞ **The Assumption,** on the ceiling, in the central octagon, painting by Domenichino, 1617

The ceiling and the painting of the Assumption were commissioned by the Cardinal Pietro Aldobrandini.

☞ **Christ with the Virgin as Empress, with Saint Peter, Popes and Saints,** in the semi-dome of the apse, mosaic, circa 1148

The mosaic represents Christ and the Madonna enthroned side by side beneath the hand of God. Christ places His arm around her, in a gesture that mirrors the position of the emperor in some imperial images. In the secular context, it signifies the emperor's confidence in his ministers; the iconography was adapted to suggest the nature of Christ's relationship with His mother as His trusted assistant.

This image emphasises Mary's grandeur. She is richly clad in crown and jewelled robes. As Queen of Heaven, she looks like an empress, a style of representation that has its origins in the changes in the status of the Virgin Mary from the time of her confirmation as Theotokos.

Brief history of the Basilica of Santa Maria in Trastevere

This is the oldest church dedicated to the Virgin Mary in Rome, believed to have been built upon the site of the first *ecclesia domestica* of Pope Saint Calixtus I, where Christians could openly worship God. The basilica was built by Pope Julius I (337-52). In a list of titular churches of AD 499 it is referred to as *Titulus Juli* and in a list of AD 595 as *Titulus Julii et Calisti.* Pope Adrian I (772-95) modernised and enlarged it, adding the lateral naves. Leo III (795-816) embellished it and Pope Gregory IV (827-44) made several major changes: he built the altar and buried below it the relics of the martyrs Pope Saint Calixtus I, Calepodius and Cornelius, venerated by means of *a fenestrella confessionis.* In the twelfth century, the basilica was rebuilt by Pope Innocent II who was from the Trastevere family of the Papareschi. Materials from the Baths of Caracalla were used to modernise it. According to a recent interpretation, the extensive use of such beautiful materials was motivated by eagerness to honour the Virgin Mary, Christ and His Church. It also indicated the restoration of freedom and justice after the long and painful years of persecution. The Baths of Caracalla were built in 216, a few years before Pope Calixtus founded the house church in Trastevere. Calixtus was martyred under Emperor Severus Alexander, who was also a member of the Severi family, from whom Emperor Caracalla was also descended. The 48 columns of the church were taken from a temple of Seraphides, having been stripped of the Egyptian figures that adorned them. The portico is an eighteenth-century addition by Carlo Fontana.

Imago Sanctae Mariae Quae per se Facta Est ('The image of Holy Mary is self-made')

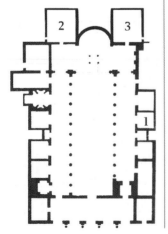

Christ and Mary hold in their hands a script considered to be from the Cantico dei Cantici, *a poem by Saint Francis of Assisi. There is a link between this representation and the miniatures contained in books of this type, in which the Church is represented as a female figure enthroned with Christ, for Mary symbolises the Church. Some people believe that the Virgin represents the Triumphant Celestial Church, while Saint Peter symbolises the terrestrial Church of which he is the head.*

On the sides, there are popes and saints, some of whose relics are kept in the basilica. On the right there are: Pope Cornelius, the martyr Caledopius and Pope Julius I; and on the left: Pope Saint Calixtus, the deacon Saint Lawrence and Pope Innocent II. The latter holds a model of the church, rich in the marbles that adorned imperial buildings.

☞ **Life of the Virgin,** below the dome, mosaics Pietro Cavallini, 1291

The cycle of images of the Life of the Madonna was commissioned by Cardinal Stefaneschi and complements the role of the Madonna in the semi-dome. From the left-hand side they are: the Birth of the Virgin, the Annunciation, the Birth of Christ, the Arrival of the Three Kings, the Presentation of Jesus in the Temple, the Assumption of the Virgin. In this last one, the soul of the Virgin, represented by the effigy of a baby, is embraced by the Redeemer. These mosaics attempt a greater degree of realism than the twelfth-century ones above; the artist's handling of space is more three-dimensional. His representations of the Virgin bring her closer to the real world than the flat, hierarchic image of the Byzantine manner.

☞ **Angels and the Marian Mysteries,** below the mosaics of the dome, paintings by Agostino Ciampelli, before 1605

These paintings were ordered by the Cardinal Alessandro de' Medici during the works carried out by Pope Clement VIII (1592-1605).

☞ **Madonna and Child with Saints Peter and Paul**

and **Bertoldo Stefaneschi,** in the centre of the apse, mosaics by Pietro Cavallini, 1291

A rainbow encircles the Madonna and Child and the two venerable martyrs present the donor, Stefaneschi, a member of a Trastevere family. The coat of arms of his family, shown at the base of the panel, includes crescent moons.

☞ **Fons Olei,** in a small *fenestella* (window), below the presbytery, between the altar canopy and the paschal candlestick, inscription

The inscription marks the spot where the fountain of oil spurted to announce the arrival of our Saviour.

Chapel of the Addolorata
third chapel off the south nave (1)

The chapel was commissioned by Cardinal Francesco Cornaro in 1652 in honour of Our Lady of Sorrow *(Addolorata)*.

☞ **Our Lady of Sorrow,** chapel of the Addolorata, wooden head, Bernini school

Altemps Chapel
to the left (north) of the apse (2)

This chapel was probably the first to be dedicated to an old image of the Virgin Mary after the Counter-Reformation; it is called the Madonna of Clemency and was previously kept in the chapel of the Sacro Cuore di Gesù.

☞ **Scenes from the Life of Mary,** on the ceiling, paintings by Pompeo Abate, 1587-89
☞ **Madonna of Clemency,** altarpiece, icon *Acheropita*, sixth to eighth century

This is one of the oldest images of the Madonna. The faithful believe it to have been produced by non-human hands. In this huge icon, the idea of the Virgin as queen is expressed in its fullest magnificence; not only is she dressed in the richest of robes, but angels stand at her side like imperial guards.

Brief history of the Chapel of the Addolorata
Built in 1652 by Cardinal Cornaro, in 1668 it was donated to the de Benedictis family. Subsequently, it was remodelled by Cardinal Cassetta, who financed the works.

Brief history of the Altemps Chapel
The chapel was commissioned by Cardinal Marco Sittico Altemps, nephew of Pope Pius IV, in honour of the Madonna of Clemency. It was built in 1584-85 by Martino Longhi the Elder.

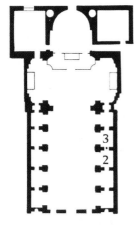

Chapel of the Coro d'Inverno

in the transept, to the right (south) of the apse **(3)**

Originally, these were the rooms of the sacristans of the basilica, converted in 1625 by Domenichino into a chapel to house an image of the Virgin, known as Madonna di Strada Cupa. The painting was found in a dark street (*cupa* means 'dark' in Italian), on the door of the vineyard of the Nobili family, at the foot of the Gianicolo. The image soon became the object of popular devotion because it was believed to be miraculous.

☞ **Madonna di Strada Cupa,** on the altar, painting, attributed to Perino del Vaga, pupil of Raphael, 16th century.

Church of Santa Maria in Traspontina

According to a traditional tale, in 1216 a miraculous icon of the Virgin and Child was brought to Rome from the Holy Land by a group of priests of the Order of Carmelites. The portrait of the Virgin Mary was named Madonna del Carmelo, from Mount Carmel in Palestine where, circa 1155, a number of devout men, apparently former pilgrims and crusaders, established themselves as Carmelites near the place where Elijah, an Old Testament prophet, made the miracle of the rain. The image of the Virgin was placed on the main altar of the old church of Santa Maria in Traspontina, where it could easily be seen and venerated by the Romans. When the church was destroyed and rebuilt further away from the river Tiber, safe from the floods, the miraculous image of the Virgin was placed on the main altar.

Outside the church:

☞ **Madonna del Carmine with Child,** on the façade of the church, statue in stucco by Filippo Tenti, 1572

The statue was commissioned by Father Arcangelo Leoni.

Inside the church:

☞ **Madonna del Carmine and Child,** on the main

altar, painting 13th century, mostly repainted

This is the icon believed to have been brought back from Mount Carmel. In 1641 the Madonna was crowned by the Vatican and in 1651 the Child received a crown as well.

☞ **Apparition of Mary and the Holy Spirit to Three Saints,** in the chapel of Santa Maria Maddalena dei Pazzi, painting by Gian Domenico Cerrini, 1639

The painting replaced an older one by Giovan Battista Ricci da Novara painted around 1626-27.

☞ **Madonna del Carmine and Child Giving the Scapular to Saint Simon Stock,** in the vault of the sacristy, painting attributed to Pietro Paolo Baldini, circa 1637

☞ **The Immaculate Conception,** on the end wall of the sacristy, painting, 18th century

The sacristy was built in 1637 by Francesco Paparelli. The area is covered in oak panels commissioned by Francesco Bidio. The works were completed in 1665-66 under the supervision of Father Girolamo Ari. The images of the Madonna del Carmine and of the Immacolata Concezione represent two of the Madonna's roles that are particularly honoured by the Order of Carmelites.

Chapel of the Madonna del Carmelo

also known as the Chapel of the Immacolata Concezione, third chapel on the left (north) side **(2)**

In 1922 a modern sculpture of the Madonna del Carmine was placed on the main altar of the chapel of the Immacolata Concezione, which was then renamed the chapel of the Madonna del Carmine. On 16th July of the same year, feast day of the Virgin of Carmel, the wooden image of the Virgin was carried in a procession. Since then a solemn procession has been organised on that day to display the Madonna del Carmine in the streets of the two boroughs.

☞ **Madonna del Carmelo,** on the altar, wooden statue by Aureliano of the Order of Fratelli della Misericordia, 1922

Brief history of the Church of Santa Maria in Traspontina
Built in the eighth century, the old church was located near Porta Sant'Angelo. Originally it was known as Santa Maria in Adrianium as it is believed that Pope Adrian I (772-95) built it and embellished it. The name Traspontina, from *transpontem*, 'over the bridge', derives from its position right at the end of Ponte Sant'Angelo. Pope Innocent II (1198-1216) put it under the jurisdiction of the Vatican Basilica. During the papacy of Innocent VIII (1484-92) extensive works were carried out by the Order of Carmelites, who also began to build a convent which was completed in 1498. Because the church was very close to the bank of the Tiber, it was often flooded by the river. In addition, its vicinity and position near the Castel Sant'Angelo, the Vatican fortress, hindered the movements of the papal artillery. In 1532 Pope Clement VII decided to move the church and the convent to a different site. In 1564 Pope Pius IV had it demolished so that the fortifications of Castel Sant'Angelo could be enlarged. Two years later the church was rebuilt in the Borgo, further away from the river, to the plan of Giovanni Sallistio Peruzzi, with the help of Ottaviano Mascherino and Francesco Paparelli.

Chapel of the Crucifix
*fourth chapel on the right (south) side from the
entrance* **(3)**

During the Middle Ages pilgrims visited this
church to venerate the miraculous statue of Christ
on the Cross, the image *Acheropita* of the Madonna
del Carmelo and the two columns where,
according to tradition, Saint Peter and Saint Paul
were flagellated. When the church was rebuilt, the
wooden sculpture of Christ on the Cross and the
two columns were moved to a purpose-built
chapel.

 **Christ on the Cross with the Virgin Mary and
Saint John the Evangelist,** altarpiece in the chapel of
the Crucifix; wooden cross, 16th century; fresco by
Cesare Conti, 1585

*When the sculpture of Christ on the Cross was
placed in the chapel, Cesare Conti was commissioned to
paint, on either side, the Virgin Mary and Saint John the
Evangelist.*

Church of Santa Maria dell'Aracoeli
also known as Santa Maria in Capitolio

According to a medieval legend, when the
Emperor Augustus was puzzled by the Senate's wish
to honour him as a god he called the Tiburtine sibyl
to his palace in Arx, Rome's first citadel, in the
Campidoglio. During the meeting, the sibyl
announced the coming of Christ and prophesied that
a virgin would bear a divine son, who would cast out
the altars of the pagan gods. The legend goes on to say
that the emperor had a vision while asleep. He saw
the sky opening up and a fantastic light coming down
towards him and a beautiful virgin above an altar
with a child in her arms. A voice said, 'This is the
Virgin who will conceive the Saviour of the world.'
Soon after, another voice said, 'This is the altar of the
Son of God.' Augustus knelt down and venerated the
forthcoming Christ.

At the suggestion of the sibyl, the emperor built a
temple on the very site where their meeting had

taken place and dedicated it to the 'firstborn of God'. Augustus raised an altar, called the *Ara Filii Dei* or *Aracoeli*; thus the name of the church became Santa Maria in Aracoeli, rather than Santa Maria in Capitolio.

☞ **Virgin and Child,** on the ceiling, painting by Girolamo Sicciolante and Cesare Trapasi, 1572-75

The ceiling was commissioned by the people of Rome as an ex voto *to the Virgin after the Victory at Lepanto, 1571. A few years later, in 1577, the ceiling of the transept was built.*

☞ **Saint Luke,** on the fifth column, to the side of the altar of the Madonna del Rifugio, fresco, 14th century

This image of Saint Luke is venerated following the tradition that he painted the icon Acheropita, *of the Madonna and Child, placed in the main altar of this church.*

☞ **Representations of the Antithesis between Mary and Eve,** on the walls of the first chapel on the left, originally dedicated to the Immaculate Conception, frescoes by Francesco Pichi, circa 1555

These are very interesting frescoes concerning the roles of Mary and Eve. They are, in the lunette: the Virgin as the woman of the Apocalypse; on the right, Antithesis between Adam and Eve and Christ and the Virgin; in the lunette: Adoration of the Virgin; in the vault: Scenes from the Old Testament.

☞ **Virgin and Child,** main altar, icon *Acheropita*, tenth century

This is the venerated image of the Madonna in honour of which, in 1348, at the end of the plague, the staircase of the Aracoeli was built. In 1948 the city of Rome was consecrated to this Madonna.

☞ **Emperor Augustus and the Sibyl,** in the middle of the vault, fresco by Nicolò Martinelli, circa 1565

The other frescoes are: Madonna with Jesus and Musician Angels, the Nativity, the Circumcision and the Evangelists.

☞ **Madonna della Gatta,** in front of the chapel of the Santo Bambino, painting by Giulio Romano, a copy of the original is kept in the Pinacoteca di Capodimonte, Naples.

Sibyls
Priestesses of Apollo, sibyls were women who had the gift of prophecy. Towards the end of the Middle Ages, the Church of the West interpreted their prophecies as foretelling the coming of Christ. They are seen as the pagan counterparts of the Old Testament prophets.

The Sibyl's prophecy
There are signs that justice will be done, soon the earth will be bathed in sweat and from the sun will descend the King of future centuries.

The Sibyl, about Christ
The Jewish son will be without sin and hostile to the pagan cult.

Voices from Heaven
Ecce ara primogeniti Dei.
This is the altar of the first born of God.

139

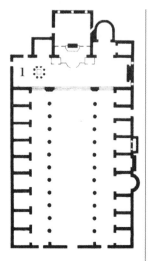

Chapel of Sant'Elena
north transept **(1)**

This is believed to be the original site where Emperor Augustus had his vision and where the first church was built. Here the icon of the Virgin and Child was venerated, before it was removed to the main altar of the church.

☞ **Augustus kneeling in front of the Virgin,** the altar, low-relief sculpture, 12th century

The altar is visible through a glass opening in the floor, as the floor level of the presbytery has been raised.

☞ **Relic of Saint Helen,** on the altar, inside an urn of porphyry, 12th century

The relic, believed to be the ashes of Saint Helen, was found in 1963 during excavations below the chapel.

Brief history of the Chapel of Sant'Elena

Built by Monsignor Girolamo Centelles, Bishop of Cavallion, in 1605, the chapel was completed in 1624. In 1833, it was rebuilt by Pietro Holl. In 1963, excavations below the chapel brought to light the remains of the old altar of Augustus and the relics of Saint Helen.

Church of Santa Maria Antiqua
also known as Santa Maria Liberatrice
a Poenis Inferni

The church of Santa Maria Antiqua was the first civilian building of the imperial period to be converted into a church. Originally dedicated to the cult of Minerva, the Roman goddess, the new building was named after the Virgin Mary. Thus the transformation into a Christian church, dedicated to the mother of Christ, stresses the contrast between the cult of the Virgin and the pagan cult of Minerva.

In the thirteenth century a new church, also dedicated to the cult of the Virgin Mary, was built upon the ruins of the old basilica, Santa Maria Liberatrice a Poenis Inferni. The unusual name, *a poenis inferni*, derives from an old superstition. Romans believed that the site was inhabited by demons, perhaps because of its proximity to the old temple of Vesta, where for centuries a fire had burned to honour the Roman goddess Minerva, or, because of the nearby pond named *Lacus Curtius*, where, during the dark centuries of Christian persecutions, 40 Christian martyrs had frozen to death. According to an old legend, with the help of

Brief history of the Church of Santa Maria Antiqua

Santa Maria Antiqua was the first civic palace of the imperial time (it dates back to the Emperor Vespasian) to be converted into a church. Originally it was dedicated to the cult of Minerva. In the sixth century AD the church was dedicated to the Virgin Mary. Remodelled and embellished by Pope John VII (705-07), Pope Zacharias (741-52), Pope Paul I (757-67) and Pope Adrian I (772-95), after a series of earthquakes it was abandoned. Under Pope Leo IV (847-55), the cult of the Virgin was transferred to the church of Santa Maria Nova.

the Virgin Mary, Pope Sylvester II (999-1003) liberated the site from the demons by killing a dragon, which clearly symbolised the power of the Devil.

In 1900, the church was demolished to restore the original structure of the basilica of Santa Maria Antiqua.

☞ **Assembly of Oriental Saints,** on the walls of the ruins, Byzantine frescoes, eighth century

This rare series of frescoes was executed by artists from Constantinople, who had fled to Rome during the period of Iconoclasm in their native city. They conform to the Byzantine tradition of showing a group of oriental saints together with scenes from the scriptures.

Church of Santa Maria sopra Minerva ✝

On 8th October 1530, during the papacy of Clement VII, the river flooded, threatening to submerge the entire city of Rome. People were scared and gathered inside the churches to pray and ask for help. When the water reached the foot of the church of Santa Maria sopra Minerva, it suddenly stopped and the flood began to recede. It is believed that the city was saved by the divine intervention of the Virgin Mary, who is venerated inside this church.

Outside the church

☞ **Inscriptions commemorating the flood of 1530,** on the right of the façade, wall inscriptions

These inscriptions list the floods of the river Tiber that have reached the church, including the one of 1530.

Chapel of the Annunciation

half-way down the nave, on the right (south) side **(1)**

Particularly strong in this church is the cult of the Annunciation of Mary. Pilgrims used to visit it on the day of the Annunciation, 25th March, to participate in the festivities in honour of Mary.

☞ **Annunciation,** altarpiece, painting by Antoniazzo Romano, circa 1508

Here the traditional iconography of the

Brief history of the Chapel of the Annunciation

Built in 1460, the chapel belonged to a Confraternity of the Annunciation, which was founded in the fifteenth century by the Dominican Cardinal Giovanni Torquemada, who also commissioned the chapel. The confraternity provided dowries for girls from poor families. In the sixteenth century, the chapel was redecorated by Carlo Maderno.

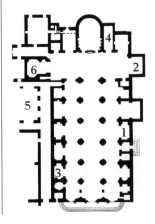

Annunciation embraces a further scene related to the Confraternity of the Annunciation. The Virgin and the Archangel Gabriel are the key figures and are therefore the largest. Between them, on a much smaller scale, are three girls receiving their dowries, introduced to their benefactress by Cardinal Torquemada. It should be remembered that Mary is the patron of brides; thus, it seems appropriate for a confraternity concerned with the provision of dowries to poor girls to have the chapel dedicated to the Virgin Mary.

Carafa Chapel
at the end of the right (south) aisle (2)

This chapel was built by the Dominican Cardinal Oliviero Carafa at the end of the fifteenth century to commemorate Saint Thomas Aquinas, the Dominican theologian, whom Carafa considered as his intercessor with the Virgin Mary.

☞ **Annunciation,** on the altar, painting by Filippino Lippi, 1488

Here Saint Thomas is introducing Cardinal Carafa, the Neapolitan cardinal who commissioned the memorable frescoes, to the Virgin and the Archangel Gabriel. In the fresco of the Annunciation, the artist has stressed the humanity of the Virgin.

☞ **The Assumption of the Virgin,** above the altar, fresco by Filippino Lippi, 1488

Mary is assisted in her ascent by a choir of musician angels. Lippi's fresco on the wall above the altarpiece makes a splendid contrast to the Annunciation since it depicts the Assumption of the Virgin, when she appears in her most ethereal guise, as she is borne up to Heaven on a cloud surrounded by musician angels. Taken together, the two representations of Mary, in the Annunciation of the altarpiece and here in the Assumption, describe the duality of her role as both a human and a celestial being. These are the two key chapters in her life: the first being the Annunciation and the last her Assumption. Filippino Lippi created an illusionistic opening in the wall: the blue sky to which the Virgin

is ascending is like an opening in the chapel itself. The Apostles are below, reunited to witness her ascension.

☞ **Sibyls,** vault of the chapel, fresco by Filippino Lippi, 1488-93

☞ **Virgin and Child between Saint Dominic and Saint Privato,** on the left of the chapel above the tomb of Guglielmo Durand, Bishop of Mende, mosaic by Giovanni Cosma

The bishop, who died in 1296, is represented kneeling on the left of the throne of the Virgin. He is introduced to her by Saint Privato.

Frangipane Chapel
also known as Maddalena Capodiferro Chapel
*second on the left (north) of the main altar **(3)***

In this chapel is buried Beato Angelico, Domenican friar and one of the most important painters of the fifteenth century.

☞ **Virgin and Child,** above the altar, painting on canvas attributed to Fra Angelico, mid-fifteenth century

The painting is now thought to be a standard or flag designed by a later follower of Frà Angelico. The image is full of poignancy, yet traces of the Byzantine style's remoteness are still present. The work can, perhaps, be seen as a bridge between the iconic style of the mosaic of the Madonna above the tomb of the Bishop of Mende and the warmer manner of the representation of the Virgins by Filippino Lippi in the Carafa Chapel.

Chapel of the Blessed Virgin of the Rosary
on the right (south) of the altar (4)

In order to commemorate the victory of the Christian fleet over the Turks at Lepanto on 7th October 1571, all the confraternities dedicated to the Virgin of the Rosary gathered in a large procession to walk through the streets of Rome. Apparently the Christian soldiers recited the Holy Rosary before the Battle of Lepanto.

Since then, the feast of the Rosary has been celebrated on 7th October.

Fra Angelico
Born in Vicchio near Florence, in 1400, as Guido da Pietro, he was also called Giovanni da Fiesole. He died in Rome on 18th February 1455. Two strands were interwoven in Angelico's life in Florence: the pious life of a monk and his continuous activity as a painter. Vasari described him as 'saintly and excellent and, not long after his death, he was given the nickname *angelico* ('angelic' in Italian), because of his moral qualities. This subsequently became the name by the word *beato* ('blessed').

Brief history of the Chapel of the Blessed Virgin of the Rosary
The chapel has been dedicated to the Virgin of the Rosary since 1579 and specifically to the Annunciation. It occupies a prestigious place near the altar of the church, where a mass is said in which the sacrifice of Christ for our salvation is re-enacted. The chapel belongs to the Capranica family, who financed its decoration in 1639.

☞ **Our Lady of the Holy Rosary with Saints Dominic and Catherine,** altarpiece, painting by Maratta, 1500

☞ **Mysteries of the Holy Rosary,** on the vault of the barrel dome, canvas paintings by Marcello Venusti and Carlo Saraceni, 16th century

The Mystery of the Crowning with Thorns is by Saraceni, all the others are by Venusti.

The Cloister (5)

The use of rosary beads to assist the faithful in their prayers derives from an Eastern habit that was introduced to western Europe in about the eleventh century.

It is possible that pilgrims who visited the Holy Land brought back the idea. In the fifteenth century, the rosary gained in popularity, finally securing papal approval from Pope Alexander VI in 1495. This gave great impetus to the practice and many confraternities were established specifically for the reciting of the rosary.

The Dominicans are closely identified with this devotional aid.

☞ **Cycle of the Rosary,** in the cloister, frescoes by various artists, 17th century

In very poor condition, they serve as a reminder that the use of the rosary was made popular by the Dominicans.

Chapel of San Domenico
from the cloister, immediately on the left (north) **(6)**

☞ **Madonna and Child with Saints John the Baptist and John the Evangelist as Children,** marble sculpture by Francesco Grassi, 1670

The charming Madonna is with the two saints as children. The vivid realism of the artist's portrayal brings these children firmly into the realm of everyday life; their sainthood is underplayed in favour of their characterisation as very young boys.

☞ **Apparition of the Virgin to Saint Dominic,** above the altar of Saint Giacinto, painting by Ottaviano Leoni, 16th century

Church of Santa Maria ad Martyres
also known as the Pantheon
and Chiesa di Santa Maria Rotonda

When, in 609, this became the first Roman temple to be converted into a Christian church, the message of the triumph of Christianity was proclaimed loud and clear. The decision to convert this temple into a church marks a major change in the attitude of Christians towards pagan temples, which were previously considered unholy. After the Edict of Milan, in 313, it became normal practice to destroy the earlier buildings and to construct churches on the same sites, reusing stone and other materials from the temples.

The interior is circular and is punctuated by eight *aediculae* (shrines) and seven chapels, many of which bear references to the Virgin Mary.

☞ **The Annunciation,** in the first chapel, on the right, fresco by Melozzo da Forlì or Antoniazzo da Romano, 15th century

Brief history of the Church of Santa Maria ad Martyres
This magnificent monument, known as the Pantheon, represented the might of ancient Rome. It was originally conceived as both a temple dedicated to all the gods and a secular imperial monument. It was built by Menenio Agrippa in AD 27. After a fire in AD 120 it was rebuilt by Emperor Hadrian. In 609, the Byzantine Emperor Foca donated it to Pope Boniface IV, who converted it into a church dedicated to the Virgin Mary. Originally the church was called Santa Maria ad Martyres because Boniface IV placed in it a large number of bones taken from the catacombs, which were believed to belong to early Christian martyrs. Only after AD 1000 was the church renamed Santa Maria Rotonda.

All Saints' Day
On 1st November 609, Pope Boniface IV dedicated the church to Santa Maria ad Martyres. From then onwards, All Saints' Day was celebrated on that date. In the past, on All Saints' Day, the pope used to say a solemn mass in front of the Roman Senate. The same ritual took place on the feast day of the martyrs Rasius and Anastasius.

Pilgrims used to flock to this church on the day of Saint Joseph of the Holy Land, patron saint of the Congregazione dei Virtuosi, and visitors to the basilica enjoyed the same indulgences as those who visited the Holy Land. On the day of Pentecost, during the ceremonies, people were showered with rose petals scattered from the cupola. In the past, on the fourth Sunday of Lent, the pope came here to bless the Golden Rose, which he presented to the Christian kings who had deserved it.

Rituals

On the feast day of the Immaculate Conception, firemen bring flowers for the Virgin and lay them at the foot of the column that bears her statue.

Brief history of the Column of the Immaculate Conception

The column was commissioned by Pope Pius IX in 1856 to commemorate the Dogma of the Immaculate Conception. The column was found in Campus Martius and Luigi Poletti redesigned it. Four statues are at the base, those of Isaiah, Ezekiel, David and Moses. It is surmounted by a bronze statue of the Madonna.

☞ **Coronation of the Virgin,** in the second *aedicula* on the right, fresco, Tuscan school, 14th century

☞ **Virgin and Saint Anne,** in the third *aedicula* on the right, statue by Lorenzo Ottoni known as Lorenzone, 17th to 18th century

☞ **Madonna with Saint Francis and Saint John the Baptist,** third chapel on the right, chapel of the Madonna of Clemency, Umbrian-Lazio school, circa 15th century

☞ **Madonna and Child,** main altar, painting, beginning of the seventh century

This image of the Virgin was crowned twice by the Vatican Chapter, in 1652 and 1697. The altar was built by Alessandro Specchi in the seventeenth century.

☞ **The Madonna del Sasso,** third *aedicula* on the left, statue by Lorenzo Lotti called Il Lorenzetto, 1524

This statue was commissioned by the artist Raphael for his tomb. The tomb of the artist was found in 1833 underneath an arch with this statue above it. Raphael is buried here, in a Roman sarcophagus, with an inscription by the humanist Pietro Bembo.

☞ **The Assumption,** on entering the church, immediately on the left, painting by Andrea Camassei, 1638

On the day of the Assumption, the image of the Virgin used to be taken up towards the roof where it disappeared through the opening in the cupola.

Column of the Immaculate Conception

On 8th December 1854, Pope Pius IX declared the Dogma of the Immaculate Conception in front of about 250,000 bishops, priests, and faithful. To glorify the dogma, a monument dedicated to the Immaculate Conception was erected in Piazza di Spagna. Following the tradition of early Christian art, a pagan column was converted to Christian imagery.

The inauguration took place on 8th December 1857. Since then, on this date, the Church has celebrated the feast day of the Immaculate Conception.

MARY'S MIRACULOUS INTERVENTION

Our journey next visits churches housing images of the Virgin that are said to have performed miracles.

Brief history of the Church of Santa Maria dei Monti

Work started on 23rd June 1580, under the supervision of Giacomo della Porta. The church was financed by the Farnese, Confalonieri, Orsini and Piccolomini families, and by the residents of the area where the image of the Virgin had first appeared. After the death of della Porta, Carlo Lombardi and Flamino Ponzio took over but the bulk of the works had already been completed. Between 1898 and 1899, the church underwent extensive restoration, which was necessitated by the humidity that had damaged the interior. During that time the inscription invoking the Madonna was added to the cornice of the church. In 1949, in preparation for the Marian Year of 1950, more works were carried out.

Church of Santa Maria dei Monti

In 1579, after a series of earthquakes had frightened residents of the Esquiline, a fresco, portraying the Virgin flanked by Saint Lawrence and Saint Stephen, appeared inside the stable of a large building converted from a nunnery into residential apartments. Many believed that the stable used to be the old chapel of the monastery, built in the thirteenth century and dedicated to Saint Clare. The residents of the building cleared up the stable and converted it into a chapel. On 26th April 1580 a blind woman, praying in the chapel in front of the portrait of the Madonna, regained her sight. More miraculous events took place after this, so Pope Gregory XIII suggested the removal of the image to the church of Santissimo Salvatore. Local people did not welcome the suggestion and, with the support of Cardinal Bianchetti and Cardinal Sirleto, it was decided to build a proper church to house the miraculous portrait of the Virgin.

147

Outside the church:
☞ **Madonna delle Grazie,** on the façade, *aedicula* with mosaic, 1949

This image was added during the works in preparation for the celebration of the Marian Year in 1950.

Inside the church:
☞ **Madonna and Child flanked by Saint Lawrence and Saint Stephen,** on the main altar, *aedicula,* beginning of the 15th century

This is the miraculous image of the Virgin. Above the altar there is a statue of Christ with two angels.

☞ **Scenes from the Life of Mary,** in the apse, by various artists, 1600

This is a beautiful cycle of the Life of the Madonna, produced for the Jubilee of 1600 by members of the Roman Mannerist school, pupils of Cesare Nebbia. Top register: Nativity, Presentation in the Temple, Marriages. Bottom register: Nativity, Adoration of the Magi, Presentation of Jesus in the Temple, Visitation, Pentecost, Death of the Virgin, Assumption, Coronation of Mary.

Chapel of the Madonna dell'Archetto

On 9th July 1796, while the French army was threatening to invade Rome, a large number of people gathered to pray in front of the image of the Madonna, kept inside the *aedicula* below the arch (*archetto* in Italian means 'small arch') that connected Palazzo Casati and the building of the Confraternity of Sant'Antonio, in Vicolo Marcello. As people prayed, and chanted '*Sancta Maria*', the eyes of the Madonna moved, first to the right and then to the left, to look lovingly upon her faithful people. It is said that somebody even took a ladder and reached up to the face of the portrait to measure how much the eyes had moved.

☞ **Madonna dell'Archetto,** on the main altar, painting on *pietra maiolicata* by Domenico Maria Muratori, end of the 17th century

The painting was commissioned by the Marquis Mellini Muti Savorelli from Domenico Muratori because he wanted a copy made of an image of the

Ritual
On 8th September, the date of the Nativity of the Virgin, the parish feast takes place and the miracle is remembered.

Brief history of the Chapel of the Madonna dell'Archetto
In the nineteenth century the Marquis Alessandro and Caterina Papazzurri commissioned the construction of the chapel, which was built by Virgilio Vespignani in 1851.

Madonna that belonged to a nun from the Mellini family, Mother Ersilia Mellini. Towards the middle of the nineteenth century, the aedicula was taken off the street and put in the chapel, purpose-built by Vespignani to house it. The chapel took its name, chapel of the Madonna dell'Archetto, from the painting. The image was crowned in 1946. Saint Maksymilian Maria Kolbe and Pope John XXIII (1958-63) were among the people particularly drawn to it.

Church of Santa Maria in Via
Chapel of the Madonna del Pozzo
first chapel on the right of the entrance

According to a medieval legend Cardinal Capocci, who lived in the thirteenth century, had his residence on the site of this church. In the courtyard there was a well where, one day, the image of the Madonna appeared. Subsequently a church was built around the well.

☞ **Well,** right-hand side of the altar

This is the well where the image of the Madonna appeared in 1256. It is still possible to draw drinking water from the well.

☞ **Madonna del Pozzo,** altar, painting

Church of Santa Maria della Vittoria ✝ 🕮

In the seventeenth century, in Bohemia, a group of heretics disfigured a tiny image of the Virgin. A Carmelite father saved the image from the Lutherans' hands and it was subsequently carried to the battlefield near Prague where, on 8th November 1620, the army of Duke Maximilian of Bavaria fought against the Lutheran army of Frederick of Saxony. According to a legend, the image shone so intensely that the enemy was blinded and was easily overcome. Thus, Mary helped the army of the faithful to triumph over the heretics. Since then the miraculous image has been known as Madonna della Vittoria.

☞ **Madonna della Vittoria,** on the main altar

This very small image is now kept in a reliquary

Brief history of the Church of Santa Maria in Via
The church was built in the thirteenth century. In 1594 Francesco da Volterra was commissioned to rebuild it upon a project of Giacomo della Porta. The interior of the church has a single nave. The baroque front was completed in 1670.

Prayer
Holy Virgin of the Victory, Mother of God and Our Mother, you who for centuries have fought at the side of the Church the battles of Truth and Faith, grant your children victory over errors and evils and obtain for us Grace and Love from your Divine Son.... Amen.

Brief history of the Church of Santa Maria dei Miracoli

A chapel, called Santa Maria dei Miracoli, was built on the site where the miracle had taken place, to house the image of the Madonna. Pope Clement VII (1523-34) donated it to the Hospital of San Giacomo degli Incurabili. In 1530, the chapel and the image were flooded by the Tiber. In 1598, following other floods, the portrait of the Virgin was moved to the newly-built church of Saint Giacomo in Augusta, where it has remained ever since. A copy replaced the original in the chapel of Santa Maria dei Miracoli. Owing to the frequent flooding of the river, the church was demolished and rebuilt in Piazza del Popolo, further away from the Tiber. In 1678, work started on the site of the old oratory of Sant'Orsola to a plan by Carlo Rainaldi and Bernini, which was completed by Fontana. It is centrally planned with a circular dome. The church was inaugurated on 5th August 1856, the day of the anniversary of the miracle of the snow, the feast day of the Virgin of the Snow. Visually it functions as a twin of the church of Santa Maria in Montesanto on the other side of the street, at the south end of Piazza del Popolo.

with a gilded frame. Above the altar on the vault of the apse, a fresco depicts the battle and on either side there are swords and lances used in the fight.

☞ **Triumphal Entrance of the Image of the Madonna into Prague,** above the altar, frescoes by Luigi Serra, 1883-84

☞ **Maximilian of Bavaria during the Battle,** in the sacristy, painting by Sebastiano Conca, end of the 18th century

Church of Santa Maria dei Miracoli

On 20th June 1525 a mother and child went to the bank of the Tiber, near Porta del Popolo, to gather some wood for a fire. The child leant forward and fell into the river, which was almost at flood levels. Nearby, on the side of the river bank, there was an image of the Madonna painted on canvas. In desperation, the woman turned towards the picture and prayed to the Virgin Mary to save her child. Suddenly, two men came by and rescued the little boy, who was not even scared. He told his mother that, while he was in the water, a lady dressed in white had supported him, preventing him from drowning.

☞ **Miraculous Image of the Virgin,** on the main altar, copy of the original kept in the church of San Giacomo in Augusta

Upon a background of clouds, the Virgin holds the hand of the Christ Child in one of her own, while in the other she holds the rosary.

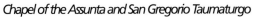

Chapel of the Assunta and San Gregorio Taumaturgo
right of the entrance (1)

☞ **Assunta and San Gregorio,** painting on canvas, 19th century

This painting was brought here from the church of Santa Chiara in 1856.

Chapel of San Giuseppe
next to the presbytery (2)

☞ **Virgin of Betharram,** statue, copy of original by Alexandre Renoir kept in the sanctuary of Nostra Signora di Betharram in Lourdes

This is a very popular statue, an object of devotion and veneration. It is also called Nostra Signora del Bel Ramo.

Chapel of the Rosary
opposite Chapel of San Giuseppe (3)

☞ **Madonna,** painting, a modern copy of the Madonna by Sassoferrato kept in Santa Sabina

Chapel of Sant'Antonio
next to Chapel of the Rosary (4)

☞ **Virgin and Child with Saints,** on the altar by Henry Gascard, 17th century

Church of Santa Maria della Pace

In the portico of the small church of Sant'Andrea de Aquarizzaris, named after the water salesmen, there was an image of the Virgin that was very dear to the people of Rome. Around 1480, after a stone thrown by a gambler in a rage hit it, the Madonna started to bleed. Pope Sixtus IV, touched by the event, renamed the church Santa Maria della Virtù (Saint Mary of Virtue) and mounted a solemn procession to visit the miraculous image. Arriving in front of the Madonna, he promised the Virgin that if the war threatened by the Florentine, Congiura de' Pazzi, an attempt to attack Rome, could be avoided, he would build a church on the site of the image. The war having been duly averted, the pope fulfilled his promise and erected the church of Madonna della

Brief history of the Church of Santa Maria della Pace
In 1482 Pope Sixtus IV commissioned the church from Baccio Pontelli. The works were completed under the papacy of Innocent VIII and in 1490 he transferred the miraculous image of Mary to the church, in honour of the peace of Bagnolo (1484) made with the Florentines. In 1656, under Pope Alexander VII, Pietro da Cortona built the façade and the beautiful little semicircular portico. His design for the surrounding buildings and the piazza was never completed.

Pace (*pace* is Italian for 'peace').

☞ **Madonna della Pace,** on the main altar, fresco, 15th century

The image is to be found among the decoration of the altar by Stefano Maderno. It still bears the sign of the impact. It was crowned by the Church in 1634.

☞ **Nativity and Annunciation,** at the side of the main altar, by D. Cresti, known as Passignano

☞ **Scenes from the Life of the Virgin,** in the central octagon below the cupola, paintings originally by Baldassarre Peruzzi, 1517

The paintings commissioned by Filippo Segardi have been destroyed and replaced; only one remains intact. From above the altar of the Crocefisso, from left to right they are: the Nativity by R. Vanni; the Presentation to the Temple by B. Peruzzi; the Visitation by C. Maratta; the Transit of the Virgin by G. M. Morandi.

Oratorio della Dottrina Cristiana

to the left of the Church of Santa Maria in Traspontina

An image of the Madonna and Child was painted on the wall of a house in the Borgo, the borough around the Vatican City. During the Sack of Rome, in 1527, the house was badly burned and for years ruins and rubbish covered the painting until it was uncovered by gushing water during a particularly bad flood. A crippled woman, who was passing by, saw it and asked the Virgin Mary to make her feel better. Soon after, she was able to walk without pain. The miracle produced excitement among the local residents, the place was cleared of rubbish and money was raised to build a church in honour of the image, which was named Santa Maria della Purità. When the church was abandoned, the image was moved to the oratory of Santa Maria in Traspontina.

☞ **Madonna della Purità,** in the convent of the oratory

☞ **The Holy Family with Saints Joachim, Elizabeth and Elias,** on the right wall, in a niche, painting by Giovanni Conca, 1717.

Brief history of the Oratory della Dottrina Cristiana
Planned by Gioacchino Maria Oldo, bishop of Narni and Terracina, for the religious institution of the Faithful of the Borgo, the oratory was built on a site donated by Cardinal Giuseppe Sacripante, parishioner of the church of Santa Maria in Traspontina. Work started in 1714 to a plan of Nicola Michetti and was finished a year later. In 1715 it was visited by Pope Clement XI and donated to the Order of Carmelites. In 1843 it was founded by the parishioner Aragon of the Confraternity of Santissimo Salvatore and of San Gabriele Arcangelo to accompany the dead. Today it is used as a place for meetings or prayer.

Church of the Santissimo Nome del Gesù

✝ 🕯 ⚱

Chapel of the Madonna della Strada
left of the tribune (2)

According to an old Roman legend, in 425, during the papacy of Celestine I, the nobleman Giulio Astalli had a church built in honour of a miraculous image of the Virgin Mary. It is believed that the image was an *aedicula*, or street shrine. It is mentioned in texts written at the end of the twelfth century as one of the most popular images of the Madonna in Rome. Many miracles are attributed to the Madonna della Strada and, in the eighteenth century, P. Carocci, a Jesuit priest, used to relate them every Saturday to the people during mass in the church of the Santissimo Nome del Gesù. In 1716 a coach driver, suffering from a painful and debilitating disease, was advised to go to the Saturday mass to pray to the Madonna della Strada. He knelt down and asked the miraculous image to save him, not for his own sake, but for his family who depended upon his salary. He immediately felt better. After one week, when he had recovered completely, he asked Carocci to tell his story during the Saturday service.

☞ **Madonna della Strada,** on the altar, fresco, repainted in the 15th century

Saint Ignatius of Loyola preached the Christian doctrine in front of this image in the little church of the Madonna della Strada. People used to flock to church to listen to him.

☞ **Scenes from the Life of the Virgin,** on the walls, paintings by Giuseppe Valeriani and Scipione da Gaeta, 16th century

The themes of the paintings are: the Conception of Mary, the Nativity, Presentation in the Temple, the Death of the Virgin Mary and the Assumption.

Church of Santa Maria del Pianto

An old Roman legend says that on 10th January 1546 two men had a fight near Via Arenula, on what is today known as Via del Pianto. They

Brief history of the Chapel of the Madonna della Strada.
In 1549, Pope Paul III donated the church of the Astalli family, known as Santa Maria de Astallis, to Ignatius of Loyola. The former street shrine of the Madonna was placed here (the name of the painting was *de Astariis, de Stara,* from which the name then became della Strada). In 1568, Cardinal Alessandro Farnese had the church Santissimo Nome del Gesù built, which included the old church of Astalli. The Madonna was placed in a purpose-built chapel, named the chapel of the Madonna della Strada.

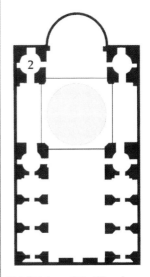

Brief history of the Church of Santa Maria del Pianto
In 1546 Pope Paul III approved the decision to build a new church in honour of the Madonna del Pianto. In 1612, the Confraternity of San Salvatore started work on the site of the old demolished church. In 1896 the church was hit by lightning and gravely damaged. It was reopened in 1907 after the Order of Oblates of the Virgin Mary had carried out extensive works of restoration.

struggled beneath the street shrine of the Madonna and Child, who seemed to look at them in great sorrow. When one of the two was killed, the eyes of the Virgin started to shed tears of blood. A large number of people rushed to see the image, which soon became very popular. Thus it was decided to take the miraculous portrait into the nearby church of San Salvatore de Cacabariis, where it could be more easily venerated. The church was later renamed Santa Maria del Pianto (*pianto* in Italian means 'weeping' or 'lamentation') in memory of the miraculous event.

☞ **The miraculous image of the Weeping Madonna,** on the altar, fresco, 15th century
When the image of the Madonna was brought to the church of San Salvatore, Nicola Acciajuoli had the task of providing it with a suitably decorative setting.
☞ **Miracle of the image of the Virgin and Gloria of the Madonna and Child,** at the beginning of the nave, banner with two sides by Lazzaro Baldi, 17th century
Representation of the miracle of the Weeping Madonna.

Church of Santa Maria in Campitelli

During the plague of 1656, Romans gathered in front of the medieval icon of Santa Maria in Portico, which is today the Register Office, to ask the Madonna to protect and save them from the epidemic. On 8th December the Conservatori of Rome (the magistracy of the city), on behalf of the entire city, promised to place the image in a better position if the city were spared by the plague. At the end of the epidemic, Pope Alexander VII decided to move the miraculous image of the Madonna to the church of Santa Maria in Campitelli.

☞ **Madonna del Portico,** main altar, icon, 11th century
This is the miraculous image of the Madonna which, saved the city from the plague in 1656, also known as Romanae portus securitas.

Church of Santa Maria dell'Orto

An old Roman legend says that, towards the end of 1488, a portrait of the Madonna suddenly appeared on a wall inside a greengrocer's house. The image was considered miraculous and became the object of the people's devotion. An old woman, suffering from an incurable illness, was cured after praying before it.

Outside the church:

☞ *Ave Gratia Plena,* inscription in the courtyard of the adjacent hospital

The inscription, a dedication to the Virgin Mary, could perhaps be from the portal of the original chapel of the Madonna dell'Orto.

Inside the church:

☞ The image of Mary, beside the altar,

This is the original wall of the greengrocer's house where the portrait of the Madonna appeared

☞ *Immacolata Concezione,* in the ceiling, fresco by Giuseppe and Andrea Orazi, 1703

☞ Assumption of Mary, in the vault of the central nave, painting by Giacinto Calandrucci, between 1703 and 1706.

Chapel of the Annunciation

first on the right from the entrance

☞ Annunciation, on the altar, painting, by Taddeo Zuccari, 1561

The painting has been extensively repainted and, according to some sources, the brother of Taddeo, Federico, received payment for it.

☞ Madonna dell'Orto with two Angels, in the oratory

The inscription of 1730 includes the symbols of the six members of the confraternity who commissioned it.

Church of Santa Maria della Scala †

A wealthy gentleman, Antonio Stinco di Ancona, left a portrait of the Virgin Mary to the

Brief history of the Church of Santa Maria dell'Orto
In 1494, the Confraternity of the Madonna dell'Orto raised enough money to build a chapel to house the image of the Virgin Mary. As the popularity of the holy portrait grew, the chapel was replaced with a church. The building was completed in the 1560s by the architect Guidetto Guidetti, and restored between 1825 and 1891.

Confraternity of Santa Maria dell'Orto
Following the miraculous events attributed to the Madonna dell'Orto, a group of the faithful gathered together and founded a confraternity, known as the Confraternity of Santa Maria dell'Orto, approved by Pope Alexander VI in 1492. The confraternity grew very large and became increasingly important. Its symbol, which is still visible in the streets of Rome on the buildings formerly belonging to it, was the Virgin and Child between two small trees. Pope Gregory XIII (1572-85) offered indulgence to each individual who would join the confraternity, and Sixtus V (1585-90) raised it to the status of arciconfraternita (arch confraternity), with the power to free, each year, one person who had been sentenced to death.

155

S. MARIA DELLA SCALA

Casa Pia in his will. This institute was founded in 1563 by Pope Pius IV, at the request of his nephew, Saint Carlo Borromeo, to help fallen women to return to an honourable life.

The portrait was placed below an outside staircase where people could see it and pray in front of it. When the first miracles began to take place, people flocked to adore the image. Pope Clement VIII (1592-1605) and Cardinal Tolomeo Gallio di Como, protector of the institute, decided to remove it to a purpose-built church.

Outside the church:
☞ **Virgin and Child,** in the portal, marble statue by Francesco di Cusart, 1633

Inside the church:
☞ **Madonna del Carmine,** on the altar, in the choir, painting by Giuseppe Peroni, 1737.

Chapel of San Giacinto
second on the right
☞ **Madonna and Child with Saints Giacinto and Catherine,** above the altar, painting, anonymous, believed to be by Trevisani, 18th century
According to old guide books a different painting was placed in the chapel, portraying John of the Cross with Christ and Other Saints by Luca de la Haye. It is not known when the present painting replaced the previous one.

Chapel of San Giuseppe
third on the right

☞ **Marriage of Mary,** on the left, painting by Antonio David, 17th century.

Chapel of the Madonna della Scala
on the left (north) of the transept

☞ **Madonna della Scala,** above the altar

The miraculous image of the Virgin is kept in this chapel. On the left there are two paintings by Luca de la Haye: right, the Coronation of the Virgin; left, Gloria of the Madonna and Child.

Church of San Giovanni dei Fiorentini ✝
Chapel of the Sacramento
on the right of the altar

On the wall of Vicolo delle Palle, near the church of San Giovanni dei Fiorentini, was a fresco of the Virgin Mary. One day, a man who was playing bowls nearby, becoming enraged with the game, threw a bowl at the image of the Madonna, hitting it in the face, below the right eye. There, the dark sign of a bruise appeared. The man immediately lost the use of his right arm, the one used to throw the bowl. Ashamed of his action, the man asked the Virgin for forgiveness and 40 days later he regained the use of his arm. The Madonna was therefore named *Misericordia* ('forgiveness' in Italian). At the request of the people of Florence, the image was moved to the Church of San Giovanni dei Fiorentini.

☞ **Madonna della Misericordia,** on the altar, fresco, 15th century

The miraculous image of the Madonna, which was crowned in 1648, is flanked by two paintings: on the left, Nativity by Agostino Ciampelli; on the right, Assumption of Mary by Anastasio Fontebuoni.

Church of San Pietro in Montorio

A dying nun of the Monastery of the Sette Dolori, on being anointed with the oil of a lamp burning below a nearby *aedicula* of the Virgin Mary,

Brief history of the Church of San Pietro in Montorio

Believed to be the site where Saint Peter was martyred, in the old circus of Caligula and Nero, the church may date back to the tenth century. Around that date the *Liber Pontificalis* of Ravenna mentioned a monastery, dedicated to Saint Peter, known as Gianicolo (today the name of the entire area). It is very likely that the monastery had a church, which could well have been the former church of San Pietro in Montorio, which the present one replaced. In 1472, Pope Sixtus IV donated it to Amedeo Menez de Sylva and to his confraternity who, with the help of the King of France, Louis XI and the royal family of Spain, Ferdinand and Isabella, demolished the old church and built a new one. On 6th June 1500, it was consecrated as the church of San Pietro in Montorio. In 1798, and again in 1809, the church was seriously damaged by French troops and in 1849 the entire apse collapsed. A further restoration took place in 1953-57. In the courtyard, Bramante built the *tempietto* for Ferdinand and Isabella of Spain on what was believed to be the exact spot where Peter had died.

instantly recovered. The news of the miraculous event spread and people started to venerate the portrait. On 9th August 1714, Pope Clement XI ordered its removal to the adjacent church of San Pietro in Montorio.

Brief history of the Church of San Rocco

The church began in the fifteenth century as a chapel of the Confraternity of San Rocco, whose members arrived in the port of Ripetta by barge. It contained the much older church of San Martino de Flumine, built in the eighth century. It was rebuilt in the seventeenth century by Giovanni Antonio de Rossi. A façade by G. Valadier was added in the nineteenth century. Beside the church there was a hospital for 50 men and later a hospital for the wives of the boatmen. Later on, it was also used for unmarried mothers. These women could live at this hospital, called Cellata, during their confinement, but had to wear a veil over their faces to hide their identity. If the mother could not keep the child it was given to the orphanage of Santo Spirito.

Chapel of the Madonna della Lettera
second chapel on the right

☞ **The Madonna della Lettera,** above the altar, painting attributed to Pomarancio but possibly by Giovan Battista Lombarelli.

This is the miraculous image set in the aedicula that was close to the Monastery of the Sette Dolori. The image shows the Virgin and Child holding a letter which, according to tradition, she sent to the people of Messina, in Sicily, as a token of her protection. Next to the miraculous image, there is a painting of the Pinturicchio school: the Coronation of Mary. In the oval altarpiece is another work of the same school: the Madonna and Child.

MARY, MOTHER OF CHRISTIANS

Our journey now takes us to the many churches dedicated to the Virgin Mary in the various roles that have been ascribed to her. The Virgin is a companion to Catholics and their intercessor in life and death. For centuries she has been invoked by the faithful to protect them from evil. The humble Virgin of the Annunciation, who became the mother of God and reached Heaven as a queen, is also the mother of Christians and she is here to protect them.

Church of San Rocco

On 26th July 1645, inside the church of San Rocco, an image of the Madonna was found below the bowl of holy water. The painting, showing the Madonna and Child, simply appeared in the church; it was called Madonna delle Grazie. Following the miraculous event, a decision was taken to build a new chapel to house the image of the Madonna.

The church of San Rocco overlooked the port of Ripetta on the river Tiber. It was a small church of the Confraternity of Barcaioli, or boatmen, whose hospital was also on the premises. The patron of the church was Saint Rocco, patron saint of the sick, particularly of the plague-stricken. He is often represented in art with the Virgin at his side while protecting and delivering people from sickness.

☞ **Madonna, Saint Rocco and Saint Antony with Victims of the Plague,** on the main altar, painting by Baciccia, 17th century

Chapel of the Madonna delle Grazie
to the right of the apse
☞ **Madonna delle Grazie,** on the main altar
This is the mysterious painting of the Madonna found under the holy water font.

Chapel of the Immaculate Conception
first chapel on the left
This chapel commemorates the vision of Marie Bernadette Soubirous, when the Virgin Mary told her that she was the Immaculate Conception.

The visions at Lourdes
Bernadette was a French saint whose visions of the Virgin Mary led to the establishment of a healing shrine at Lourdes. Between 11th February and 16th July of 1858, at the age of 14, she had a series of visions in a grotto on the river Gave, outside the village of Lourdes. The Virgin revealed her identity with the words, 'I am the Immaculate Conception'. Bernadette steadfastly maintained the authenticity of her visions in the face of hostility from all those around her, and she faithfully passed on Mary's messages. In 1866 she was admitted to the Convent of the Sisters of Charity at Nevers. She spent the rest of her life there, loved for her kindliness, holiness and wit, despite almost constant sickness and pain. She died in agony, willingly accepting her great sufferings in faithful fulfilment of her 'Lady's' request for penance. On 8th December 1933, she was canonised by Pope Pius XI. Celebration of her feast is optional in the Roman calendar.

Brief history of the Chapel of the Madonna delle Grazie
The chapel was commissioned by Gaspare Morelli in honour of the Virgin.

Ritual
On the Feast Day of Our Lady of Lourdes, 11th February, Bernadette's first vision of the Virgin is commemorated in the Chapel of the Immaculate Conception.

Feast day of Our Lady of Lourdes:
11th February
Feast day of Saint Bernadette:
16th April, sometimes
18th February in France

Brief history of the Church of Santa Maria in Campo Marzio
In the tenth century a monastery was built for the Byzantine nuns, which was dedicated to the Virgin. Towards the end of the seventeenth century, Cardinal Gasparre Carpegna decided to build a church to house the Madonna Advocata. The church overlooks a courtyard with medieval houses that belonged to the original monastery. It was built in 1685 by Antonio de Rossi, with a Greek cross plan.

☞ the replica of the grottoes at Lourdes
☞ **Miracle of the Madonna at Lourdes,** on the left of the tabernacle, marble relief by Ascanio Angeloni, 17th century

Church of Santa Maria in Campo Marzio

In 750, the Byzantine nuns of the Monastery of Saint Anastasia fled Constantinople owing to the iconoclastic persecution of Emperor Leo III (717-41) and Emperor Constantine V (741-75). They took refuge in Rome under the papacy of Pope Zacharias. The nuns took with them several relics, among which were those of Saint Gregory Nazianzus and the icon of the Virgin Advocata, named after her gesture of intercession shown in the painting. The icon was the object of a strong cult as it was believed it had been painted by Saint Luke.

Ritual
In this church services are said in the Aramaic language which, according to some scholars, was the language spoken by Christ.

☞ **Virgin Advocata,** over the main altar, painting, reproduction of the original by P. Bombelli, 18th century
The original is kept in the Fondazione Cini in Venice.
Advocata *means 'called upon' and refers to the gesture of this Madonna, represented with the right hand pointing upwards and the other on her breast. The gesture indicates that the Madonna has the affairs of the Christians close to her heart and that she is willing to become the one to put their interests before God.*

Brief history of the Chapel of the Madonna della Salute
Originally known as chapel of the Conception, it was renamed after the image of the Madonna della Salute. In 1718 the chapel was redecorated by Francesco Ferruzzi.

Church of Santa Maria Maddalena ✝
Chapel of the Madonna della Salute
The Madonna della Salute, *Salus Infirmorum*, was venerated by the Romans for her healing power over the weak and sick.

☞ *Salus Infirmorum,* on the altar of the chapel, painting by unknown artists, 16th century
This image of the Madonna and Child was crowned by the Vatican in 1668.

Church of Santa Maria dell'Anima
A sacred image of the Madonna, now lost, was venerated inside this church. The Madonna

dell'Anima (in Italian *anima* means 'soul') was portrayed seated with two souls of the faithful kneeling in front of her, one on each side. This image was regarded as a means of intercession for souls in Purgatory. Catholics believe that on the day of Judgement the Virgin will sit on the right of Christ and will intercede for them.

Outside the church:

☞ **Madonna Seated between Two Souls from Purgatory,** in the tympanum, marble group by Antonio Sansovino, 1530

This group derives from the original image venerated in this church, from which it derived its name.

Brief history of the Church of Santa Maria dell'Anima
The church owes its origin to the hospice for German pilgrims built after the Jubilee in 1350. In 1400 the chapel of the hospice, dedicated to the Madonna dell'Anima, was completed. The church was rebuilt, probably by Giuliano da Sangallo, in 1499, in time for the Jubilee in 1500. It had a triple nave, a plan inspired by German architecture and unusual in Rome. In 1843 it was completely restored. It is the church of the German congregation.

Church of Sant'Agostino

This church, which is dedicated to Saint Augustine, contains many Madonnas: the Madonna del Parto, the Madonna of Pellegrini, the Madonna of the Roses and the Madonna of the Belt.

It is traditional to light oil lamps and place them in front of the Madonna del Parto when a woman is having a difficult delivery (*parto* in Italian means 'delivery'). This Madonna is a version of the very rare type known as the Madonna Expectant or the Pregnant Madonna. She, herself a mother, understands the spiritual depth of motherhood and intercedes for all women and children at the moment of birth.

Outside the church:

☞ **Madonna del Parto,** on the right side of the central door, marble statue by Iacopo Sansovino, 1516-18

The statue was commissioned by the heirs of Giovanni Francesco Martelli. It is lit by a blaze of candles and is surrounded by banks of flowers; on the walls are numerous silver ex voto plaques giving thanks to the Virgin from women whose prayers have been answered with the birth of a child. The Madonna del Parto is shod in gold to protect her from the kisses of her supplicants. Newlyweds, pregnant women and mothers visit her to touch her foot.

Brief history of the Church of Sant'Agostino
The church was built in the 1420s and enlarged towards the end of the century by Giacomo di Pietrasanta and Sebastiano Fiorentino for Cardinal d'Estouville. The travertine used for the church is supposed to have come from the Coliseum. The exterior has barely been touched, although the interior was redecorated in the eighteenth century by Vanvitelli.

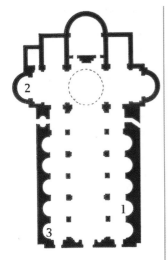

Inside the church:

☞ **Virgin and Child with Saint Anna,** third pillar on the left of the central nave, marble statue by Andrea Sansovino, 1512

The statue is below a painting by Raphael (1512) showing the Prophet Isaiah.

☞ **Virgin and Child,** on the altar, main chapel, painting by Barnaba da Modena or Nicola da Voltri, 14th century

This image is believed to have come from Santa Sophia of Constantinople.

Chapel of San Giuseppe
second on the right (1)

☞ **Madonna delle Rose,** on the altar, painting by Avanzino Nucci, 16th century

This is a copy of the Madonna del Velo by Raphael.

Chapel of the Madonna della Cintura
to the left of the main altar (2)

According to an old tradition, Saint Monica, mother of Saint Augustine, asked the Virgin for help because she was concerned that her son was leading an impious life.

The Virgin of Consolation appeared to her dressed in black with a shining belt. She donated the belt to Saint Monica and told her to keep it and promote her cult, promising to help those who pledged their devotion to her.

☞ **Madonna of the Belt with Saints Augustine and Monica,** on the altar, painting by Gottardi di Faenza, 1765

The Madonna della Cintura or della Consolazione (Madonna of the Belt or of the Consolation) is venerated by the Order of Augustinians. Following the vision of Saint Monica, Augustine converted and became devoted to this Madonna. In 1439, Pope Eugene IV granted to the hermits of Saint Augustine the right to form a religious association with the title 'Cinturati della Beata Maria Vergine'.

Chapel of the Madonna dei Pellegrini or of the Madonna di Loreto
from the entrance, first chapel on the left (3)

Loreto is a town in the Italian region of Marche near Ancona. In the town there stands the house in which Mary and Joseph are said to have lived in Nazareth. The Archangel Gabriel visited this house to announce the birth of Christ and Jesus spent His childhood here. It is believed that, in 1291, the house was borne away from Nazareth by angels to save it from the Saracens. First it landed in Dalmatia and then it was placed in Loreto, Marche.

☞ **Madonna dei Pellegrini,** on the altar, painting by Caravaggio, 1604-05

The painting represents the Madonna on the threshold of her house in Loreto. She looks like a village woman, carrying the Child on her hip, opening the door to some local peasants with bare feet dirty from the dust of the roads. It is a human and earthly image of the Madonna and Child, yet the inner meaning of the picture is that she has her door open to welcome the souls of pilgrims on their spiritual journey.

Basilica of Saint Peter
Chapel of the Pietà

One of the most moving images of the Madonna is the great *Pietà* created by Michelangelo in 1497-1500. The Virgin is represented holding the body of her dead Son across her lap. It is a deeply reflective, almost meditative subject, a devotional image of profound sorrow and humanity. Mary's humble acceptance of the will of God is eloquently conveyed through her expression and gesture.

☞ *Pietà,* first chapel on the right-hand side of the entrance, marble sculpture by Michelangelo Buonarroti, circa 1500

Michelangelo made this extraordinary work for the French ambassador, Cardinal Jean Bilhères de

Michelangelo Buonarroti
The son of a Florentine magistrate, Michelangelo (1475-1564) began his career as an apprentice to the fresco painter Ghirlandaio. His interest in sculpture drew him into the circle of Lorenzo de' Medici, who had a collection of antiques in the Medici Garden in Florence. From 1490-1492, he lived in the Medici household, where he would have met leading neo-Platonists and other intellectuals. He came to Rome for the first time in 1496, where he carved the first of his major works, the Bacchus (now in Florence) and the Saint Peter's *Pietà*. The latter immediately established his reputation; when he returned to Florence in 1501 he was much in demand. In 1505, Pope Julius II summoned the artist back to Rome to design and execute his own tomb. This huge project was to occupy Michelangelo for the next forty years of his life; it was never fully completed. In 1508, Julius persuaded him to agree to paint the vault of the Sistine Chapel in the Vatican. He carried out the logical conclusion to this work when, in 1536-41, he painted the Last Judgement on the altar wall of the same chapel. The breadth, range and quality of this extraordinary artist is well represented in Rome, where he settled permanently in 1534. Whether in painting, sculpture or architecture his originality was so great that it led his contemporaries to call him 'divine'.

163

Representation of the *Pietà* in art
In the Middle Ages the body of Christ was represented lying across the Virgin's lap, a form continued by artists of the Renaissance. Later, Christ might be seen on the ground, wrapped in a sheet, with only His head in the Virgin's lap. This model was preferred during the Counter-Reformation.

Brief history of the Church of Santa Maria Annunziata
The church was built during the second half of the eighteenth century by the Confraternity of Santo Spirito, opposite the hospital. In 1940 it was moved to a new location because of changes to the plan of the area and in 1950 it was entirely rebuilt.

Lagraulas. Critics said the Madonna seemed impossibly young, considering the age of her Son. To this, Michelangelo replied that her youth was due to her eternal purity. It is the only marble sculpture that Michelangelo signed.

Church of Santa Maria Annunziata
also known as Nunziatella

In this church the Madonna del Latte was venerated as *Refugium Peccatorum*, a sacred image portraying the Madonna in her role of loving mother, symbolically feeding her baby (*latte* in Italian means 'milk'). On 8th December 1926 the image was crowned.

☞ **Madonna del Latte,** on a small altar on the left of the entrance, fresco by Antoniazzo Romano, 15th century
It is likely that this fresco came from the quadriportico of the old basilica of Saint Peter. It was removed to the north altar of the church of San Michele Arcangelo, which was decorated by Valadier. When the church was demolished, in 1939, it was moved to the church of Santa Maria Annunziata.

Basilica of Santa Sabina

Saint Dominic, founder of the Order of Dominicans or Black Friars, is closely identified with the Madonna. It is believed that the rosary was handed to him in a vision by the Virgin Mary, which is why he is frequently depicted in the act of receiving it either from the Virgin or from Baby Jesus sitting in her lap.

Elci Chapel
in the left aisle *(1)*

☞ **Madonna of the Rosary with Saints Dominic and Catherine,** in the Elci Chapel, painting by G. B. Salvi, known as Sassoferrato, 17th century
In 1643 the Princess of Rossano commissioned the painting in memory of the vision of Saint Dominic. In 1901 the painting was stolen, only to reappear the following year. During the remodelling of the 1930s it was placed in the Elci Chapel.

Church of Santi Bonifacio e Alessio ✝

The Madonna venerated by Saint Alessio is housed in this church. It is said that the saint used to fall in prayer in front of this image in the city of Edessa. The painting was then brought to Rome by Sergio, Archbishop of Damascus, in the tenth century in order to preserve it during the period of Iconoclasm, when all religious images were ordered to be destroyed.

☞ **Madonna of the Intercession,** in a chapel, next to the main altar, painting on canvas

This Madonna follows the stylised manner of Byzantine art. However, her large almond-shaped eyes look at us with a gaze charged with warmth and attention. Her hands, pointing upwards, seem to indicate the path that she opens up for Christians on the way to Heaven.

Church of Santa Francesca Romana ✝
also called Santa Maria Nova

In 1950, Professor Cellini discovered an early-Christian image of a Madonna painted underneath the image of the Virgin of the Consolation. The painting is thought to have come from the old church of Santa Maria Antiqua. The church, known to the Romans as Santa Francesca Romana, the patron saint of motorists, is also dedicated to the Blessed Virgin Mary and named Santa Maria Nova. Besides the early-Christian Madonna, images of the Virgin are conspicuously present in the church.

☞ **Madonna and Child with Saints Agnes and Cecilia,** ceiling of the nave, painting

The Madonna is surrounded by a luminous mandorla and holds the emblem of the Order of Olivetans: a red cross and two branches of olive trees on three hills.

☞ **Madonna and Child Enthroned with Saints James, John, Peter and Andrew,** in the semi-dome of the apse, mosaic, 12th century

She is crowned and wears lavish robes, as does the Christ Child. She is seated on a jewelled throne

Brief history of the Church of Santa Francesca Romana
Formerly the oratory of the Church of Santa Maria in Antiqua, this building became a church in its own right when the latter was abandoned because of structural damage in 847. It was enlarged and reconsecrated in 1116, and the façade was added during further reconstruction in 1615. It has a Latin Cross plan with a central nave and eight side chapels.

Brief history of the Church of Santa Maria in Via Lata

The church was built in the seventeenth century on the site of an earlier church. The façade was completed by Pietro da Cortona in 1662.

beneath a gilded Heaven lush with exquisite flowers and fruits.

☞ **Virgin of the Consolation or Santa Maria Nova,** in the apse, above the main altar, painting, Tuscan school, 12th century

This is a greatly venerated image housed in a wooden painted tabernacle.

☞ **Virgin and Child,** in the sacristy, fifth century

This is one of the earliest Christian paintings to survive. The Madonna is the Mother Amabilis, the 'mother who loves'.

The Lady of Sorrows

The feast day of the Blessed Virgin of Sorrows is 15th September. The feast was established in the thirteenth century by the Order of Servites from Cologne. They meditated on the Madonna and her Seven Sorrows.

Church of Santa Maria in Via Lata

The Mater Dolorosa, or Lady of Sorrows, grieves for her son. Her breast is pierced with seven swords, each representing one of Seven Sorrows. In the thirteenth century, the monastic Order of Servites fixed the number of her Sorrows at seven; previously it had fluctuated between five and fifteen.

☞ **Madonna Advocata,** altar, panel painting, 13th century

The image of the Madonna Advocata is believed to have been painted by Saint Luke.

☞ **Mater Dolorosa,** statue, high altar

Simeon said to Mary during her Presentation in the Temple:
'And a sword shall pierce your own soul too.'
(Luke 2:35)

The Lady of Sorrows is a tall statue of the Virgin, her body pierced with seven swords to represent all her sorrows.

Church of Santa Maria della Quercia

Craftsmen's guilds frequently organised themselves into religious confraternities to worship, to do charitable works and to ask for divine guidance in their professions. Many of them chose the Madonna as their protector. Usually they adopted, as their emblem, the image of the Virgin surrounded by the coat of arms of the guild.

Brief history of the Church of Santa Maria della Quercia

This church was first dedicated to Saint Nicola de Curte and in 1507 it was given to the Maremmani, or horse merchants, in the nearby Campo dei Fiori. Then in 1523 the butchers founded, in this church, the Confraternity of Santa Maria della Quercia. It was recognised officially as their own in 1532 by Clement VII.

☞ **Image of Virgin and Child,** high altar, tabernacle

The image of the Madonna is linked to the devotion of the Roman butchers' guild. She wears a crown and her image is surrounded by oak leaves (quercia in

Italian means 'oak'). On the gilded frame, just below her image, there are the emblems of the butchers' guild: the ox and the sheep.

Church of Santa Maria dell'Orazione e Morte

In 1577, Duke Cesare Glorietti donated a much-venerated image of the Virgin Mary, that had been placed on the wall of his stables, to the Confraternity of Orazione e Morte, which undertook to bury the dead and pray for their souls. The image was placed on the main altar of the old church of Santa Maria dell'Orazione e Morte, inserted into a composition by Filippo Zucchetti. It represents Saint Carlo Borromeo in adoration before the Christ Child, and the Archangel Michael, patron of the confraternity, in the act of freeing souls from Purgatory.

☞ **Madonna dell'Orazione,** in the main altar, fresco
The painting is supported by angels.

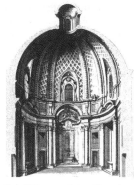

Brief history of the Church of Santa Maria dell'Orazione e Morte
The church was built by the confraternity of the same name between 1575 and 1576. Next to it, in 1594, an oratory was built. The vast cemetery was situated below the church, near the river. Demolished in 1733, the church was rebuilt to the plan of Ferdinando Fuga and consecrated in 1737.

Sacre Rappresentazioni per l'Ottavario dei Defunti
The confraternity, instituted by Pope Julius III in 1552, sold illustrations in order to raise funds. The representations were reproduced in a series of prints, which were distributed to the visitors of the cemetery in exchange for donations. They showed scenes from the Old Testament or allegorical scenes.

THE MADONNA
IN THE STREETS OF ROME

Our journey will now take us away from the churches and basilicas into the streets of Rome. We shall discover the many shrines dedicated to the Madonna that are located at the corners of the streets, on the doors and house walls of Rome.

They are simple tabernacles with painted or sculpted images of the Virgin which have, through the centuries, offered a focus for popular and collective devotion. They also represent the need of the faithful to have images of the Virgin as intercessor and protector close to them, in the space where they conduct their daily lives. People would flock to them and fall to their knees in prayer to implore a grace from the Madonna of the shrine.

In pagan times *aediculae*, erected at the city crossroads, were shrines dedicated to the divinities who protected the wayfarers: the *Lares Compitales*. This is why many of the shrines also offered a sheltered area and seats where the pilgrims could rest. In the fourth century AD in Rome there were about 423 of these shrines dedicated to the Wayfarers.

With the arrival of Christianity, and as pagan temples were converted and dedicated to the Virgin Mary, more images of her went up in the streets of Rome to invoke her protection for the city and its citizens. Many of these shrines bear the inscription *posuerunt me custodem*, 'they put me to protect'.

On special feast days these *aediculae* became the focus of devotional celebrations: during the Christmas festivities the fifers came from the countryside and gathered to play in front of them. The major feast days, such as the Annunciation (25th March), the Assumption (15th August), the Nativity of Mary (8th September) together with the day of the celebration of the Madonna del Rosario (2nd October) and of the Madonna del Buon Consiglio (26th May) were occasions to adorn the shrines and make them into special sites for prayers.

Few shrines remain out of the many that once existed. Their positions in the open air made them vulnerable to the devouring agents of time and weather. The ones that remain are usually the miraculous ones that enjoyed particular devotion and care from the faithful.

Madonna and Child

in Via dei Querceti

The medieval historian Gregorovius narrates a story related to this *madonnella* (street shrine).

In the ninth century a young woman arrived in Rome from Magonza. She was wearing men's clothing and she wanted to be taken as a man. She entered the Papal Curia and, thanks to her intelligence, was eventually elected as Pope Giovanni VIII.

Her true sex was discovered exactly on the spot where this image is. The female pope was riding back to the Vatican when, to the amazement of her companions, she gave birth to a child

Since then the gender of future popes has been checked carefully. A marble chair with a hole in the middle, was devised and placed in the portico of the Lateran to perform this task.

☞ **Madonna and child enthroned,** at the corner with Via dei Santissimi Quattro, at eye level, fresco

This image looks like a small chapel. It is believed to have been a pagan aedicula *transformed into a Christian one during the early Middle Ages. It is simple, with a small platform roof. On the left-hand side it bears a rhymed inscription which translates as, 'The smile of Mary, will cheer up this place, if the passer-by, will greet her with Ave, O Mother'.*

Madonna dell'Arco dei Pantani

When, in July 1796, many street images of the Madonna started to move their eyes, this particular one caused some dried lilies to revive and stay fresh for a month in the scorching heat of a Roman summer. Among the devotees of this Madonna was the noble Prince Rospigliosi. After being restored to health, thanks to her intercession, he entered in a horse competition and won. He dedicated the banner

Mary to Gabriel
Ecce ancilla Domini.
('I am the Lord's servant';
Luke 1:58)

169

he won to this *madonnella*. This *palio*, or banner, is now in the Museum of Rome.

☞ **Madonna and child with crowns**, on the building at civic number 1, fresco

Until the beginning of the twentieth century, this image was surrounded by a wooden baroque frame, inset in a tabernacle, sheltered by a baldachin. At one point in its history it displayed 89 ex voto hearts, but now there are only a few left.

Madonna of the Piety
in Vicolo delle Bollette

All Rome was very excited by the news that the Madonna of the Archetto had apparently moved her eyes. The Marquis del Bufalo was going to witness the phenomenon with his own eyes when he was informed by his friend, the Marquise Barbara Palombara, that the Madonna here had started moving her eyes as well. He changed his route and came instead to the Madonna della Pietà.

In the process that took place afterwards to verify the reality of this phenomenon, the Marquis stated that: 'This Madonna della Pietà started moving hers [eyes] as well. Both eyes moved and slowly rolled up until they were almost hidden behind her opened eyelid's. The possibility that an optical illusion was being created by reflection on the glass that covered the canvas was discarded by the removal of the glass. Meanwhile, the eyes kept moving until 25th November.

Since then, this image has been much venerated and many silver *ex votos* or coral necklaces and bracelets were positioned around her as signs of devotion. Unfortunately, this wealth of gifts attracted robbers. In 1853 the covering glass was broken and the valuable *ex votos* were stolen.

☞ **Madonna della Pietà,** at civic number 10, painting, 17th century

Surrounded by a simple wooden frame, this Madonna raises her eyes up to Heaven whilst her hands

are folded on her heart.

The inscription refers to the miracle of 1796: Die IX Iulii MDCCXCVI Posuit oculum suum Super corda illorum Ostendere illis Magnalia Operum Suorum. *'On the 19th July 1796 Her light was made to shine in their hearts and showed them the majesty of her deeds'.* (Eccles chap. XVII)

Immaculate Conception
in Piazza delle Rotonda

The dogma of the Immaculate Conception was formalised in 1854, but this large eighteenth-century *madonnella*, shows us that its cult was dear to people's heart well before that date.

☞ **The Immaculate Conception,** at the civic number 5, fresco, 18th century,

Framed in an elegant stucco decorated with the dove of the Holy Spirit, this fresco depicts a Virgin clad in a blue robe, standing on a globe, with a crescent moon and a snake.

On the base, a cartouche contains an inscription taken from the Cantico dei Cantici: 'Tota pulchra es, amica mea, et macula non est in teo' *(You, my friend, are entirely beautiful and no stain is in you).*

Immaculate Conception
in Piazza del Collegio Romano

This lovely *aedicula* was built under the spell of the religious fervour of the Marian miracles that took place in the summer of 1796. The noble family of the Doria Pamphili commissioned this work and placed it on the corner of their palazzo. In the family's archive all the bills paid for the construction of this *aedicula* are still preserved.

☞ **The Immaculate Conception,** on the corner, overlooking Via della Gatta, painting by Antonio Concioli, 18th century

In a gilded stucco frame with delightful floral motifs by Francesco Toma, this oil painting was executed by a follower of Pompeo Batoni. Here the Virgin is seated

Prayer
Alleluia, alleluia!
Hail Mary, full of grace; the Lord is with thee!
Blessed art thou among women.
Alleluia!

171

among clouds and underneath is a crescent moon, traditional symbol of the Immaculate Conception.

Our Lady of Sorrow
in Piazza del Gesù

Originally hanging on the wall of a palace which is now demolished, this *madonnella* is one of those whose eyes were said to move, in 1796. Pius VI even granted indulgences to who went to pray in front of her, as the inscription testifies.

☞ **Our Lady of Sorrow,** oil painting, 18th century
The bust of the Madonna still has her own silver crown and also some ex votos *can be seen behind the covering glass.*

Madonna of the Rosary
in Via dell'Arco della Ciambella

Here we find another Virgin whose eyes moved in 1796, a miracle that lasted for three weeks. This *aedicula* belonged to the Capparucci family. They were very devoted to this Virgin and every first Sunday in October they organised a feast in her honour. On these occasions the *aedicula* was decorated with hanging tapestries, branches of myrtle, and lights. This continued until one day in 1873 when the *aedicula* was vandalised. Since then, the Capparucci have removed the image every night. When they moved house they took the image of the Virgin with them. A carpenter paid for a copy of it to be installed here.

The Holy Rosary
Rosary comes from the Latin word *rosarium,* 'a rose garden'. A rosary is a string of beads that functions as a mnemonic device to assist the recital of a sequence of prayers to the Virgin. It is perceived by Christians as a succession of contemplative thoughts on the Life of Jesus and includes meditative prayers such as the *Pater Noster,* the *Ave Maria* and the *Gloria.*

☞ **Madonna of the Rosary,** under a ruined Roman arch from the Baths of Agrippa called 'della ciambella', by Pietro Campofiorito, end of 19th century
The Madonna holds the child and in her right hand holds a rosary. A stone bears the following devotional inscription which translated as: 'Oh Virgin, whoever thinks and meditates about your Mysteries, you make him have only pure thoughts. And you light up love in his soul, when he gives up his heart for you'. The aedicula *also includes a kneeling bench.*

Assumption of the Virgin

in Piazza Tor Sanguigna

This tabernacle is positioned unusually high up. This is because it was vandalised by French soldiers in 1798.

When Pius VII entered Rome in June 1800, the Grosso Gondi relocated the Madonna of the Assumption higher up, for safety, near the first-floor windows of his palazzo.

☞ **Madonna of the Assumption,** on the walls of Palazzo Grossi Gondi, at first-floor level, painting, 18th century

The oil painting is inserted within a beautiful tabernacle richly decorated with lilies, cherubs and hovering clouds. Angels hold a crown of lights at the top and candelabra. The whole shrine is surmounted by a baldachin.

Coronation of the Virgin

in Via dei Coronari

In the 15th century this was the house of Vincio di Stefano Vincio and an image of the Virgin decorated its walls. When the house passed into the hands of Cardinal Alberto di Monferrato a new image was planned. In 1523 he commissioned the tabernacle from the sculptor and architect Antonio da Sangallo the Elder, whilst the image of the Coronation was executed by a pupil of Raphael, the artist Pierino del Vaga.

The cardinal was a notary of the Apostolic Chamber. It is said that this cardinal was one of the victims of the Sack of Rome in 1527. He is said to have died of fright!

This *madonnella* was nicknamed 'Image of the bridge' because it hung at a point where the pilgrims had to pass it in order to cross on the bridge leading to Saint Peter's. This passage was once crowded with rosary (or crowns) sellers, hence the name of Via dei Coronari.

☞ **Coronation of the Virgin,** next to the Vicolo Domizio, fresco by Pierino del Vaga, 16th century

The tabernacle that Sangallo devised is a small temple with two columns. The fresco by Pierino del Vaga is not in good condition, but on the tympanum of the temple the inscription can still be read: 'Instaurata fuit quam cernis Imago Pontis.' *I was made in the image of the bridge.*

Madonna of Providence
in Via delle Botteghe Oscure

Another Madonna in which the phenomenon of moving eyes occurred in 1796. This Virgin was once called Virgin of the Elm, because of a large elm tree that was nearby.

☞ **Madonna of Providence,** opposite the Torre Argentina, painting

The half-length image of the Virgin, with her hands folded on her breast, is surrounded by many silver ex votos that testify her popularity among the faithful.

Madonna of the Lamp
on the Isola Tiberina

In 1577 the river Tiber flooded covering an image

of the Madonna that occupied the same site as this one. The small lamp that lit under it was also submerged, but miraculously kept on burning. In the twentieth-century a copy of this *madonnella* was placed here to remind us all of the prodigious event.

☞ **Madonna of the lamp,** at the base of the bell-tower of San Giovanni Calibita, twentieth-century copy

The Virgin and the child are accompanied by two angels.

Madonna in Prayer

in Viale Trastevere

This Madonna dates back only to the middle of the twentieth century, but it is deeply venerated nonetheless. It is full of *ex votos* that carry dates up to 1993.

☞ **Madonna in prayer,** opposite the Place of the Ministry of the Public Education, high relief in coloured terracotta, in a semicircular niche

This is a simple image, but its simplicity speaks to many people who come and pray in front of her.

Our Lady of Sorrow

in the Vicolo del Bologna

Vicolo del Bologna, in Trastevere, was named after a carpenter from Bologna who lived here and built the wooden structure of the church of Santa Maria dell'Aracoeli. Near number 40 there is an *aedicula* dedicated to Our Lady of Sorrow (Madonna Addolorata). This was one of the 26 images of the Madonna that appeared to be moving their eyes and crying during the French occupation of the city in 1796, which forced the pope to sign the Peace of Tolentino.

☞ **Our Lady of Sorrow,** *aedicula,* 18th century,

Underneath the image, an inscription says that each person who recites the litanies of Saint Mary in front of the image will receive 200 days of indulgences for his or her soul in Purgatory.

The Seven Sorrows
These are the different moments of revelation to the Virgin of the death of Jesus.
They are:
Simeon's prophecy of a sword piercing her at the time the Virgin was presented to the Temple;
The Flight into Egypt;
The disappearance of Jesus for three days when He went into the temple;
Christ's Walk to Calvary;
The Crucifixion and the last farewell;
The Descent from the Cross;
The Entombment.

IV

ROME, CITY GUARDED BY ANGELS

The Apostle Paul travelled to Rome from Asia Minor. His journey was long, tortuous and full of danger. He sailed across the Mediterranean Sea, risking the turbulent weather. At that time shipwrecks were very common and on his voyage Paul experienced three. He survived the last one thanks to the intervention of an angel. When all the other passengers aboard the ship had given up hope and were ready to die, Paul rallied them by describing his vision: at the height of the tempest, a beautiful angel had reassured him that they would survive the peril.

In 590 the plague was ravaging the population of Rome. The people were scared and without hope. As the epidemic raged, Pope Gregory the Great decided to organise a special procession as a form of prayer to God for the deliverance of the city. The procession stopped at each of the seven basilicas and culminated at Saint Peter's. When the pope was about to cross Ponte Elio, the bridge that leads to the Vatican area, he suddenly saw, on the top of the fortified papal palace, the Archangel Michael returning his blood-stained sword to its sheath. Gregory interpreted this gesture as a sign that the sinners had been punished and that the Black Death had finally been brought to an end. Rome did indeed become free of the plague and in memory of his vision the pope renamed the fortified palace Castel Sant'Angelo, 'the castle of the holy angel'.

Catholics believe that angels are the messengers of God and in the tale of Christianity they play supporting roles. The Archangel Gabriel

Paul to his companions

For there stood by me this night the angel of God, whose I am, and whom I serve, saying, Fear not, Paul; thou must be brought before Caesar: and, lo, God hath given thee all them that sail with thee.
(Acts 27:22-24)

Angel

The term angel is derived from the Greek word *angelos*, meaning 'messenger'; in Hebrew, *mal'akh*. However, to the Greeks the word *angelos* applied only to the spirits who protected the dead.

Pre-Christian angels

Belief in spiritual beings that mediate between the transcendent realm and everyday reality in time and space has been common to religions throughout history. In Eastern cultures these beings can be both good and bad, their nature depending on their situation. With the advent of monotheism, angels took up their familiar identity as beings clearly distinct from the Divinity itself. In contrast to the Eastern tradition, however, in Western religions a benevolent spirit is identified as an angel whereas a malevolent spirit is described as a demon.

The Annunciation to the shepherds

And there were shepherds abiding in the field, keeping watch over their flock by night. And the angel of the Lord came upon them, and the glory of the Lord shone round about them, and they were sore afraid. And the angel said unto them, Fear not: for, behold, I bring you good tidings of great joy, which shall be to all people ... For unto you is born ... a Saviour.
(Luke 2:8)

brought to Zacharias the news of the imminent birth of John the Baptist to his parents and was the carrier of the most famous message of all: the Annunciation.

From the beginning to the end, the earthly life of Christ was marked by angelic mediation. The Gospel tells us that an angel brought the news of Jesus' birth to the shepherds.

An angel appeared to Joseph in a dream to warn him to take his family to Egypt and to stay there until it was safe to come back. Joseph followed the advice and remained in Egypt until Herod died. Only then was he called back by another angelic vision.

During the temptation of Christ in the wilderness, Satan attempted to exploit the compassion of angels, using it as a weapon against Jesus. He took Him to the top of the Temple of Jerusalem and demanded that He prove that He was the Son of God by throwing Himself off the Temple.

Escape into Egypt
The angel of the Lord appeareth to Joseph in a dream saying, Arise, and take the young child and his mother, and flee into Egypt, and be thou there until I bring thee word: for Herod will seek the young child to destroy him.
(Matt. 2:13)

The Temptation of Jesus
Then the devil leaveth him, and, behold, angels came and ministered unto him.
(Matt. 4:11)

'The angels of God will come and rescue you,' said the devil to Jesus, but Christ reminded him that he could not tempt God. Then the devil took Him to the top of a high mountain and showed Him all the kingdoms of the world and offered them to Him if He would prostrate Himself in front of him. Christ told him to go away, saying that there is only one God to worship. Once the devil had been banished, the angels came to take care of Christ.

During the Resurrection, an angel moved the boulder that sealed Christ's sepulchre. Amid a great earthquake, the angel came down from Heaven and rolled back the stone and sat upon it. He was shining and radiant. The keepers of Jesus' burial place started to shake in fear. The angel then turned to the women and told them not to be afraid because Christ had come back to life.

During Christ's final journey to Heaven angels acted as witnesses.

When angels bring good news or are in the presence of God, they frequently play musical instruments. Praising God with music is at least as old as the Hebrew Bible and angels are seen as members of the celestial orchestra. Catholics hear their voices

The Resurrection
And, behold, there was a great earthquake: for the angel of the Lord descended from heaven, and came and rolled back the stone from the door and sat upon it. His countenance was like lightning, and his raiment white as snow: And for fear of him the keepers did shake, and became as dead men. And the angel answered and said unto the women: Fear not ye, for I know that ye seek Jesus which was crucified. He is not here: for he is risen, as he said. Come, see the place where the Lord lay.
(Matt. 28:2-6)

The Ascension into Heaven
And while they looked steadfastly toward heaven as he went up, behold, two men stood by them in white apparel; Which also said, Ye men of Galilee, why stand ye gazing up into heaven? this same Jesus, which is taken up from you into heaven, shall so come in like manner as ye have seen him go into heaven.
(Acts 1:10-11)

in the Gospel, and in medieval manuscript illuminations they sing carols at the Nativity. Dante wrote that the spheres of Heaven themselves ring in harmony to the sound of divine praises.

Although the primary role of angels was to act as God's messengers, they occasionally played the leading role in the narrative. An angel rescued Daniel from the lions' den, an angel stopped Abraham from slaughtering his son Isaac and the scripture tells us that Michael guards the gates of Heaven against Satan. Nevertheless, the deeds of angels took place in the name of God. Michael, the prince of the celestial army, for example, always acted as God's representative or delegate.

Catholics believe that angels have responsibilities to the individual; they act as personal guardians. An example of the active intervention of a guardian angel occurred during Saint Peter's imprisonment in Jerusalem. The night before Herod was going to pass judgement on him, Peter was visited in a dream by an angel who led him out of prison.

Saint Thomas Aquinas, dubbed by his contemporaries 'Doctor Angelicus' for his interest in angels, affirmed that everyone, whether Christian or not, has a guardian angel. Traditionally, guardian angels have been seen as a form of protection against evil, but Saint Thomas recognised their importance in the role of fostering and promoting goodness in men. They are seen to encourage humanity to aspire to do good, in contrast to Satan, who tempts men to do evil. Guardian angels are also seen as a type of confidant, someone to whom the faithful can turn in order to express hopes and desires in the expectation of enlightenment.

Messengers between Earth and Heaven, angels inhabit an intermediate realm. Because of this, Saint Augustine defined them as *corpus, non caro*, 'body, but not flesh' that is, although they are embodied, they are not material. Angels have wings, float in the air and visit people in dreams. These characteristics, which facilitate and speed their journeys between Heaven and Earth, are linked to their role. In Saint Augustine's view, it is the angels' office and deeds that characterise them, not their nature or their being.

Saint Thomas Aquinas denied that angels had any corporeal existence at all, arguing that they are purely immaterial and spiritual beings.

It is to artists that we owe our visual concepts of angels. Their earliest interpretations were based on accounts in biblical texts and the Apocrypha. Angels first became a popular artistic subject during the Middle Ages and it is no coincidence that Dante's *Divine Comedy*, which contains a great literary exposition of angels, was written at that time. This provided painters with an inspirational starting point; from there the symbiotic relationship between literature and the visual representation of angels continued to evolve throughout the centuries.

Having a spiritual essence, angels are immortal. They came into being at the Creation and will survive until the end of time. However, this does not give them parity with God since He transcends time. Their immortal status can, nevertheless, be revoked by God, who can dispose of angels if He so chooses. The idea of the fallen angel does not appear in the

And Jesus answered and said unto him, Get thee behind me, Satan: for it is written, Thou shalt worship the Lord thy God, and him only shalt thou serve.
(Matt.4:10)

Categories of angels in art
Angels are represented in many shapes and sizes. The most common are:
1. The young adult version, which is fully clothed and of somewhat indeterminate gender. This type derives from the Victory or Nike figures found in the art of ancient Greece and Rome. During the medieval period it was this version that served as the artistic prototype.
2. The putto or cherub, which looks like a small child. These angels are usually naked or semi-naked and although their gender is not usually made plain, they are normally presumed to be male. Their lineage is just as ancient as that of their adult kin, since they derive from representations of the Classical god of love, Cupid.

Old Testament but is clearly described in the Book of Revelation. Here, large numbers of angels were cast down to Earth together with Satan, who had been a great angel himself. Some believe that he can be identified as the Angel Lucifer, before his fall, but this seems to depend on a mistranslation of the Book of Isaiah.

As the prince of evil spirits, Satan can be disguised as an angel of light. He tempts humanity, trying to draw men towards him away from the love of God. During His 40 days and nights in the wilderness, Jesus was repeatedly tempted by Satan.

The Book of Revelation states that when Christ returns from Heaven to rule on earth, Satan will be bound by a chain for a thousand years and then be utterly defeated.

The Old Testament contains many references to angels but does not provide us with a coherent order of the celestial hierarchy. In Genesis there are mentions of groups of angels, including the cherubim and the seraphim, and also single angels that are simply called 'the angel of the Lord'. It is not until the Book of Daniel that angels are referred to by name. Here Gabriel makes his first entrance as the interpreter of Daniel's cryptic vision concerning the ram's horns and the kingdoms of Media and Persia (Dan. 8:16-27). It is somewhat disconcerting to find that not all Old Testament angels had wings and that they ate and drank like mortals. For example, the two angels who were entertained by Lot at Sodom behaved exactly like men; Lot 'made them a feast, and he did bake unleavened bread, and they did eat' (Gen.19:1-28). For the avoidance of confusion, angels were later given wings and a less corporeal identity.

The rich variety of angels performs a wide range of tasks. In the *Summa Theologiae*, Saint Thomas Aquinas attempted to understand the hierarchy of angels. He divided them into three main groups, each representing a different relationship to the Almighty. The first group in the hierarchy, the Cherubim and Thrones, are involved in the

Angels in and out of favour
The early Christians were somewhat ambiguous in their attitudes. Nevertheless, in 325, at the Council of Nicaea, it was decreed that belief in angels was part of the Christian dogma. However, only 18 years later, at the Synod of Laodicea, the same belief was declared idolatrous. Saint Augustine (354-430) asserted the existence of angels but it was not until the Seventh Ecumenical Synod of 787 that the cult of angels and archangels was formally re-established. In 1986 Pope John Paul II stated that to doubt the existence of angels 'is radically to revise Holy Scripture and with it the whole history of salvation'.

individual worship of God; the second, the Dominations, Virtues and Powers, are concerned with arriving at a knowledge of Him through an awareness of the universe; the third, the Principalities, Archangels and Angels, deals with the more general interaction between God and man. It is in this last group that we find the angels with which we are most familiar.

According to the Book of Enoch, which was probably written during the last two centuries BC, archangels are above angels. Their superior status is accorded to them by virtue of the fact that they enter into the presence of God. In addition to Michael, there are two other archangels, Gabriel and Raphael. Gabriel (feast day: 24th March), who in the Old Testament explains Daniel's vision to him, is considered by both Jewish and Christian writers to be an archangel. In the Old Testament Book of Tobit, Raphael (feast day: 24th October) appears in human guise to accompany Tobias on his journey. In the Book of Enoch he is the 'angel of the spirits of men' and it is his responsibility to heal the world.

Although the word 'archangel' can apply generally to all angels above the rank of ordinary angel, some texts refer to specific numbers of archangels. Exactly how many archangels there are is not entirely clear; numbers vary from three to nine or even twelve. Similarly, the names of the archangels are not beyond dispute but most sources agree that Gabriel, Michael and Raphael should be numbered among them.

After a somewhat tentative start, the story of the angel in Rome has been one of increasing success. From the Middle Ages onwards representations of angels proliferated, reaching a peak in the explosion of art and architecture that followed the Counter-Reformation in the seventeenth century. We can appreciate them in mosaics, in frescoes, in oil paintings or in sculptures which may be in marble, gilt, bronze or stucco. They greet the visitor in every basilica, church and chapel in Rome.

Prayer to Michael, the Archangel
Saint Michael, defend us all in our struggles against evil and the temptations of the devil. O Lord, we humbly pray You, to order Saint Michael, prince of the heavenly army, to chain in Hell Satan and all the other evil spirits that are abroad in the world.

The Celestial Hierarchy

This text is a comprehensive classification of angels. Long thought to be the work of Dionysius the Areopagite, who was converted to Christianity by Saint Paul in Athens, the book was written around 500. Inspired by Saint Paul, who in his letters refers to angels by nine different names, the writer, a Syrian monk, arranged angels into three hierarchies, each in turn divided into three, to reflect the Holy Trinity. Angels who flank Christ's throne comprise Seraphim, Cherubim and Thrones. Below them are the governors of the stars and the elements, who include Dominions, Virtues and Powers. The third hierarchy is that of messengers, who alone intervene in the affairs of humankind; it is composed of Principalities, Archangels and Angels.

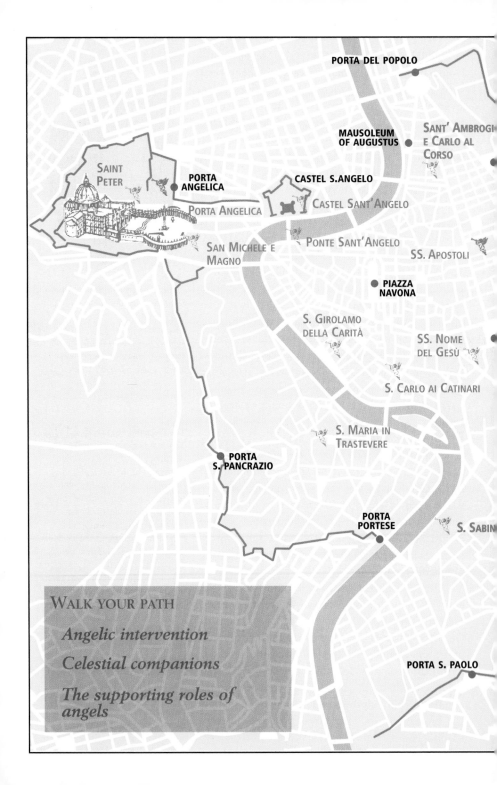

PORTA DEL POPOLO

MAUSOLEUM
OF AUGUSTUS

SANT' AMBROGIO
E CARLO AL
CORSO

SAINT
PETER

PORTA
ANGELICA

CASTEL S.ANGELO

PORTA ANGELICA

CASTEL SANT'ANGELO

SAN MICHELE E
MAGNO

PONTE SANT'ANGELO

SS. APOSTOLI

PIAZZA
NAVONA

S. GIROLAMO
DELLA CARITÀ

SS. NOME
DEL GESÙ

S. CARLO AI CATINARI

S. MARIA IN
TRASTEVERE

PORTA
S. PANCRAZIO

PORTA
PORTESE

S. SABIN

PORTA S. PAOLO

WALK YOUR PATH

Angelic intervention

Celestial companions

*The supporting roles of
angels*

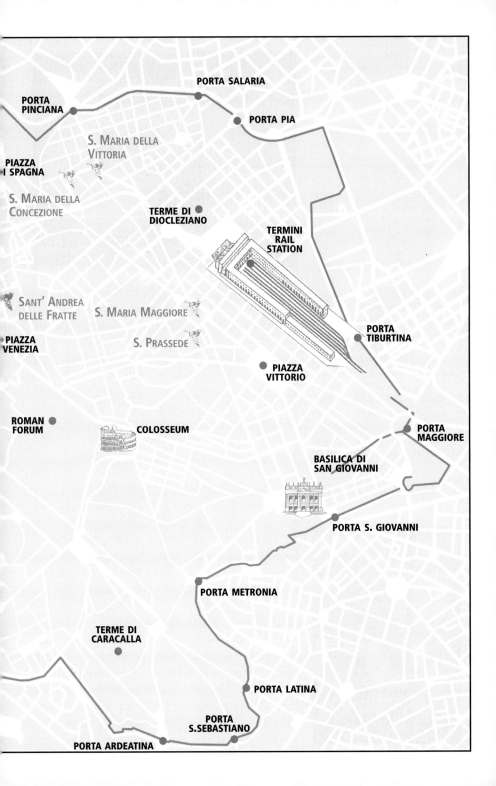

*And, behold, the angel of the Lord
came upon him, and a light shined
in the prison: and he smote Peter
on the side, and raised him up,
saying, Arise up quickly. And his
chains fell off from his hands. And
the angel said unto him, Gird
thyself, and bind on thy sandals.
And so he did. And he saith unto
him, Cast thy garment about thee,
and follow me. And he went out,
and followed him; and wist not that
it was true which was done by the
angel; but thought he saw a vision.*
(Acts 12:7-9)

WALK YOUR PATH

Our walk will introduce us to a variety of angelic duties and deeds, ranging from dramatic interventions, such as the saving of Rome from the plague, to their many supporting roles in the story of Christianity.

From the Middle Ages onwards representations of angels increased in numbers, assuming a particular importance in the iconography of the Counter-Reformation. Angels became the *alter ego* of pilgrims, showing their grief, their sorrow or their joy on the journey towards understanding.

ANGELIC INTERVENTION

Our journey starts at Ponte Sant'Angelo and continues via Castel Sant'Angelo, the site of Pope Saint Gregory's vision, to end at the basilica of Saint Peter. The main subjects are the bridge guarded by angels, which links the city of Rome to the Vatican, and the Archangel Michael.

Ponte Sant'Angelo

This bridge was the most direct and convenient link between the city of Rome and the Vatican. In the fifth century, when Ponte Neroniano was demolished, Ponte Sant'Angelo became the only bridge giving access to the basilica of Saint Peter and the Vatican palaces. Because of its strategic position, it has been the scene of many events in the history of the papacy.

Brief history of Ponte Sant'Angelo

The Ponte Sant'Angelo was originally called the *Pons Aelius* after Hadrian, whose full name was Publius Aelius Hadrianus. Hadrian had it built in AD 134 in order to provide a suitably noble approach to his mausoleum, the present Castel Sant'Angelo. After the fifth century it was renamed *Pons Sancti Petri*, to underline its role of providing access to the basilica of Saint Peter. After the vision of Pope Saint Gregory it was called Ponte Sant'Angelo, in honour of the angel of deliverance. It was given a new appearance by Gian Lorenzo Bernini when Clement IX, soon after his accession in 1667, decided to modernise the bridge and embellish it with ten marble angels, each meditating over the instruments of the Passion.

On Christmas Eve 1075 Cecius, the son of the prefect of Rome, kidnapped Pope Gregory VII while he was saying mass in Santa Maria Maggiore and imprisoned him in a tower he had had built on Ponte Sant'Angelo. The following morning, the people of Rome destroyed it completely in order to free the pope.

A few years later, Pope Paschal II (1099-1118) was leading a procession on the bridge when he was attacked by Pietro, son of Pierleone, and his men, who wanted to force the pope to confirm his illegal nomination as prefect of Rome.

After their coronation in the basilica of Saint Peter, German emperors stopped on the bridge to invest their followers as knights, before proceeding towards the basilica of San Giovanni in Laterano.

In 1450, during the last day of the Jubilee, the bridge was crowded with pilgrims who had just left Saint Peter's to venerate Saint Veronica when Cardinal Pietro Barbo lost control of his horse. In the ensuing mayhem over 300 people died. The following year, in memory of the people who had tragically perished, Pope Nicholas V had two small chapels built dedicated to Saint Mary Magdalene and the Santi Innocenti. In 1534, Pope Clement VII had them replaced with two statues of the Apostles Peter and Paul.

In the seventeenth century, amid a flurry of studies on Christ's Passion, Pope Clement IX decided to embellish the bridge with a procession of angels carrying

Gian Lorenzo Bernini

By the early 1620s Gian Lorenzo Bernini was established as the greatest sculptor since Michelangelo. He was a man of hot temper, described by his son as *'terribile nell'ira'* ('terrible in his anger'), but also of true piety, who practised the spiritual exercises of the Jesuits. As an artist of genius exactly in step with the mood of his time, he was able to give full expression to the new religious confidence and militant faith that were identified with the Counter-Reformation. He was employed by eight popes, several monarchs (including Louis XIV of France) and many cardinals and princes.

Michael

As the leader of the heavenly hosts, Michael is the warrior archangel. In the struggle against paganism Michael came to be seen as the champion of the Church's army against the heathens. He has a further role as one who weighs the souls of the dead in order to measure their good and bad deeds. Thereafter he presents the souls to God.

the symbols of the Way of the Cross. Bernini was nominated director of the project and the most prominent sculptors in Rome were invited to participate under his guidance. Each of the ten angels carries one of the symbols of the Passion and each object gives the keynote to the spiritual expression of the angel. These angels portray, with great eloquence, the grief they feel as witnesses of the suffering of Christ.

☞ **Angels with the instruments of the Passion,** marble statues;

to the left starting from the statue of Saint Peter:
☞ **Angel with flagellation instruments,** by Tommaso Morelli
In flagella paratus sum ('I am ready to be flagellated')
☞ **Angel with the crown of thorns,** replica by Paolo Naldini of the original by Bernini, now in Sant'Andrea delle Fratte
In aerumma mea dum configitur spina ('In my painful breath while the thorn is inflicted on me)
☞ **Angel with the tunic of Jesus and the dice,** by Paolo Naldini
Super vestem meam miserunt sortem ('They have thrown dice to gamble for my tunic')
☞ **Angel with superscription,** replica by Bernini and Giulio Cartari of the original by Bernini, now in the church of Sant'Andrea delle Fratte
Regnavit a ligno Deus ('The Lord reigned even as He hung on the wood of the Cross')
☞ **Angel with the sponge,** by Antonio Giorgetti
Potaverunt me aceto ('They gave me vinegar')

to the right leading on from the statue of Saint Paul:
☞ **Angel with the column,** by Antonio Raggi
Tronus meus in columna ('My throne in the column')
☞ **Angel with the sudarium,** by Cosimo Fancelli
Respice in faciem Christi tui ('Behold the symbol of your Lord')
☞ **Angel with the nails,** by Girolamo Lucenti

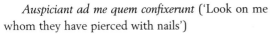

Auspiciant ad me quem confixerunt ('Look on me whom they have pierced with nails')

☞ **Angel with the Cross,** by Ercole Ferrara

Cuius principatus super humerum eius ('His kingdom is on His shoulders')

☞ **Angel with the lance,** by Domenico Guidi

Vulnerasti cor meum ('You have hurt my heart')

The Angel with the crown of thorns *and the* Angel with the superscription *are copies. The originals, carried out by Bernini himself, were finished in 1669 and were never displayed on the bridge. The other statues were executed by eight eminent sculptors under Bernini's overall direction, from 1668 to1671.*

Castel Sant'Angelo

The castle acquired its association with angels and its name Castel Sant'Angelo in 590, following the vision of Pope Saint Gregory the Great. Over time, it has become a shrine to the Archangel Michael, prince of the celestial army.

Michael is chief of the archangels, the angel of repentance and righteousness, the prince of light. He leads the angels of light in the battle against the forces of darkness. Most of the angels portrayed in Castel Sant'Angelo are, in fact, of a warrior type, carrying swords and wearing armour of some sort. This type-casting may have arisen from the fortified nature of the building that they help to defend. During the centuries, many popes have taken refuge inside its walls.

Michael is the angel who spoke to Moses, the angel who prevented Abraham from slaying Isaac, the angel who slew the fire-breathing dragon. He is frequently represented in art in the latter guise: he can easily be distinguished from Saint George, another dragon-slayer, by his angel's wings. Because of his fearlessness in facing the dragon, Pope Pius XII, in 1950, appointed Michael the patron of policemen.

☞ **Colossal angel,** at the summit of the building, bronze statue, by Peter Anton Verschaffelt, 1752

This is a huge bronze angel on the very top of the

The instruments of the Passion
The instruments of the Passion are the objects associated with Christ's suffering and His death on the Cross. Most frequently represented are: the crown of thorns, the nails, the lance, the column of flagellation and the sponge from which He was given vinegar to drink on the Cross.

Feast of the apparition of the Archangel Michael: 8th May

Feast day of Archangel Michael: 29th September

First biblical appearance of Michael
The highest ranking of all the archangels, he makes his first appearance in the Bible in the Book of Daniel. 'Then there came again and touched me one like the appearance of a man, and he strengthened me. Then said he, Knowest thou wherefore I come unto thee? ... I will show thee that which is noted in the scripture of truth: and there is none that holdeth with me in these things, but Michael, your prince.'
(Dan. 10:18-21)

Emperor Hadrian
Hadrian, who was emperor from AD 117 to 138, was the nephew and adopted son of Emperor Trajan. He was renowned as a strong ruler who had unified and strengthened Rome's vast empire. He was widely travelled, a poet and patron of the arts. Many examples of his patronage of architecture survive, including his villa at Tivoli and the Pantheon, which he rebuilt in about AD 119.

Grotesque style

The grotesque style of fresco painting derives from Roman wall and ceiling paintings found in the *Domus Aurea* of Nero, which are dated AD 37-68. In about 1480 artists began to explore this ancient palace, which was by then beneath ground level, in grottoes, hence the name 'grotesque'.

Brief history of Castel Sant'Angelo

This extraordinary circular monument is the old *Hadrianeum*, a mausoleum built by Emperor Hadrian for himself and the members of his family. Erected in AD 130, it was used as a burial monument until 217, when Emperor Caracalla was the last emperor to be buried here. The core of the building, with its square base and cylindrical body dates from this time. However, much of the appearance of the building is of a later date. Indeed, Hadrian would have difficulty recognising his tomb were he to revisit it today.

The dominant position of the building on the banks of the river Tiber no doubt suggested its use as a fortress. In the fourth century Emperor Theodosius turned it into a prison. During the Middle Ages, with the development of Saint Peter's basilica and the palaces of the Vatican, it gained yet more importance. When the papacy returned from Avignon in 1377 the building was extensively altered in order to make it into a safe retreat for the pope.

building. It is over four metres high and replaces a sixteenth-century marble angel, which is now housed within the citadel.

☞ **Archangel Michael,** in the Courtyard of the Angel, marble statue by Raffaello da Montelupo, 1544

In 1348, when the icon of Santa Maria dell'Aracoeli was taken in a procession to seek deliverance from the plague, 60 people on the Ponte Sant'Angelo said they saw this marble angel, then on top of Castel Sant'Angelo, bow several times in a gesture of adoration for the holy icon.

Opening off the Courtyard of the Angel is the Sala dell'Apollo, one of the 16th century state rooms decorated for Pope Paul III (1534-49), who was a Farnese.

☞ **Grotesque decorations,** in the Sala dell'Apollo, fresco, 16th century

The frescoes recreate the style known as the grotesque, which imitates the interior decoration of the Domus Aurea, *the 'golden house' of Nero. It is characterised by fantastic figures and animals linked together to form a continuous decorative pattern. Although angels,* per se, *are not introduced into the scheme, it is interesting to note the proliferation of winged creatures, which can perhaps be viewed as remote ancestors of the Christian angel.*

Walk through the Farnese Apartments with their labyrinthine layout and then climb to the next floor to view the most sumptuous rooms, the Sala della Biblioteca and the Sala Paolina. The decorative schemes of both these halls rest on the significance of the Archangel Michael as a warrior guardian of Christianity.

☞ **Archangel Michael,** upper floor, in Sala della Biblioteca, fresco by Luzio Luzzi, 1545

As in the Sala dell'Apollo, the decoration is primarily in the grotesque style. However, in this state room it incorporates a fresco representing the Archangel Michael. The curiosity of the Christian angel's inclusion in a design of pagan origin is underscored by the presence of stucco angels in the corners of the room: this combination of ancient and Christian culture was clearly quite acceptable to Pope Paul III.

From the Library, a door on the far side of the room opens into the Pompeian Corridor, which leads to the most elaborate and grandiose of all the rooms of the Farnese Apartments, the Sala Paolina.

☞ **Archangel Michael and Emperor Hadrian,** facing each other across the hall, in Sala Paolina, frescoes respectively by Pellegrino Tebaldi and Girolamo Siciolante da Sermoneta, 16th century

In commissioning this decorative scheme, Pope Paul III clearly wished to associate himself with Michael, one of the most powerful angels, and Hadrian, one of the most powerful emperors. Paul himself is represented in the room by the repetition of his motto 'festina lente' in the painted decoration. The interior thus gives the impression of an act of self-aggrandisement on a major scale. In case the message was not sufficiently obvious, monochrome scenes from the life of Alexander the Great have been included for good measure!

Church of San Michele e Magno ⚜

Towards the end of the eighth century, the citizens of Rome accused Pope Leo III of promoting and carrying out the interests of the

Paul III

Pope Paul III (1468-1549) was born Alessandro Farnese. As a young man he lived the colourful life of a Renaissance nobleman. He had wide-ranging interests in the arts and philosophy, nurtured by the time he spent in Florence in the circle of Lorenzo the Magnificent. He was not ordained into the priesthood until 1519, by which time he was already both a bishop and a cardinal. In the same year he commissioned the Palazzo Farnese, in the Via Giulia, from the architect Antonio da Sangallo. As pope he was both a lavish patron in the Renaissance tradition and a determined reformer. He set in motion what was to become known as the Counter-Reformation by calling the Council of Trent in 1545.

Brief history of the Church of Santi Michele e Magno

The church was built in the second half of the ninth century; it is first mentioned in a Bull of Pope Leo IV of 10th August 854. In the seventeenth century it was dedicated to the Archangel Michael and Saint Magnus, when the relics buried in the cemetery were found and displayed. It was modernised under Benedict XIV (1740-58) and Clement XIII (1758-69).

German emperor, Charlemagne. The strongest defenders of the pope were members of the *Schola Frisonis*. After a series of brutal fights, the bodies of the dead members of the Schola were buried in a cave, on the Gianicolo hill. Years later, in 846, another group of Frisians were buried in the same place, after fighting the Saracens who had invaded Rome.

According to an old legend a group of Frisians, who had miraculously escaped the Saracens, arrived near Fondi, a village between Rome and Naples, and found the relics of Saint Magnus, who had died there in 251 a short time after being arrested by the soldiers of Emperor Decius. Saint Magnus's relics had been stolen by the Saracens, who had offered them as a ransom to the inhabitants of the city of Anagni. They were brought back to Rome by the Frisians.

In honour of the heroism of the Frisians and of Saint Magnus, a church was built on the site of the burial and dedicated to the Archangel Michael, defender of Rome.

 **Vision of Archangel Michael,** at the end of the central nave, painting by Nicolò Ricciolini, 17th century

The painting shows the archangel returning his sword to its scabbard. Michael is flanked by Saint Magnus and Pope Saint Gregory the Great, beneath the Castel Sant'Angelo, with scenes of people dying of the plague.

Church of San Michele Arcangelo
demolished in 1939

This church was dedicated to the Archangel Michael and to all the angels. Adjacent to it there was a hospital, Hospitale Angelorum of Sant'Angelo of the Confraternity of San Michele Arcangelo. The church was also known as *'al corridoio'* for its position adjacent to the curving corridor, called *passetto*, linking the papal palace and Castel Sant'Angelo. In 1939 the church was demolished. The interior decoration was moved to the church of Santa Maria Annunziata.

Church of Santa Maria Annunziata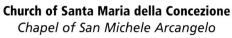
also known as Nunziatella

☞ **Archangel Michael with Lucifer,** on the right of the entrance, bronze sculpture by Albert Lefeuvre

This statue was donated by Pope Leo XIII (1878-1903) to the church of San Michele Arcangelo.

☞ **Procession of Pope Saint Gregory the Great,** on the left wall of the church, fresco by Giovan Battista Montano, 16th century

The fresco shows the solemn procession during which the pope had a vision of the Archangel Michael on Castel Sant'Angelo.

☞ **Gloria of the Divine Dove with the double Cross of the Holy Spirit donated by an angel,** above the altar, on the vault.

Church of Santa Maria della Concezione
Chapel of San Michele Arcangelo

Michael is the champion of the angels, the main defence against the Devil and the protector of men and women from evil.

☞ **San Michele Arcangelo,** on the altar, painting by Guido Reni, 16th century

The painting shows the Archangel Michael, dressed as a warrior, defeating evil.

☞ **God the Father surrounded by cherubs,** in the vault, painting by unknown artists.

Brief history of the Church of Santa Maria della Concezione
In 1626 Pope Urban VIII allowed the Capuchin friars to purchase the land for the church and the convent of Santa Maria della Concezione. In 1631, when construction was complete, the friars moved to the new convent. During the same year the bones of the friars buried in the cemetery of Santa Croce e Bonaventura dei Lucchesi were transferred to the new cemetery adjacent to the new complex. In 1890, after the opening of Via Veneto, the entrance to the church and the convent was modified.

Church of Santissimi Apostoli

Lucifer, the prince of angels, enticed some of the other angels to revolt against God. In punishment for his rebellion he was cast from Heaven, together with his mutinous entourage, who were transformed into demons.

☞ **Rebellious angels,** on the vault, fresco by Giovanni Odazzi, 1709

The effect of the angels tumbling down is very realistic. As the angels fall from Heaven, where God is enthroned, they acquire a bestial appearance with claws and tails; they become demons. Heaven is at war.

Church of Sant'Ambrogio e Carlo ✝

As ruler over the fallen angels, Lucifer continues the struggle against the Kingdom of God in three ways: he seeks to seduce man into sin; he tries to disrupt God's plan for salvation; and he appears before God as slanderer and accuser of the saints, so as to reduce the number of those chosen to enter the Kingdom of God.

☞ **The Fall of the Rebellious Angels,** on the vault, main nave, fresco by Giovanni Brandi, 1667-69

The vault is decorated with gilded stucco and acanthus leaves; in the centre the fresco stands out, suffused with golden light. God and His angels at the top banish, with invincible authority, the angels of Lucifer who fall from Heaven.

Church of Santissimo Nome del Gesù

Chapel of the Angels

☞ **Expulsion of the Rebellious Angels,** on the wall, fresco by Federico Zuccari, 16th century

The other frescoes representing angels are: on the walls, Angels who free the souls in Purgatory; on the altar, Archangel Saint Michael and angels adoring the Trinity.

☞ **Angels,** in the niches, statues by Giacomo Silla Longhi da Viggiù, 16th century

CELESTIAL COMPANIONS

At every turn in Rome, angels direct us, protect us and enlighten us. They act as our companions, offering a sympathetic presence to the pilgrim and the tourist. Although we may not always be aware of their proximity, the city is given a more benevolent aspect through their existence.

Porta Angelica

The German emperors who came to Rome to be crowned by the pope entered the Leonine city from the Porta Angelica and met their escorts in front of the church of Santa Maria in Traspontina. They then carried on in a procession, to be met by the pope at the entrance of the basilica of Saint Peter, where the solemn coronation took place.

☞ **Angels,** on the gate facing Via di Porta Angelica, statues, marble

Brief history of Porta Angelica
Pope Pius IV (1559-65) had this gate built, together with the fortified wall that stretched all the way to Castel Sant'Angelo. Its name derives from the pope himself, whose name was Angelo, and who dedicated the gate to the guardian angels. On the sides of the door there were two marble low reliefs of angels.

Basilica of Saint Peter

On entering the basilica, the pilgrim is dwarfed by the soaring scale of the interior, which immediately creates an impression of the insignificance of man and his small part in the scheme of things. However, to the left and right of the entrance are four angels who greet us, each pair supporting a golden marble shell of holy water.

☞ **Holy water stoop and cherubs,** to the left and right of the main entrance on the first piers of the nave by Francesco Moderati, marble, circa 1725

Although larger than lifesize, these figures nevertheless act as intermediaries between the vast, heavenly scale of Saint Peter's and the more humble scale of the visitor. Although the saints, high in their niches, dominate the nave, the smaller angels are less intimidating to the visitor. They help to make pilgrims feel welcome in the awesome spaces of the basilica.

As well as having a mediating role between the human scale and the divine, angels can serve to unite disparate parts of the interior. For example, throughout Saint Peter's basilica, small cherubs form a leitmotif to the decoration, surrounding cartouches, adorning cornices, supporting coats of arms or carrying the papal keys.

☞ **Angels holding up portraits of popes or papal tiaras,** in the nave on the entrance wall and piers, designed by Bernini, 17th century

Among these are 56 portraits of popes, from Saint Peter to Saint Benedict I, carved in relief on white marble medallions. These were designed by Gian Lorenzo Bernini and executed by his assistants in the late 1640s. Together, the various angels and cherubs give the effect of a cheerful chorus of intimates, a crowd of familiar friends who warm every surface that they adorn.

Larger angels can also serve to harmonise the decoration.

☞ **Tomb of Queen Christina,** in the south aisle on the first pier, by Fontana, 1689

☞ **Monument to Countess Matilda of Tuscany,** in the south aisle on the second pier, by Bernini, 1635

Although the two monuments were not conceived as a pair, the similarity of the angels found in both provides homogeneity to the schemes. As well as drawing them together visually, the repetition of the supporting angels underlines the common theme of the two monuments, both of which commemorate famous women: a rarity worthy of notice!

☞ **Tabernacle and angels,** in the chapel of the Santissimo Sacramento by Bernini, 1673-74

A gilt-bronze ciborium designed by Bernini, which he based on the Tempietto at San Pietro in Montorio by Bramante. The work, as we see it today, is only a part of Bernini's original scheme in which many angels were planned to be supporting the tabernacle. The splendid flanking angels were conceived as part of this unfinished scheme of 1673-74. It is recorded that, though by now an old man, Bernini insisted on making the full-scale models for these himself. The tabernacle, rich and glowing with lapis lazuli and gold, symbolises the perfect beauty of God. The original notion of creating a tabernacle for the sacrament dated back to Urban VIII but it was actually commissioned from Bernini by Clement X. He required more than an ordinary altar tabernacle; it needed to be a grand conception worthy of the scale of Saint Peter's and the homage of its many pilgrims. In this instance Bernini has introduced the angels to express the adoration and faith experienced by the pilgrim: the angels are used as vehicles for the expression of human emotions.

☞ **Cherub and cornucopia,** on the right-hand side of the aisle, beyond the Gregoriana Chapel, by Bracci, 18th century.

This is the tomb of Pope Benedict XIV (1740-58). Here the cherub, with his cornucopia, once again provides us with an introduction to the towering figures of the saints and pope above.

☞ **The Angel of Death,** in the archway, beside the tomb of Clement XIII (1758-69), by Antonio Canova, 18th century

A sculptor in the neo-classical tradition, Canova conceived a funerary monument very differently from Bernini. The baroque master conveys his certainty of the Resurrection; in contrast, Clement appears to be praying for his own future rather than being assured of it. Canova's angel is the Angel of Death, who leans on the tomb awaiting his moment. This solemn neo-classical figure serves to underline the cheerful optimism of the

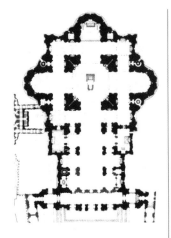

earlier baroque angels of Saint Peter's and to stress the friendliness of the huge majority of his winged companions.

☞ **Tiny angels amongst the vines of the twisted** columns of the baldachin, at the very heart of the basilica, above the tomb of Saint Peter, by Bernini, 1623-33

The baldachin was designed by Bernini as part of his scheme for Urban VIII (1623-44), the greatest patron of sculpture in Vatican history. As Cardinal Barberini, he had been a close friend of Bernini since the artist's childhood. This huge suspended canopy is a tour de force of gilt bronze (the metal was taken from the portico of the Pantheon), in which angels play a major role. Four large angels appear to hold up the canopy on ropes of flowers as they dance on the four corners of the baldachin, bringing vitality to an otherwise massive design. Between them, sitting on the edge of the canopy, are more angels, this time little cherubs, who take their duties as bearers of the papal keys and tiara very lightly: they might topple down amongst us at any moment! Beneath them, cherubs share with the Barberini bees the honour of decorating the tasselled hangings of the canopy. Even smaller angels climb in the vines that encircle the monumental columns, clinging on tightly as they make their ascent.

☞ **Angels in primary positions to left and right of the chair of Saint Peter,** in the apse, chair of Saint Peter, by Bernini, 17th century

The baldachin serves as a frame for the visual explosion of Bernini's chair of Saint Peter. It was commissioned by Pope Alexander VII (1655-67) and realised from 1657 to 1665. Conceived as the throne of the Vicar of Christ, this was Bernini's magnificent finale in Saint Peter's. It has the dual role of acting as the symbol of the triumph of the newly reformed Catholic Church and as the focal point of the pilgrim's journey in the basilica. The chair was believed to have been the episcopal throne of Saint Peter, but is now thought to be of medieval construction. Bernini made it the centre of a highly theatrical design, in which it appears to be suspended between the founding fathers of the church below and a billowing cloud of angels above. The fertility of Bernini's conception of angels is magnificently underscored by the crescendo of angelic activity in the upper part of the scheme that surrounds the dove, known as 'the Glory'. It is probable that the artist was influenced by the writings of the Syrian monk know as Dionysius the Areopagite, in his description of angels in the celestial hierarchy circa 500. This early-Christian text had been published in 1634 in a Latin translation, with a title page by Rubens; it seems very likely that it fuelled Bernini's imagination in the creation of these gilded stucco angels.

On the way out of the basilica the visitor will notice some grieving angels.

☞ **Canova's grieving angels,** north aisle, on the last pier

This monument is dedicated to the last of the Stuarts: James Francis Edward Stuart (the 'Old Pretender' and son of the deposed James II); Charles Edward Stuart, 'Bonnie Prince Charlie' (the 'Young Pretender' and grandson of James II); and Henry Stuart, Cardinal of

Antonio Canova
The most famous sculptor of the Neoclassical style, Canova (1757-1822) began his career in Venice. His earliest work is in the French eighteenth-century tradition but, following a visit to Rome in 1780, he adopted the Neoclassical manner and made it his own. In the following decade he received two important papal commissions, firstly for the Monument to Pope Clement XIV in Santissimi Apostoli, and then for the Monument to Pope Clement XIII, in Saint Peter's basilica. In 1802 he was persuaded by the Vatican to travel to Paris to work for Emperor Napoleon. One of his most celebrated works is a portrait of Napoleon's sister Pauline Bonaparte Borghese as Venus, which is in the Borghese collection in Rome.

York, brother of 'Bonnie Prince Charlie', who are all buried in Rome. (George IV, King of England, paid for this memorial to his historical enemies.) These guardian angels are unusual in combining the attributes of the two angel categories, being both adult and naked. Their body language speaks of their sorrow and mourning, yet they are noble in their grief.

Church of Sant'Angelo in Gianicolo
demolished

According to an old tradition, while Peter was being crucified two angels knelt next to him to give him comfort during his martyrdom. The print of their knees remained on the marble stone where they knelt and were housed in a church built on the site of the martyrdom, the church of Sant'Angelo in Gianicolo, also known as Sant'Angelo in Ginocchio (*ginocchio* in Italian means 'knees'). The church was probably built before 1000, when it is first mentioned in the Catalogue of Cencio Camerario. The relic was moved by the Bishop de Datis to the church of Santa Dorotea, for the Jubilee of 1500 and, in 1731, it was moved to the church of Santa Maria in Trastevere from where it was lost.

According to some researchers, the church of Sant'Angelo in Gianicolo was on the exact site where Bramante built the *tempietto* between 1502 and 1510.

Church of San Girolamo della Carità ✝
Spada Chapel
first chapel on the right

This is believed to be the site of the house of Saint Paula where Saint Jerome resided in 382 after being summoned to Rome by Pope Damasus.

☞ **Two angels, on the balustrade,** marble statues by Antonio Giorgetti, 17th century

The two angels function as guardians of the altar of the small chapel and at the same time they welcome people. They kneel and hold a cloth made of diaspore, a mineral. The right angel's wings, made out of wood, then turn on themselves to open up and let the faithful enter the space of the chapel.

Brief history of the Spada Chapel
The chapel is a polychrome jewel of marbles, yellow, chrome and black. It was designed by Francesco Borromini between 1660 and 1662, to the commission of Cardinal Virgilio Spada, a follower of Saint Filippo Neri. The cardinal wanted a family burial chapel. On the side walls, resting on two yellow and black marble chests, are portrayals of two members of the Spada family: Giovanni, who died in 1274, and Bernardino Lorenzo, Bishop of Calvi, who died in 1543. Above the chests are medallions representing other members of the family.

THE SUPPORTING ROLES OF ANGELS

The third part of our journey will enable us to appreciate the abundant variety of Rome's angels and the many roles they played in the Christian story.

Basilica of Santa Maria Maggiore

The basilica of Santa Maria Maggiore is of primary importance to the pilgrim interested in the Virgin Mary, but it is also a rich store of angels of every type.

☞ **Angels and Christ Pantocrator,** through a large door to the left of the main entrance, and up a wide staircase in the loggia, mosaics, early 14th century

It is possible to gain unprecedented close proximity to the mosaics that decorate the original entrance, which lies behind the present eighteenth-century façade. The story of the founding of the basilica, the Miracle of the Snow, is related here. The upper section describes Christ Pantocrator (or Christ blessing) with angels and saints. Below are four scenes that describe the miracle.

☞ **Four large angels**, in the loggia, statues by Pietro Bracci, 18th century

The illogical juxtaposition of the mosaic angels with the statues of angels in the loggia is delightful. Neither type was meant to be viewed at such close quarters; their proximity serves to accentuate the difference in their media. The two dimensions of the mosaic contrast with the three of the sculpture, the small scale with the large, the static with the dynamic, the colour versus the plain monochrome.

Cappella Sistina
or Chapel of the Holy Sacrament
to the right of the altar apse **(2)**

This magnificent chapel, the size of a small church, was commissioned by Pope Sixtus V from Domenico Fontana in 1585.

☞ **Gilded tabernacle,** above the altar

Amid the richly coloured marbles of this lavish interior, the gilded tabernacle, held aloft by four torch-bearing angels, dominates the chapel.

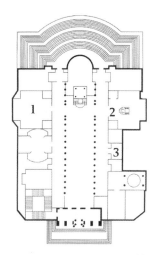

The Annunciation
And the angel said unto her: Fear
not Mary, for thou hast found
favour with God. And behold, thou
shalt conceive in thy womb, and
bring forth a son, and shalt call his
name JESUS.
(Luke 1:30-31)

☞ **Angels swinging and holding the candelabra,** in
the frieze and on the four candelabra
*In the frieze, high-relief angels swing among the
garlands and swags, or support the papal tiara. Angels
punctuate the design and help to bind the decorative
scheme together. They also hold the four candelabra;
these angels are very different from the ones that
support the tabernacle. They have a softer, more
feminine identity, which is characteristic of nineteenth-
century angels.*

☞ **The layers of painted cherubs,** in the cupola
*The crowning glory of the Capella Sistina is its
extraordinary vault, which is frescoed with layer upon
layer of receding cherubs.*

☞ **Angel,** on the gate of the small subsidiary chapel
to the right of the entrance
*This gilt example affords a rare glimpse of the
modern angel in Rome.*

Borghese Chapel
*known also as Paolina Chapel **(1)***

Much of the design and decoration of the
Borghese chapel echoes that of Sixtus's chapel.
Commissioned by Pope Paul V, it was designed by
Flamminio Ponzio in 1611. Although it is not
identical, Paul's version also takes the form of a
domed Greek cross, with an interior of
multicoloured marbles and an angel frieze.

☞ **The Madonna and Child altarpiece,** above the
high altar
*The focal point of this scheme is a reverent
portrait of the Madonna and Child once believed to
have been painted by Saint Luke 'with the assistance
of angels'. This beautiful and modest painting is set in
a frame of ostentatious luxury that is rather at odds
with the image. Unfortunately, the work is now
thought to date from the twelfth or thirteenth century,
so Saint Luke is ruled out as the artist.*

☞ **Mosaic angels,** nave and apse
Mosaics form a spectacular aspect of the decoration

of the basilica. These include many angels, who for the most part play the lesser roles in the stories described. The main apse, for example, contains numerous fine angels with dazzling fluttering wings; they are grouped to the left and right of the central scene, which focuses on Christ's crowning of Mary.

☞ **The Angel Gabriel greeting the Virgin Mary,** between the left side of the apse and the first window, mosaic by Giacomo Torriti, 13th century

However, in the lower scenes, which describe the Life of the Virgin, they play a more significant role, particularly in the enchanting Annunciation on the left-hand side. All the mosaics in the apse were commissioned by Pope Nicholas IV (1288-92) from a Franciscan friar, Giacomo Torriti.

Basilica of Santa Prassede

The entrance to the basilica of Santa Prassede is inconspicuous and easily overlooked, giving no hint of the treasures it holds.

☞ **Angels greeting the faithful,** chancel arch, mosaics, ninth century

The subject of the mosaics is the New Jerusalem. In the centre of the arch two angels flank the Saviour, each with one wing tidily folded back so as not to inconvenience Him. The gates to the New Jerusalem are guarded by two more angels (with both wings folded) and the faithful queuing outside are welcomed by two further angels (with wings raking up to heaven). The saints in the heavenly city seem rather dour, some having furrowed brows or solemn expressions; the angels provide a welcome contrast with their open gestures and benign demeanour.

Chapel of San Zeno (1)

☞ **Angels supporting Christ the Saviour,** in the vault, mosaic, 9th century

On the walls are represented six saints in heaven: Prassede, Pudenziana and Agnes on the left and Andrew, James and John on the right. Above them, in

Brief history of the Chapel of San Zeno

This small chapel was built by Saint Paschal from 817 to 824 as a mausoleum to his mother, Theodora. The interior is entirely covered with mosaics of exquisite simplicity, in a scheme that was known as 'the Garden of Paradise'.

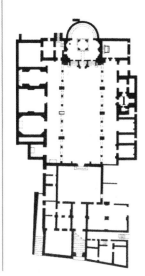

the vault, the circular portrait of Christ is carried, shoulder high, by four angels. The smooth, clean, classical lines of these ninth-century angels makes an interesting comparison to the swirling curves of a Bernini angel; the earlier type appears to be a simpler being than his dramatic and emotional seventeenth-century counterpart.

☞ **Dancing angels,** in the nave, frescoes, late 16th century

These enchanting trompe-l'oeil frescoes portray colourful angels with swirling skirts and fluttering ribbons who dance to a lost melody. They make a surprising contrast to the mosaics at the end of the nave.

Church of Santa Maria della Vittoria ✝ 🔯
Cornaro Chapel
last chapel on the left, off the main altar

Christians believe that angels are messengers of God and as such they bring news of His love to men and women.

☞ **Angel with a spear,** above the altar, marble group by Bernini, 1644-48

The angel is represented in the act of transfixing Saint Teresa's heart with the spear of the ardour of the faith. The angel delicately swivels his body, his expression is sweet and the hand holding the spear is gracefully positioned.

Saint Teresa
... It pleased God to make me have this vision ... Next to me there was an angel in body form. It is rare to me to see angels in such a way. But this time God wanted me to see it as such. ....The angel was not large, but small and very beautiful... he looked like those sublime spirits ... that I believe are called Cherubs. (from Life of Saint Teresa, chapter 29)

204

Church of Sant'Andrea delle Fratte

At the request of Clement IX (1667-69), the two marble angels carved by Bernini himself for Ponte Sant'Angelo were never displayed on the bridge. The pope had seen them in the artist's studio and decided to preserve them from exposure to the elements; they remained in the studio until they were finally donated to this church by Bernini's grandson.

Outside the church:

☞ **Angels holding flaming torches,** on the bell-tower, marble statues by Borromini, 17th century

The bell-tower, enriched with curves and counter-curves, is seen at its best from Via Capo le Case.

Inside the church:

☞ **Angel with the crown of thorns and Angel with the superscription,** by the altar, marble statues by Bernini, 1669

These are the statues originally created for the Ponte Sant'Angelo, which the pope considered too fine to join the other angels on the bridge.

Church of San Biagio e Carlo ai Catinari ✝
Chapel of Santa Cecilia

Musician angels accompany the celebration of Christianity with celestial melodies. They sing the joy of faith and the love of God for his children.

Brief history of the Church of Sant'Andrea delle Fratte

Originally built in the twelfth century, it was named '*delle fratte*' because it was then on the edge of the city; *fratte* means 'thickets'. The church belonged to the Scottish community before the Reformation and was rebuilt by Borromini in the seventeenth century.

The superscription INRI

An inscription was put first around the neck of a condemned man, then later it was attached to the top of the cross to state the nature of his offence, hence 'superscription', or 'text written above'. Christ's was written by Pontius Pilate and read '*Iesus Nazarenus Rex Iudeorum*', or 'Jesus of Nazareth King of the Jews'. On the inscription the abbreviation in Latin - 'INRI' - is used.

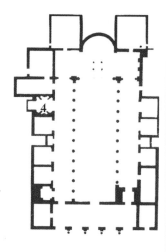

🖙 **Angels playing musical instruments,** central dome, marble statues, by Antonio Gherardi, turn of the 18th century

Dedicated to Saint Cecilia, the patron saint of music, this chapel rises to a central dome encircled with angels playing musical instruments.

Church of Santa Maria in Trastevere
Avila Chapel

🖙 **Four angels,** in the dome, marble statues by Antonio Gherardi, turn of the 18th century

Suspended from the centre of the dome, as if ascending to Heaven, these dour angels are carrying between them a tempietto, *or miniature temple, intended perhaps as a metaphor for the offering up of prayer through the medium of the Church.*

Basilica of Santa Sabina

In 1222 Saint Dominic brought the Regula (the law) to Pope Honorius III, who had moved to the fortified church of Santa Sabina. According to an old legend, Dominic arrived at night and when he knocked at the door, two angels came to let him in.

The pope donated the church and part of the adjacent building to Saint Dominic and the Order of Dominicans. In 1248 the Dominicans consecrated a chapel of the church to the angels, but this was unfortunately demolished in the nineteenth century.

🖙 **The Legend of the Two Angels,** in the portico, on the lateral door of the convent, paintings, 1624

This door was used during the Middle Ages to gain access to the convent.

🖙 **Saint Dominic,** in the portico, near the door of the convent, statue

An old legend tells that one day, while Saint Dominic was praying inside the church, the Devil, angered by his devotion, threw a stone at him. His hands blackened the stone and his fingers, from which emanated flames, perforated it, forming three holes. The stone flew towards the priest but an unknown force, stronger than that of the Devil, changed its course, preventing it from hurting the saint.

☞ **Black stone, on the left,** as soon as you enter the church

This column marks the place where Saint Dominic used to pray. The black stone, originally a measure of weight, has three neat holes across it. It is believed to be the one thrown at the saint by the Devil.

The Convent of Santa Sabina

Saint Dominic founded a convent on the Rocca Savella, adjacent to the church. Here Saint Thomas Aquinas was made a Dominican priest. From 1874 to 1936 it was used as a hospital for the sick.

☞ **Angel opening the door to Saint Dominic,** in the hall of the convent, glass, 1937

Dominican Order

Like the Franciscans, the Dominicans are not a monastic order, but mendicant friars; their lives are spent in the wider community rather than in the monastery.

In 1215, Saint Dominic, with the support of sixteen men he had gathered together, applied to Rome for permission to found an order which was to be based on the teaching of Saint Augustine and Saint Thomas Aquinas. In 1216, Pope Honorius III officially recognised the order. The primary aim of Saint Dominic was to preach the Christian doctrine, a task which had previously been undertaken only by bishops and their appointees.

The first house was established in Toulouse and, within a few years, there were sixty houses, some in university towns such as Oxford and Bologna. Dominic placed great emphasis on theological study; as early as 1218, he had sent seven of his followers to the University of Paris.

The order was more centralised than those that had preceded it, with control being maintained by a master general.

The individual friar owed his loyalty to the whole order rather than to his house and was obliged to serve the Dominican cause wherever he was sent.

This emphasis on the importance of the order as a whole entity was taken up by many later orders.

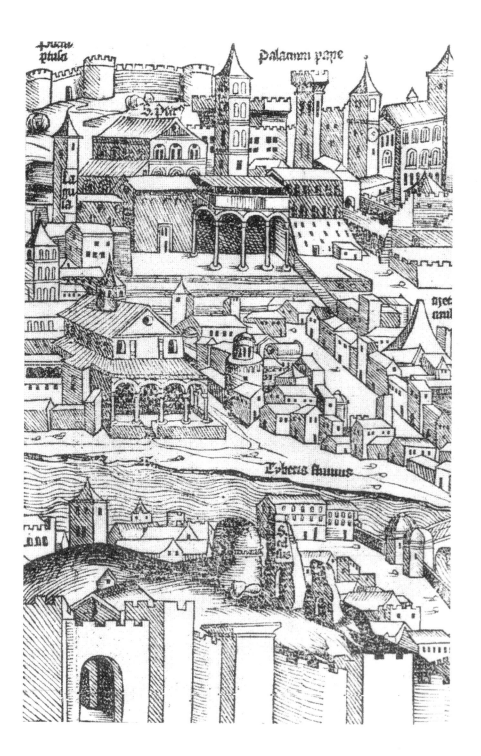

V

ROME, CITY OF POPES AND JUBILEES

W hen Jesus asked His disciples who they thought He was, Peter answered, 'You are Christ, son of the living God'. 'And you are Petrus,' replied Jesus, 'and on this rock I will build my church, and the powers of death shall not prevail against it. I will give you the keys of the kingdom of heaven, and whatever you bind on earth shall be bound in heaven, and whatever you loose on earth shall be loosed in heaven.' (Matt.16:18-19). Thus Peter was accorded his apostolic primacy.

Invested by Jesus, Peter headed towards Rome, *Caput Mundi*, where he laid the foundations of Christ's Church, a task that would lead to its transformation into *Civitas Domini*, the capital of Christianity.

Until Emperor Constantine formally ended persecution in 312, Rome was the main battlefield in the struggle between Christianity and paganism. Thus, it was only in the early part of the fourth century that Christians were finally free to worship God, to honour their martyrs and build monuments, churches and altars to their memory. After three centuries spent underground or in hiding, Peter's successors were able to come out into the open to lead the faithful. Rome was their city, the one chosen by Peter and by Christ Himself before him.

A new institution emerged from Peter's legacy, one that would withstand the test of time: the papacy.

In 330, Constantine abandoned Rome and made Constantinople capital of the Roman Empire. Stripped of its imperial status, Rome

Jesus to Peter
Feed my lambs. (John 21:15)

Saint Ambrose of Peter
Where there is Peter, there the Church is.

Papal primacy
Having nominated Peter as His successor, Christ conferred upon him the position of leader of the Apostles and head of the Church. Known as the Petrine primacy, this supreme position was not merely honorary, but carried with it full jurisdiction. It is handed on, in perpetuity, to all those who follow Peter as Bishop of Rome, investing them with the authority of papal infallibility in issues of morality or faith

The papacy
The word describes the organisation of the government of the Church under the direct authority of the pope. It derives from the Latin *papatia*, which in turn stems from *papa*, a term once used by all bishops, but reserved from 1073 for the bishop of Rome. The papal office encompasses a wide range of differing roles. Amongst these are the universal ones of Vicar of Christ, successor of the Prince of the Apostles and *Pontifex Maximus* (supreme head) of the Church. More regionally, the papal titles include, as well as Bishop of Rome, that of the Metropolitan Bishop of the Roman province and the Primate of Italy. In combining the role of bishop with that of the successor to Saint Peter, the papal office raises the pope to a unique and lonely pre-eminence.

nevertheless retained its position as the capital of the Christian Church. The city was the *Sedes Apostolica* and the core of the *Ecclesia Mater* and the pope was its sole and official voice. The transition from *Caput Mundi* to *Civitas Domini* was complete. From then on, the destiny of the institution of the papacy and the fate of the city of Rome were conjoined. Thus, Rome became the Eternal City.

In 640, Jerusalem was conquered by the Moors and became a city alien to Christians. Rome, with its many churches and Christian monuments erected in memory of martyrs and saints, was immediately perceived as the 'New Jerusalem', the holy city of Christianity. As the Christian world set out to liberate the birthplace of Christ from Muslim domination, swarms of warriors, heading for Palestine, stopped in Rome to be blessed by the pope. On their way back from the Crusades, the survivors brought a wealth of holy relics rescued from the Moors. Soon, new churches began to be erected to house those relics and to honour the martyrs and saints related to them.

Sedes Apostolica

Pope Damasus (366-84) defined the Roman Church as *Sedes Apostolica*, conferring on it primacy over all other churches. The Council of Rome (369) and the Council of Antioch (378) together established that a bishop, in order to be legitimised, has to be accepted and recognised by the bishop of Rome. In 382 the Council of Constantinople officially declared that Peter was the founder of the church '*voluntas domini*' (at God's will).

Pilgrims

On their route pilgrims carried distinguishing symbols: a shell, an image of Christ's face or a palm leaf. The shell of Saint James symbolised the pilgrimage to Santiago de Compostela, in Spain, where in the ninth century the burial ground of the Apostle was found. According to tradition, a star appeared to mark its exact location. Since then pilgrims have flocked to Santiago de Compostela. Pilgrims used the shell of Saint James to drink water during their journey and it became widely recognised as the symbol of a pilgrim.

The image of Christ was carried for protection and at the same time represented the final aim of any Christian pilgrimage: to find the word of Jesus inside oneself by visiting the sacred places.

The palm leaf was the emblem of the Christian martyrs and the symbol of Jerusalem. Pilgrims were called *Palmieri* (palm bearers), or *Conchiglieri* (shell bearers), or *Campustelliani* according to which symbols they carried.

Following in the footsteps of the Crusaders came Christian pilgrims who felt the need to visit the New Jerusalem, to pray for the liberation of the Holy Land, for the salvation of their souls and, above all, to honour the pope, the Vicar of Christ. The city embraced them with enthusiasm. Hospitals, hostels and *scholae* were built to house them. Pilgrims were grateful to the Eternal City for its care and hospitality. The stories of martyrs told inside Roman churches, the tales of the Apostles Peter and Paul and the wealth of holy relics fascinated them. Although Rome was not Bethlehem or Jerusalem, it was the city chosen by Christ to build His Church, the city that alone embodied the full Christian mystery.

As the Crusades continued, century after century, the holiness of the city became more and more tangible. Armies of soldiers and pilgrims flocked to Rome to be blessed by the pope. Jerusalem and the Holy Land had not lost their great appeal, but, in the eyes of the Christian pilgrims, Rome and the papacy began to symbolise a stronger and better link with

God. The Church appreciated this change of perception and responded by incorporating the holiness of the city into the Christian doctrine.

On 22nd February 1300, the feast day of Saint Peter Cathedra, a multitude of pilgrims crowded into the basilica of Saint Peter and overflowed into the square outside. They had gathered to hear Pope Boniface VIII deliver the text of the Bull *Antiquorum Habet Fida Relatio*, a revolutionary religious document. Plenary indulgence was offered to all Christians who would visit the basilica of Saint Peter and Saint Paul during 1300, renamed *Annus Benignitatis*, a special year of penance and forgiveness. The pilgrimage to Rome was definitively linked to the divine power of washing away centuries of sin. It was the beginning of the tradition of the Jubilee year.

The inner message of the Jubilee is one of forgiveness and, as such, it represents the central theme of the Christian faith. It gives people a chance to start again, to cancel all sin and to embark on a new road of hope. This gesture of pardon was initially conditional upon the pilgrim's visit to the Roman basilicas of Saint Peter and Saint Paul, the two Apostles martyred in Rome. To be eligible for the indulgences Roman residents had to visit the basilicas at least once a day on each of 30 consecutive or alternate days. Visiting pilgrims had to do the same for only 15 days. In the eyes of the world, Rome was not only the burial place of the Prince of the Apostles, the Eternal City and the capital of the Christian world, it was also a holy place, a city of grace, where sins could be washed away. The gate of salvation through which, 13 centuries earlier, Peter and Paul and the multitude of martyrs had passed, was now completely open. Beyond it was a glimpse of the path to eternal life. Rome was the first step, the threshold to salvation.

The Jubilee gave the city a new identity. No longer perceived as the 'New Jerusalem', Rome became a magnet for Christian pilgrims in its own right. They came from all over the world to be forgiven, to perform the rituals and processions suggested by the Church, to kneel and pray in its churches and to meditate in front of its relics. Rome was transformed into a city of pilgrimage, a holy city, God's largest temple on earth.

In 1350, the year of the second Jubilee, Pope Clement VI and the papal court were in Avignon, France. Rome was not only a city without a pope, it was a place in ruins. Raided by brigands and murderers, with a population ravaged by the plague of 1348 and the earthquake of 1349, the city had lost much that had attracted the pilgrims of the first Jubilee. Nevertheless, the faithful flocked to Rome to celebrate the Holy Year, among them Louis I of Hungary and Saint Bridget.

Pilgrims came to visit the basilicas, to honour martyrs and saints and to adore the relics. Some of these were displayed only during the Jubilee, for example the handkerchief of Veronica with the imprint of the face of Christ, which was shown in Saint Peter's every Sunday or feast day. Seeing the relics often inspired the crowd to ecstasy. Inspired by the vision of Veronica, Pope John XXII (1316-34) wrote a hymn, which pilgrims used to sing during the Jubilee.

In 1377 Saint Catherine of Siena convinced Pope Gregory XI, the last of seven French popes, to leave Avignon and return to Rome. The city was a desolate site, almost uninhabited, with much of its small population living among heaps of debris and rubbish. Its glorious and virtuous past seemed gone for ever. A year after his return, Pope Gregory XI died. Amid demands from the Roman populace for 'a Roman or at least an Italian' pope, the archbishop of Bari was elected as Urban VI (1378-89). He decided to remain in Rome even though the city was ravaged by epidemics and overrun by criminals. This decision so appalled the cardinals, who had assumed great powers during the years spent in Avignon, that 13 of them, 12 French and one from Aragon, left Rome and went to Anagni, a small town south of Rome. Pope Urban VI remained in Rome with the four Italian cardinals. In Anagni, the rebellious cardinals elected

The Jubilee
The word derives from the Hebrew '*yobel*', the blast of a ram's horn. In the Old Testament it is said that every fifty years the Hebrews introduced a year of rest dedicated to God, which was announced by the ram's horn. However, the Christian Jubilee was first introduced in 1300 by Pope Boniface VIII and does not appear to have been based on the practices of its Old Testament predecessor. To differentiate the Christian from the Hebrew, the words 'Holy Year' were often used in conjunction with 'Jubilee'. When Pope Boniface VIII established the tradition, it was to mark the passage of a century of religious observance. However, in 1342 Pope Clement VI reduced the interval to 50 years and in 1470 Pope Paul II reduced it yet further to 25 years. From 1500 the Jubilee has been conceived as a worldwide event to be celebrated during the whole of the following Holy Year. Since the sixteenth century several special Jubilees have been celebrated. For example, in 1965, at the close of the second Vatican Council, a Jubilee was declared in order to promote the council's reforms, and there have been many others, such as the Jubilee of the Madonna in 1983.

A song for the pilgrims
on their way to Rome
Annus centus - Romae semper est
iubileus.
Crimina laxantur - cui poenitet ista
donatur.
Hoc declaravit - Bonifacius et
roboravitur.

Pope Urban VI   (1378-89)

one of their number, Robert of Geneva, as Pope Clement VII (1378-94), claiming that the election of Pope Urban VI had been invalid because it was made under duress, in fear of popular pressure. Clement VII then took up residence in Avignon. This act marked the beginning of the Schism, a painful dispute that lasted until 1417.

Europe was torn in its support for the two popes. Because the followers of one or the other were divided along national lines, the rivalry fuelled already existing political conflicts. Germany, central Europe and most of Italy supported Pope Urban VI, while France, Burgundy, Naples, Scotland, Spain and Portugal supported Pope Clement VII. To make matters worse, in 1383 another epidemic of plague hit Rome. The pope left the city in great secrecy and on his return he found it yet more devastated.

In 1389, Pope Urban VI announced that, exceptionally, 1390 would be a Holy Year, 33 years after the last one, as many as the years of the life of Jesus. The purpose of this Jubilee was to heal the city, both spiritually and materially. That same year, emotionally and physically worn out, the pope died. Pope Boniface IX (1389-1404), his successor, approved the decision and went ahead with the celebrations. It was a Jubilee of great fervour. The Order of Flaggellati Bianchi ('White Flagellants') came barefoot from France, followed by flocks of pilgrims. Unfortunately, the plague killed a large number of them. During the epidemic in Rome, the sick people received great comfort from a young Italian monk, later to become Saint Bernard of Siena.

As Gregory XI had suggested in the 1370s, to obtain indulgences pilgrims were expected to visit the basilica of Santa Maria Maggiore, because the Virgin Mary played an important role in the protection of souls. Pope Boniface IX established that indulgences could be purchased by paying certain sums of money to *ad hoc* functionaries placed all over Europe. Pilgrims could choose between travelling to Rome or paying the authorities. Most of the vast sums of money collected were channelled to Rome, where they were used to rebuild the Holy See.

In 1399, Pope Boniface IX declared the following year a Holy Year, which coincided with the 50-year recurrence of the Jubilee. This gave Rome new hope

The Great Western Schism

The election of two popes seriously weakened the Church. Early attempts to heal the breach were fruitless, owing to the entrenched positions of the popes, which were reinforced by nationalistic concerns. Neither pope would resign. In an attempt to end the deadlock, a Council at Pisa, which met in 1409, elected a third pope, Alexander V, who was succeeded shortly afterwards by John XXIII (1410-15). Emperor Sigismund forced John to call the Council of Constance in 1414. The result of this Council was that all three popes were either deposed or resigned, thus clearing the path for the election of Pope Martin V in November 1417. A member of the Colonna family, Martin succeeded in restoring papal authority in Rome.

Hymn

Salve, sancta facies - nostri Redemptoris
in qua nitet species - divini splendoris
impressa pannicula - nivei candoris
dataque Veronicae - signum amoris.
Salve vultus Domini - imago beata
Salve nostra gloria - in hac vita dura.

The Holy Doors

The main symbols of the Jubilee are the Holy Doors, which are found in the four major basilicas in Rome. They symbolise God's mercy, which is open to all comers. The Holy Doors are opened for believers at the beginning of the Holy Year. Throughout the centuries their opening has taken place amid glorious celebration, in an atmosphere of awed expectancy.

Verily, verily, I say unto you, I am the door of the sheep. ... I am the door: by me if any man enter in, he shall be saved, and shall go in and out, and find pasture. (John: 10:7-9)

for revival. Many penitents came for the centenary Jubilee to gain absolution for their sins and to pay homage to the sacred relics. Unfortunately, the hunt for indulgences turned into a sort of market that was subject to abuse and the pope had to act to put a stop to it. In 1402 he declared ineffective all indulgences previously granted.

In 1417, in an atypical conclave held during the Council of Constance, Cardinal Oddone Colonna, a nobleman from a Roman family, was elected pope, to be named Martin V. The election of Cardinal Colonna, who was backed by all the European powers, marked the beginning of the end of the Schism.

Pope Martin V, fearing the consequences of the Schism, decided to re-establish the papal residency in Rome. On 29th September he reached the city, where a joyful crowd welcomed him. It had been more than one hundred years since a Roman had been elected pope and Romans wanted to show their approval. They followed the new pope in procession to Castel Sant'Angelo. It was a strong and positive sign that the Schism was over.

In 1422, Martin V announced that a Jubilee would take place in 1423, 33 years after the one of 1390, a precedent established by Pope Urban VI. During the Jubilee he introduced the ritual of the opening and closing of the Holy Door in the basilica of San Giovanni in Laterano to mark the beginning and the end of the Jubilee.

With the abdication of the last antipope, Felice V, the Schism finally ended and the papacy entered a century of rejuvenation and renaissance, serenity and peace. Once again, Rome blossomed.

From Pope Martin V to Pope Alexander VI, all the popes of the fifteenth century saw, in the institution of the Jubilee, an opportunity to stress the holiness of the Eternal City. They relaunched the concept of Rome as *Sedes Apostolica*, the geographical and spiritual centre of Christianity.

On the evening of 24th December 1449, Pope Nicholas V inaugurated the Jubilee, which was to be known as the Golden Year, with a new ceremony. While he was opening a golden door in the basilica of Saint Peter's, three cardinals chosen by him carried on the same ritual in the other three basilicas.

Throughout the centuries the tradition of the opening of the door has remained unchanged. The Christian Jubilee still begins on Christmas Eve, with the simultaneous opening of the Holy Doors in the basilicas of Saint Peter's, San Giovanni in Laterano, San Paolo fuori le Mura and Santa Maria Maggiore, and ends with their closing on the following Christmas Eve. The four basilicas, it is said, are compared to the four parts of the Christian world. Saint Peter's corresponds to the patriarchate of Constantinople, San Paolo to the patriarchate of Alexandria, San Giovanni to that of Rome and Santa Maria Maggiore to that of Antioch.

The sixteenth century began with a luxurious Jubilee under the Borgia pope, Alexander VI. On Christmas Eve 1499, he opened the door in Saint Peter's with a golden hammer. He then crossed the threshold on his knees holding a candle. At the same time, in the basilicas of San Giovanni in Laterano, San Paolo and Santa Maria Maggiore, the three cardinals delegated by the pope, performed the same ritual.

In the sixteenth century, the spectre of many national churches supplanting a unitary Christian

Ritual of the Holy Door

On Christmas Eve of the Jubilee year the pope opens the Holy Door in Saint Peter's using a hammer. He removes the bricks and cement with which it has been sealed since the end of the last Jubilee. The ritual symbolises Moses' gesture when he saved his people from thirst by striking a rock from which water then flowed. After the opening, pilgrims take home pieces of bricks and cement as relics. Pope Sixtus IV (1471-84) increased the number of Holy Doors to four to coincide with the major Roman basilicas.

The roots of Protestantism

Protestantism originated in the Reformation, a movement that was initiated by Martin Luther. His initial intention was to correct abuses and reform the Church; when he began to argue for change he had not envisaged a total break with Rome. However, from the reform of abuses, Luther gradually moved to a more radical position, challenging and then rejecting episcopal and papal authority. His repudiation of all the sacraments except the Baptism and the Eucharist further distanced him from Rome. His doctrine of justification by faith, in which he stated that salvation could only be granted by God, underlined the distance between Luther's beliefs and those of the papacy: an unbridgeable gulf had opened up between the reform movement and the Church in Rome. Luther's anti-papal stance was popular with the German princes for a number of reasons. It gave them a pretext for taking over ecclesiastical power in their territories, for ceasing to pay dues to Rome and for the absorption of the wealth and land of the monasteries. At the same time, his beliefs appealed to the growing merchant class, who found that the papal ban on usury, or the lending of money for interest payments, an irksome inhibition.

Church became a grim reality. The Reformation shook the institutions of both the Church and the papacy with alarming force and speed. What neither heresy nor dispute had been able to do before, namely, to divide Western Christendom permanently, was achieved by a movement that professed loyalty to the orthodox creed and abhorred schism.

In 1525, during Luther's rebellion, Pope Clement VII opened the Jubilee. It was a low-key celebration with fewer pilgrims than during the previous Holy Years, owing to the threat of plague and the religious revolution that was shaking Europe. Two years later the city suffered what has become known as the Sack of Rome.

The challenge of the Protestant Reformation became the occasion for a resurgent Roman Catholicism, an opportunity to clarify and reaffirm its principles. Emerging from the Council of Trent was a new vision of the Jubilee. The emphasis of the celebration of the Holy Year had shifted away from the indulgences towards a more spiritual gift. Pilgrims began to flock to Rome to be blessed through prayers, fasting, and caring for the sick and needy. The joy of the mercy of God and Christ were coupled with spirituality, humility and the mysticism of the faithful.

Christian pilgrimages to Rome also became a way of discovering the secrets of the city. This was facilitated by the opening of several museums to house relics and religious works of art. In 1734, Pope Clement XII founded the Capitoline Museum and a year before the Jubilee of 1750, Pope Benedict XIV established the Sacro Museo in the Vatican.

In 1796 the Papal State was occupied by French troops and Rome was declared a republic. Pope Pius VI was sent into exile and taken to France, where he died on 29th August 1799. On 30th September 1799, Pius VII was elected pope. No Jubilee took place in that year. Italy was in the middle of a revolutionary struggle, which eventually was to result in its unification as a state. In 1825, the twentieth Holy Year was inaugurated amid fears of political demonstrations.

In the twentieth century the Jubilees were interspersed with the tragedies of two world wars. In the second half, the Second Vatican Council (11th October 1962 to 8th December 1965) proposed a vision of the Church as a Church of the people. The concept of the Church as *societas perfecta* (the 'perfect society'), founded by Christ working through the Apostles and their successors, to which one belongs through subjection to the hierarchy, was integrated into a vision of the Church as a community in which all possess the sacramental mission to live and proclaim the Gospel, and all have a function in the service of the whole. The vision of the people of God as *sacramentum mundi*, a sign of redemption for all mankind, gave a new insight into the relationships with the Protestant Church, the other world religions and atheistic and non-religious humanist movements.

During the last 50 years pilgrims have flocked to Rome for four Jubilees: in 1950, in 1975, in 1983 for the extraordinary Jubilee that brought back into focus the concept of Redemption and in 1987 for the Jubilee dedicated to the Virgin Mary, *Redemptoris Mater*. They came from all over the world, from Africa, Latin America, southern Asia, East Africa, Australia - from everywhere that the word of Christ had been spread by the work of His missionaries. Many more will come in 2000 to celebrate the Jubilee in honour of Christ, the saviour of humanity.

The Apostles, martyrs, saints, popes and, above all, the people, the masses of faithful individuals - have been our companions in our Roman journey of discovery of Christianity. They have contributed to building, upon that first stone laid by Peter, the modern Church - ecumenical, global and without boundaries. Rome is ready for a new chapter and prepared to continue the tale of Christianity into the third millenium.

...to increase the splendour of the city and witness the truth of religion through the sacred places of the Christians
(Benedict XIV, about the establishment of Sacro Museo in Vatican)

Saint Carlo Borromeo on a pilgrimage to Rome
He started his visit to the churches on foot and barefoot ... he walked with devotion, humility ... praying aloud and mentally ... he was in communion with God and nothing would have distracted him ...

During the Jubilee of 1725, under the papacy of Benedict XIV, Queen Maria Casimira Zobieski was among the pilgrims. She entered Saint Peter's barefoot and for the length of the Holy Year she visited the churches clad in the habit of a penitent. At the Hostel of Santissima Trinità she assisted pilgrims, washed their tired feet and fed them.

The Second Vatican Council
Pope John XXIII called the Second Council Vatican in 1962. The theological and organisational changes made at the Council significantly revitalised the Church and opened it to new reform, ecumenical dialogue and the increased participation of bishops, clergy and laity.

They will say what they want: this Jubilee must be done.
(Pope Leo XII (1823-1829))

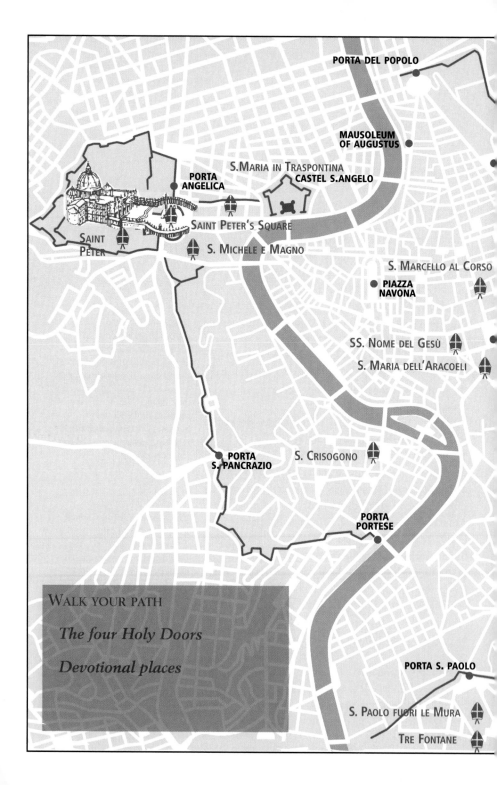

PORTA DEL POPOLO

MAUSOLEUM
OF AUGUSTUS

S. MARIA IN TRASPONTINA
CASTEL S. ANGELO

PORTA
ANGELICA

SAINT PETER'S SQUARE

SAINT
PETER

S. MICHELE E MAGNO

S. MARCELLO AL CORSO

PIAZZA
NAVONA

SS. NOME DEL GESÙ

S. MARIA DELL'ARACOELI

PORTA
S. PANCRAZIO

S. CRISOGONO

PORTA
PORTESE

WALK YOUR PATH

The four Holy Doors

Devotional places

PORTA S. PAOLO

S. PAOLO FUORI LE MURA

TRE FONTANE

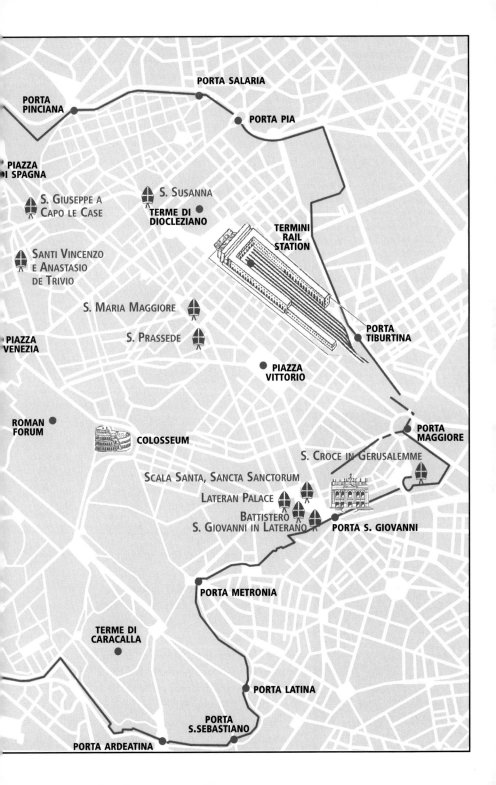

Pilgrimage to Rome

The pilgrim would visit the tombs of the Apostles; would tramp on the same earth red from the blood of the martyrs; would see the image of the face of Christ impressed on the cloth of Veronica ...; he would go into the Sancta Sanctorum, a small site, but full of celestial grace; he would visit the Vatican and the tiny cemetery of Callisto, with the bones of the beati; he would see the crib in Santa Maria Maggiore; he would contemplate the head of Saint John the Baptist and the grid iron of San Lorenzo; he would admire the cross where Peter was crucified and the springs of water that spurt out of the blood of the decapitated head of Saint Paul, and the place built where the snow fell in summer...

(Petrarch, Epistole Familari, IX, 13; of his visit to Rome in the Jubilee 1350)

WALK YOUR PATH

Our journey will take us to the major sites of the Jubilee's pilgrimage. The Holy Years generated large revenues for the Church, much of which was used to embellish the City of God with fine monuments and works of art and also to prepare it to receive the pilgrims. Architects were employed to enlarge streets, reinforce bridges and build churches. Artists were commissioned to immortalise the ceremonies of the Jubilee, such as the opening of the Holy Doors. Obelisks, steeples and bell-towers were erected in strategic positions to guide the religious crowd; hospitals were constructed to look after those in need. Even little *borghi*, foreign enclosures within the city areas, centred around *scholae*, were built to house pilgrims. Regardless of nationality and language, Rome became, for every Christian, *communis patria*, the homeland.

THE FOUR HOLY DOORS

The majority of pilgrims entered the city from the Via Trionfale, the road leading to Monte Mario, a more secure route than the Via Cassia, which is on flat land and therefore often flooded by the river Tiber. Their first glimpse of the city was from the top of Monte Mario, renamed *Mons Gaudi*, the hill of joy, in recognition of the breathtaking view of Rome and the sense of achievement and reward that pilgrims felt in reaching it after a long, and often painful, journey across Europe.

As they proceeded towards the city, they arrived at the church of San Lazzaro, originally dedicated to Saint Mary Magdalene and renamed in 1480 after the construction of a *lazzaretto*, a hospital for the quarantine of sick people. Annexed to the church was a hostel where pilgrims could rest, eat and drink before entering the city walls. If emperors, kings, princes or the clergy were travelling, the papal emissaries would wait to welcome them in front of this church, to accompany them to Rome.

Most pilgrims entered the city wall at Porta Peregrini ('pilgrims' in Latin), named after them, a small passage constantly crowded with people, animals and carts. As soon as they stepped inside the Leonine walls, they saw in front of them the façade of Saint Peter's. Their spiritual journey started here, inside the Borgo Leonino, the fortified enclosure built by Pope Leo IV (847-55) to protect the *Civitas Domini*.

...in the name of the Father, of the Son and of the Holy Spirit...

The Vatican

Imagine the joy, the emotion, the reward of the Christian pilgrim as he lifts his head above the crowd, upon entering Porta Peregrini, and finally sees the basilica of Saint Peter. It does not matter if this sight takes place at dawn, in the middle of a hot summer day or at dusk, in the reddish light of the Mediterranean sun. Whatever the conditions, the image of the shrine of Saint Peter, Prince of the Apostles, is breathtaking and that first glance is magical.

The pilgrim can stop for an instant only. He may step aside from the flow of people and reflect on what lies ahead of him. This is where Peter preached and died, where he passed through the Gate of Salvation, where he is buried along with 147 of his papal successors and where millions of previous pilgrims have come to share the joys of the Jubilee. This is the *Ecclesia Mater*, the core of Christianity, the common heart that beats for all its followers.

Resuming his march towards Saint Peter's, he suddenly understands the deepest meaning of his pilgrimage, why he has come all the way to Rome: to be part of the wonderful tale of salvation.

Saint Peter's Square

The square is the architectural embrace of the Christian Church. As the pilgrim walks towards the basilica, the colonnade closes behind him, two caring arms that seem to have waited impatiently for his arrival. Pillar after pillar, the distance between the three rows of columns gets smaller and smaller, until it disappears altogether by the time he reaches the centre of the square and steps on to a square stone near the obelisk.

☞ Obelisk in Saint Peter's Square

The obelisk is the second tallest in Rome after the one in front of the Lateran basilica; it is 25.5 metres high. It has no inscriptions and comes from Heliopolis, the Egyptian city built by Akhenaton, the semi-legendary pharaoh. In AD 37, it was taken to Rome by Emperor Caligula, to embellish his circus, later on renamed the Circus of Nero. Saint Peter was crucified in front of it.

In medieval times, when it was referred to as the legendary aguglia, *people believed the obelisk contained the ashes of Julius Caesar, on the top, inside a bronze sphere. Until 1586, when Sixtus V had it moved to the middle of Saint Peter's Square, it stood at the side of the basilica, in front of the Vatican sacristy.*

While Domenico Fontana was directing the lifting of the obelisk, a complex manoeuvre that involved 900 men and 150 horses, the horses suddenly became stuck and were unable to pull the ropes. The obelisk remained suspended in mid-air, in danger of crashing down at any moment. A sailor from Liguria, who was one of a large crowd of people watching the operation, realised that the ropes were about to catch fire because of the friction. Remembering that water would shrink them, he cried, 'Water on the ropes!'. This saved the lives of several people, who would have been crushed by the obelisk if it had fallen. To thank the sailor, Pope Sixtus V granted to his home town, Bordighera, the monopoly of supplying palm fronds to the Vatican on Palm Sunday.

☞ **Relics of the True Cross,** on top of the obelisk, inside an urn

When the obelisk was moved, Pope Sixtus V had the bronze sphere on top of it replaced with an urn containing a relic of the True Cross. It is this holy urn that is admired by pilgrims from the foot of the obelisk.

☞ **The colonnade,** on both sides of the square, of semi-circular shape, by Bernini, 1656

The colonnade, commissioned by Pope Alexander VII in 1656, was completed in 11 years. It embraces the square: these are the arms of the Church, and Saint Peter is its heart. Built by Gian Lorenzo Bernini, the colonnade is a masterpiece of theatrical effects. There are 284 columns and 88 pillars altogether, and the columns in the three outer curved rows disappear behind the columns of the inner curve. This effect was obtained by increasing the diameter of the columns from the inner to the outer rows while maintaining the same distance between them.

☞ **The Benediction loggia,** on the façade, the middle balcony, by Carlo Maderno, 17th century

This is the balcony from which popes have, century after century, given the solemn 'Urbi et Orbi' blessing. It is also the place from which the election of a new pope is announced to the people and where he is presented to the Christian world.

Basilica of Saint Peter

Standing in the portico, the Christian pilgrim faces five doors, and will very likely be overcome with emotion at this spot, a few steps away from the entrance of the primary temple of the Christian faith. The first door on the right-hand side is the Holy Door, bricked up most of the time and open only during Jubilees. Before passing it, the pilgrim will pause to read, and be moved by, the Christian story written on its panels.

Outside the basilica:

☞ **The Holy Door,** first door on the right of the entrance

Brief history of the Basilica of Saint Peter

The first basilica was built around 320 by the Emperor Constantine, after his victory over Maxentius, on the site where Saint Peter was buried. This basilica was consecrated by Pope Sylvester I in 326 and finished in 349. It had five naves divided by columns and a vast atrium with the *cantharus*, a large pool, in the centre. In the fifteenth century, Pope Nicholas V asked Bernardo Rossellino to modernise it, but the artist's death brought the works to a halt. The modernisation was carried out under Pope Julius II (1503-13), who asked Bramante to supervise the work. He demolished more than half of the northern part of the church.

The remodelling of Saint Peter's started on 18th April 1506 and was finished more than a century later. On 18th November 1626 Pope Urban VIII consecrated the new basilica, exactly 1300 years after the first one. The basilica had the dual function of *martirium* and *aula funeraria*.

This explains its vast dimensions and why it was no longer divided into five naves, as cathedrals usually were, but instead had a long nave with a triumphal arch.

The basilica has an area of 22,067 square metres, is 218 metres long, including the portico, and has 11 chapels and 45 altars. The diameter of the dome is 42 metres and it is 136.5 metres high, including the cross on top of the dome.

The panels treat the theme of salvation, the core of the celebration of the Jubilee.

☞ **Inscription tablet,** above the Holy Door, on the left

This records the Bull Antiquorum Habet Fida Relatio dated 22nd February 1300, with which Boniface VIII opened the first Jubilee.

☞ **The bronze door,** main entrance, third door in the middle of the portico, by Filarete, 1450

Pope Eugene IV commissioned the artist Filarete to build a large bronze door for the main access to the basilica. A fitting entrance for so special and important a place as the shrine of Peter, the door is made of bronze, the lustrous material used since ancient times for imperial buildings. It has six panels, which show: Christ enthroned, the Madonna, Saint Peter, Saint Paul, the martyrdom of Paul and the martyrdom of Peter. In between the panel scenes there are narrative strips concerning the papacy of Eugene IV.

☞ **Jesus Giving the Christian Flock to Saint Peter**, above the bronze door, low relief by Bernini, 1633-44

☞ **The Navicella: Jesus and Saint Peter Fishing on Lake Tiberias,** above the central gate in the portico, mosaic, copy of mosaic by Giotto, 1300

Christ rescues Peter who has been thrown into the stormy sea when the Apostles' boat almost capsized (Matt. 14:26, 33). The original mosaic, now lost (only fragments remain), was commissioned by Cardinal Stefaneschi on the occasion of the first Jubilee in 1300. The cardinal is portrayed praying in the middle of the sea. The message contained in the mosaic, to be read by the pilgrim who is about to enter the shrine of Saint Peter is that, during their lifetime, Christians' faith is constantly under challenge. The Church and Christians sail in a perennial boat, but Christ is always there, ready to save the faithful.

A fragment of the original Giotto mosaic representing an angel in a tondo is in the Vatican Grottoes.

☞ **Equestrian statue of Constantine**, at the foot of the staircase, on the right-hand side of the atrium, marble statue by Bernini, 1670

The statue is in honour of Constantine, the emperor

who legitimised the Christian religion in Roman times and founded the church of Saint Peter.

☞ **Equestrian statue of Charlemagne,** at the left end of the atrium, marble statue by Cornacchini, 1725

Pope Leo III was accused by a group of Roman nobles of conspiring with Charlemagne. In November 799, the king came to Rome with his son, 'to restore the state of the Church, which was greatly disturbed'. On the night of 2nd December, in front of Charlemagne and a crowd of nobility and clergy gathered in Saint Peter's, the pope took the Bible and called God as his witness to affirm that he had not committed any of the crimes of which he had been accused. This statement was considered sufficient to lift all suspicions from the pope. His accusers were sentenced to death but the pope asked for the sentence to be suspended. On Christmas Eve, at the end of the celebrations, just as Charlemagne was about to stand up, the pope moved over to him and put a splendid golden crown on his head. The crowd inside the basilica watched mesmerised as Leo III pronounced the following words: 'to Charles, the pious Augustus crowned by God, to the great emperor who brings us peace, life and victory!'. According to the Liber Pontificalis, *this gesture was inspired by 'God and Saint Peter, the gatekeeper of Heaven'.*

The pilgrim finally enters into the glory of the basilica, which resonates with centuries of reverence and veneration. The atmosphere is warm and the light that filters into the church is full of dazzling reflections from the materials employed to decorate its interior: coloured marble, gilded stucco, polychrome mosaics and stained glass. Immediately one feels part of it, drawn into its mysticism. This is a place of worship that is as much a delight to the soul as it is a feast for the eyes. The white verticals of the marble floor are the first detail to catch the visitor's attention. In the central nave, marked on the floor, are the dimensions of the largest churches in the world.

Festivities

Five festivals in the calendar of the Roman Catholic Church involve honour paid to Peter. The name of Paul is also associated with each of them. On 22nd February the festival of the *Cathedra Petri* is celebrated in Rome. 29th June marks the feast day of Peter and Paul, ranking among the 12 most important celebrations of the Roman Catholic Church. Peter's escape from his chains is remembered in the feast of 1st August. Lastly, the dedications of the basilicas of Peter and Paul, commemorating their construction by the Emperor Constantine, are celebrated in the festival of 18th November.

One of the major events in Rome is the feast day of Saint Peter and Saint Paul on 29th June. On the night of 28th June, the pope blesses the *pallium*, or cloth banner, and goes to pray at the tomb of Saint Peter. On the morning of the 29th, the time of the Holy Mass is announced to the crowd of the faithful assembled in Saint Peter's Square using 'a fishing basket' hanging on the main gate of Saint Peter's. The same rituals are followed for the evening service.

Inside the basilica:

☞ **Saint Peter,** at the end of the nave, on the right, bronze statue, by Arnolfo da Cambio, 13th century

A fine filigree halo hovers over the head of the saint. His right hand is raised in the act of benediction, his left is holding the key symbolising the key received by Christ. His foot has been worn away by the devotion of the pilgrims who have touched it.

☞ **Medallion of Pius IX,** above the statue, put in place in 1871

This commemorates the traditional claim that Pius IX (1846-78) was the only pope to have equalled Peter's legendary 25 years of papacy.

☞ **The baldachin,** in the centre of the church, by Bernini, 1624

Commissioned by Pope Urban VIII, the baldachin covers the papal altar like a celebration canopy. It rests on four twisted columns like the ones in the temple of Solomon in Jerusalem. The columns are decorated with the coat of arms of the Barberini (barberini *in Italian means 'bees'), to remind us of the great patron of the baldachin, Pope Urban VIII of the Barberini family.*

☞ **The Glory of the Cathedra,** in the domed apse, gilded sculpture by Bernini, 1666

The wooden throne is traditionally called the Cathedra Petri *and it dates from around the ninth century. It was believed to have belonged to Peter, but it is in fact the throne of Charles the Bold. Bernini, the great artist and intellectual of seventeenth-century Rome, created a stunning piece of gold and bronze sculpture called the Glory, which encapsulates it. It is a golden triumph of joyful angels on clouds, with the dove of the Holy Spirit hovering over it, shining with heavenly light. It symbolises the Pentecost, the day when the Holy Spirit came to the disciples to give them knowledge of all the languages, so that they could spread the message of Christ all over the world. Below, supporting the throne, are four large statues representing the Doctors of the Church: Saint Athanasius and Saint John Chrysostom, representing the union of the Eastern churches with the Romans, and Saint Ambrose and Saint*

Augustine, that of the Western churches.

☞ **Inscription,** central nave

This inscription refers to Saint Peter as shepherd and it is taken from the Gospel of John (21:15-17).

☞ **The *confessio*,** central nave, in the middle, by Carlo Maderno and Ferrabosco, 1600

The site of Saint Peter's tomb is marked with 89 silver lamps that are lit to indicate the spot.

☞ **Portraits of popes,** in the piers, 56 medallions

These are the popes who have been canonised.

Basilica of San Paolo fuori le Mura

After visiting the basilica of Saint Peter and having rested in one of the *scholae*, the Christian pilgrim will now set out for the second largest basilica in Rome, the one dedicated to Saint Paul. In the famous Bull *Antiquorum Habet Fida Relatio*, Boniface VIII (1294-1303) had granted plenary indulgences *ad limina apostolorum*, that is, to all the pilgrims who visited the shrines of the two Apostles.

The church of San Paolo, built upon the site where Saint Paul was beheaded, is outside the Leonine walls, hence the designation *'fuori le Mura'* (outside the city walls). To reach it, pilgrims leave the Leonine enclosure at Porta San Paolo and walk along the Via Ostiense. In the Middle Ages, this stretch of road was one of the marvels of Rome with a portico built in the 870s by Pope John VIII that sheltered the pilgrims on their journey to the basilica. The portico

Early life of Saint Paul
Born a Jew and a Roman citizen, probably in about AD 10, at Tarsus in Southern Turkey, Paul trained as a rabbi in Jerusalem. He used the Jewish name Saul when in the Jewish community, and the Roman name Paul when speaking Greek, in which he was fluent. He was bitterly opposed to Christian teaching, regarding it as a threat to Pharisaic Judaism. His conversion to Christianity occurred when he had a vision on the way to Damascus, where he was to have arrested some converts. This experience shaped the rest of his life, which he devoted to preaching the Gospel to the Gentiles of the Northern Mediterranean.

A small church was probably built at the time of Constantine on the site where the Apostle had been buried and was consecrated by Pope Sylvester I in 324. The popularity of Saint Paul, renamed *doctor scientiae* by the people of Rome for his intellectual and philosophical nature, persuaded Pope Damasus (366-84) to build a basilica as beautiful and as large as that dedicated to Saint Peter. Work started in AD 380, during the rule of Emperor Valentinian II, and continued under Theodosius and Arcadius. The basilica had three naves and was lit by 42 windows. The altar marked the site of the tomb of the Apostle. In the ninth century, a crypt was built underneath; it was circular and had two entrances to allow the flow of pilgrims in and out.

In the fifth century Pope Symmachus built a hostel for pilgrims and poor people next to the basilica to house the large number of people wishing to visit it. Pope Saint Gregory the Great (590-604) performed a ceremony of consecration over the tomb of Saint Paul to stress its role as *martirium*. In 846 the basilica was fortified against the threat from the Saracens, surrounded by protective walls and temporarily renamed Giovannopolis, after Pope John VIII who had built it. The basilica was partly destroyed and rebuilt several times, the last time in 1823 when it was damaged by fire. The existing building dates from the reconstruction after this fire.

was supported by 800 marble columns and was 1.5 kilometres long.

Right outside Porta San Paolo was the walled suburb of Giovannopoli, a small citadel built around the church by Pope John VIII to protect him from the attacks of the Saracens. The Normans destroyed it in 1084.

Before reaching the basilica, pilgrims were able to glimpse a large necropolis, the Sepolcreto Ostiense, where many believed Saint Paul had been buried.

Outside the church:

☞ **Saint Paul,** in the centre of the quadriportico, statue, marble, by Giuseppe Obici, 19th century

A colossal statue of Saint Paul represents the Apostle with the sword in his hands.

☞ **The Holy Door,** on the left-hand side of the quadriportico, by Straurachios de Scio, 1070

This is the original bronze door of the basilica, with panels inlaid in silver, showing scenes from the Old and New Testaments. It was brought back from Constantinople in the eleventh century.

Inside the church:

☞ **Scenes from the Life of Saint Paul,** along the walls of the nave, in between the windows with alabaster shutters, and along the walls of the transept, 36 frescoes, by Pietro Gargliardi, Podesti, Guglielmo de Sanctis, Francesco Coghetti and Cesare Mariani, 19th century

The scenes, taken from the Acts of the Apostles, are framed and carry a border at the top with the title of the scene represented. The Latin title of the scenes is at the bottom of the frescoes. The stories are arranged chronologically, starting from the transept.

☞ **Portraits of 265 popes,** in a frieze along the nave and aisle, mosaics of popes from Saint Peter onwards

According to a Roman tradition, the world will come to an end when there is no more room for a new pope's portrait. There are only eight spaces left after John Paul II. The first 40 survived the fire of 1823.

☞ **The mosaic of Galla Placida,** on the triumphal

arch, mosaics, fifth century

These mosaics were commissioned by Galla Placida, sister of Emperor Honorius and daughter of Emperor Theodosius. The name of Galla Placida is around the arch and above it are the names of Theodosius and Honorius. The mosaic was remade in the eighth and ninth centuries and has since undergone many restorations.

☞ **The triumphal arch,** on the inner face of the arch, mosaics attributed to Pietro Cavallini, 13th century

The mosaics were originally on the façade.

☞ **Christ with Saint Peter, Saint Andrew, Saint Paul, Saint Luke and Pope Honorius III,** in the apse, mosaics, Venetian school, 1220-30

These mosaics were commissioned by Honorius III. They are similar in style to the ones in the basilica of Saint Mark in Venice. The figures stand on a pretty ground enlivened by flowers and animals. In the register below Hetimasia is represented, flanked by two angels. Hetimasia is an empty throne surmounted with a cross and the instruments of martyrdom.

☞ **Ciborium,** over the high altar, marble canopy, Arnolfo di Cambio and Pietro Cavallini, 1285

☞ **The confessio,** below the canopy, by Arnolfo di Cambio, 1285

Saint Paul is buried here. The bronze sarcophagus that contained his relics was looted by the Saracens in 846, when they stole about 5 tonnes of gold from the basilicas of Saint Peter and Saint Paul. Inside the confessio, *next to the inscription* Paulo Apostolo Mart, *carved in a stone slab, there are two holes where pilgrims inserted pieces of cloths,* brandea, *to be made sacred by the proximity of the saint's relics.*

☞ **Paschal candlestick,** at the point where the right transept joins the nave, marble, by Nicolò d'Angelo and Pietro Vassalletto, 12th century

It is more than five metres high and covered in sculpture representing scenes from the Passion and Resurrection of Christ. It was used to hold the candle near the altar during the ceremonies of vigil at Easter.

☞ **Conversion of Saint Paul,** on the altar of the

The collection of indulgences
Pope Boniface VIII specified in the Bull introducing the ritual of the Jubilee that, in order to collect indulgences, pilgrims had to visit the tombs of Saint Peter and Saint Paul not once, but 15 times, if they were *Romei* (foreign pilgrims who had come to Rome for the Holy Year), or 30 times if they were *Romani* (residents of Rome).

When Saint Stephen was stoned to death in Jerusalem, the murderers 'laid down their garments at the feet of a young man named Saul'. (Acts 7:58)

He who had set me apart before I was born, and had called me through his grace, was pleased to reveal his Son to me, in order that I might preach him among the Gentiles. (Gal. 1:15-16)

Brief history of the Basilica of San Giovanni in Laterano

Lying just within the Aurelian wall, the site originally belonged to a Roman noble named Plautinus Lateranus, executed by Nero for plotting against him. The property was later owned by Fausta, wife of Constantine and sister of Maxentius. In AD 313 the emperor used Fausta's palace, where the baptistery is today, for a church council with Pope Miltiades. This became the residence of the bishop of Rome. Constantine donated the surrounding land to the Church and the place soon became a cult centre for the Christian religion. The church was built on the nearby barracks of the imperial guard, confiscated and destroyed by Constantine after the victory over Maxentius in the Battle of Milvian Bridge. Destroyed twice by fire, the basilica was rebuilt several times.

The last time the interior was reconstructed was in 1646. The façade dates from the early eighteenth century. However, the church has managed to retain its original fourth-century shape.

transept, on the left-hand side of the main altar, painting by Camucci, 18th century

☞ **The cloister,** by Vassaletto school, 1214

The cloister was spared in the nineteenth-century fire and is one of the most beautiful pieces of medieval architecture in Rome. Commissioned by Cardinal Pietro da Capua and the Abbot Caetani, it has columns of different shapes with inlaid mosaic decorations in gold, red and black.

Oratory of Saint Stephen

According to *De Locis*, a seventh-century pilgrims' guide, there was an oratory dedicated to Saint Stephen next to the church of San Paolo fuori le Mura. Stephen had been stoned to death in Jerusalem in front of Saul, a young Jewish man who later became Saint Paul. An important relic, one of the stones used to kill the martyr, was kept here.

San Giovanni in Laterano Square

Pilgrims reach San Giovanni Square from Porta San Giovanni, an ancient gate in the Aurelian wall built in 1574. The much more ancient Porta Asinara, built between AD 271 and 275, is still visible in the small garden on the left-hand side of the square.

In this square the newly elected pope, riding a white mule, headed a joyful procession. At the end of the ceremony, the pope took possession of the keys of the basilica. This ritual ended when the papacy was moved to Avignon.

Basilica of San Giovanni in Laterano

The pilgrim cannot but admire the basilica of San Giovanni in Laterano and feel that this is the mother and supreme church of Rome and of the world. This was the first church built by Constantine after his victory at the Milvian Bridge, as a gesture of thanks to Pope Sylvester (314-35) for saving him from leprosy.

In the sixth century, the basilica was dedicated to Saint John the Baptist and Saint John the Evangelist by Pope Saint Gregory the Great (590-604). It is also known as the basilica of the Saviour, after the sacred icon of Christ kept in the nearby Sancta Sanctorum. An old legend says that, on the day of the consecration of the church, the face of Christ appeared inside it. This miraculous event is shown in a fresco in the transept, on the left-hand side.

Before the popes moved to Avignon, the church and the annexed Lateran Palace together formed the chief papal residence. In the Middle Ages, it was regarded as the Vatican is today. Five Councils of the Church were held here and, until the nineteenth century, popes were crowned inside this church. Important people came to participate in religious ceremonies. In 774, Charlemagne chose to be baptised inside this basilica.

Through the centuries the church had its ups and downs. In 455, it was ransacked by the Vandals of Genseric and rebuilt by Pope Saint Leo the Great (440-61). By 1300, when Boniface VIII declared the first Jubilee, it was one of the great wonders of its time. Fifty years later, it lay in ruins. It fell into another decline just before the Jubilee of 1650.

Cathedral
The name cathedral derives from the Latin word *cathedra*, the chair of the bishop of Rome.

The trial of the corpse
In 897 Pope Formosus was tried here posthumously. The trial was conducted in the basilica before Pope Stephen VII, who had the corpse exhumed and dressed in full pontifical regalia. The papal lawyer cross-questioned the dead pope for hours. Formosus, although given time to respond, failed to defend himself. Declaring him a usurper, Stephen VII cut three fingers from his benedictory hand and tossed the rest of the body in the river Tiber.

22nd February is the feast day of the *cathedra* of Saint Peter, a ceremony first introduced in the fourth century to commemorate the Prince of the Apostles. On the Thursday before Easter, the day consecrated to the Eucharist, the pope says a special mass, *Missa in Coena Domini*, in this basilica in honour of the institution of the Eucharist during the Last Supper. After the singing of the Gospel, the pope renews the ritual of *mandatum* reintroduced by Pope John XXIII (1958-63). He washes the feet of 12 students from the ecclesiastic schools. From the basilica, a procession heads for the chapel of San Francesco, where the hosts are left until the communion of Good Friday.

The day of the birth of Saint John the Baptist, 24th June, is preceded by a festive vigil, which includes a meal of snails in the piazza. Inside the sacristy another ancient ceremony is carried out. The cloves are blessed. This tradition was first introduced in the fourth century, when this exotic spice was sent to the pope. The festivities include, an important ceremony of vespers, mass and the chanting of hymns.

Outside the church:

☞ **The Holy Door,** in the portico, second door on the right

This is the door of Redemption and is opened for each Jubilee.

☞ **Scenes from the Life of Saint John the Baptist,** above the doors, by various artists, reliefs, 18th century

The scenes are: The Beheading of Saint John the Baptist, by Filippo della Valle, 18th century; The Naming of Saint John the Baptist, by Bernardino Ludovisi, 18th century; John the Baptist Preaching, by G. B. Maini, 17th century; John the Baptist Facing Herod, by Pietro Bracci, 18th century.

The inscription
There is an inscription on both sides of the main entrance, below the stylobate where the keys of Saint Peter are. It reads 'Sacros Lateran Ecclesia, Omnium Urbis et Orbis, Ecclesiarum Mater, et Caput'. *(Sacred church of the Lateran, mother of the Church and head of the Church everywhere)*

Inside the church:

☞ **The Jubilee of Boniface VIII**, behind the first pier on the right, fresco, attributed to Giotto, 14th century

Pope Boniface VIII gives his blessing from the balcony for the opening of the first Jubilee in history. This fragment of fresco survived the fire of 1360 and was originally in the loggia of Pope Boniface VIII. Borromini placed it where it is now in the seventeenth century.

☞ **Memorial to Pope Sylvester II,** on the next pier, commissioned by a rich Hungarian patron in 1909

Sylvester II crowned Saint Stephen, first king of Hungary, in 1001. An old inscription originally on the tomb of Sylvester II, has been incorporated in the memorial. According to a medieval legend, the pope's tomb used to sweat and rattle when a pope was about to die. The legend was linked to Sylvester's fame as a magician.

☞ **Altar of Santissimo Sacramento,** in the transept, by Pietro Paolo Olivieri, 16th century

The artist used four bronze columns believed to be from the Temple of Jerusalem.

☞ **Statues of the Apostles and Prophets,** in the *aedicolae,* along the pillars, statues of the Apostles by various artists, 18th century; above them, oval stucco low relief showing the faces of the Prophets

From the right the statues represent: Saint Taddeus, by Lorenzo Ottono, and Nahum, by Domenico Maria Muratori, 1712; Saint Matthew, by Camillo Rusconi, and Jonah, by Marco Benefial, 1715; Saint Philip, by Giuseppe Mazzuoli, and Amos, by Giuseppe Nicola Nasini, 1715; Saint Thomas, by Pierre Legro, and Hosea, by Giovanni Odazzi, 1711; Saint James the Great, by Camillo Rusconi, and Ezekiel, by G. Paolo Melchiorri, 1718; Saint Paul, by Pierre Monnot, and Jeremiah, by Sebastiano Conca, 1706. Walking back on the other side: Saint Peter, by Pierre Monnot, and Isaiah, by Francesco Trevisani, 1709; Saint Andrew, by Camillo Rusconi, and Baruch, by Francesco Trevisani, 1709; Saint John, by Camillo Rusconi, and Daniel, by Andrea Procaccini, 1713; Saint James the Less, by Angelo de Ross, and Joel, by Luigi Garzi, 1715; Saint Bartholomew, by Pierre Legros, and Obadiah, by Giuseppe Chiari, 1712; Saint Simon, by Francesco Moratti, and Micah, by Pierleone Ghezzi, 1719.

☞ **The *cathedra,*** at the end of the apse

This is where the pope sits after his election when he comes to the basilica to take possession of his diocese. This ceremony gives him full authority over the Church all over the world.

☞ **The cloister,** by Vassalletti, father and son, between 1215 and 1223

Cola di Rienzo

After the pope moved to Avignon, Rome was abandoned to the rule of the local nobility and experienced a period of internal fighting and turmoil. In 1342 the Senate was destroyed and a new government of 13 people, *boni homines,* from the 13 corporations, was formed. Cola di Rienzo, the son of a publican and a washerwoman, was chosen to go to Avignon and present the case for the changes in the Roman political landscape. In 1344 he came back to Rome with the title of Notary of the Municipal Chamber.

He was a mystic dreamer who wanted to restore the spirit of the Roman Empire and bring in popular liberties, freeing the city from the feudal chains of nobility. In 1344, during the revolts, he was nominated head of the city. In 1347, with a citizen army, he conquered the Capitol and established a new regime. Nominated senator of the city and *tribunus populi* ('representative of the people'), he began a major work of reorganisation.

Concerned about the reforms, the pope, from his seat at Avignon, excommunicated him. This triggered the hatred of the nobility and Cola di Rienzo was forced to run away from Rome to plead for justice before Emperor Charles IV. Arrested, he was brought before Pope Innocent VI, who absolved him from all the accusations and sent him back to Rome with responsibility for special tasks. In Rome the population welcomed him.

However, Cola di Rienzo's second government was tyrannical and on 8th October 1354 the people, incited by the nobility, rebelled against him.

Inscription on the architrave
... mergere, peccator, sacro
purgande fluento... Virgineo foetus
genitrix ecclesia natos, quos
spirante Deo concipit amne parit...
Fons hic est vita, et qui totum diluit
orbem, sumens de Christi vulnere
principium.
('... dive into the holy font, you
sinner, to come out purified. The
mother Church gives birth, in this
water, to the newborn conceived
when Christ died ... This spring is
the life, from the wounds of Christ,
and it washes all the world.')

Brief history of the Baptistery
Originally known as San Giovanni
in Fonte because it was built on a
thermal spring (*fonte* refers to a
spring), the baptistery was a
circular building with a baptismal
bath in the centre. Constantine had
it built in AD 320. The monument
was the first to honour a Christian
sacrament. During the papacy of
Pope Sixtus III (432-40), the
architecture of the baptistery was
altered. Pope Hilarius (461-68)
added three chapels dedicated to
Saint John the Baptist, Saint John
the Evangelist and the Sacred
Cross. In the seventh century, Pope
Theodore I added the chapel of
Saint Venantius (or Fortunatus).

This is a medieval jewel of revived classicism.
Twisted columns and inlaid marble mosaics create
the setting for this peaceful corner. All around the
walls there are fragments from the earlier
incarnation of Saint John.

Battistero

Walking below the *logge* (balconies) of Pope
Sixtus V (1585-90) and Leo XIII (1878-1903), the
visitor reaches the baptistery, originally known as San
Giovanni in Fonte. This is the first baptistery in
Christendom, built by Constantine in the 320s in an
octagonal form which was later on copied in
baptisteries all over Italy.

In the fourteenth century, in this holy place, Cola
di Rienzo took a bath in the baptismal font and spent
the night in vigil, to emerge in the morning, dressed
like a Liberace in golden spurs, and christened
himself 'Knight Nicholas, Friend of the World'.

☞ **Baptismal bath,** in the centre of the baptistery
According to the Liber Pontificalis, *the bath was*
surrounded by two silver statues of Christ and John the
Baptist, a golden ampulla and seven silver deer that
poured water into the bath.
☞ **Two bronze doors,** on either side of the
octagonal room where the basin is
One is from 1196, etched with scenes that show how
the Lateran basilica looked at the turn of the first
millennium. It opens into the chapel of Saint John the
Evangelist. The other door, from the baths of Emperor
Caracalla, 'sings' with a low, harmonic sound when it is
opened slowly.

The Lateran Palace

The Lateran Palace, known as Patriarchio, was the
official papal residence until it was moved to Avignon
in 1309. Most of the palace was destroyed in a
massive fire during the same year. It remained in ruins
for more than two centuries. When the popes came
back to Rome, they established their residence in the
smaller Vatican Palace because the Lateran was

Giouanni inLaterano

Pope Paul V (1605-21) made it the residence of the *arciprete* and *canonici* (archpriests and canons) of the basilica. Pope Urban VIII (1623-44) transformed it into a hospital. In 1693 Pope Innocent XII donated it to the apostolic hospice of Saint Michael. In 1805 Pope Pius VII used part of it as an archive and in 1838 Pope Gregory XVI made it the base for the Gregorian Museum. The museums have since been moved to the Vatican and the palace is the residence of the vicariate of Rome.

Pope Sixtus V (1585-90)

Famous for redesigning large sections of Rome, Pope Sixtus V, Felice Perretti, was a man with a vision. He enlarged roads and opened up the city to facilitate the flow of pilgrims visiting the Seven Churches. As *Civitas Domini*, Rome had to be able to embrace the faithful coming from all over the world. The city assumed a new look, more suitable to its renewed role as the capital of Christianity. The final touch was the erection of the obelisk in Piazza San Giovanni in Laterano, the building of Santa Maria Maggiore e San Pietro and the completion of the dome of Saint Peter's by Michelangelo in 1590.

uninhabitable. It was only in 1586 that Pope Sixtus V had it rebuilt by Domenico Fontana, although he himself continued to reside in the Vatican and Quirinale Palaces.

☞ **Obelisk,** in front of the palace

This is the tallest obelisk in the world, just over 31 metres high, made of red granite from the Temple of Amon, in Thebes. The obelisk was erected by Thutmose IV, 15 centuries before the birth of Christ. In AD 357, Emperor Constantius II, son of Constantine, brought it to Rome. A special ship had to be built to carry it across the sea. In 1587, it was found in the Circus Maximus, broken into three pieces. The following year Domenico Fontana placed it in the square. Between 1603 and 1607 a fountain was built next to the obelisk. Unfortunately, the statues and the lilies that adorned it were destroyed during the last century.

Papal residences

Pope Paul II (1464-71) had Palazzo San Marco built where Piazza Venezia now stands and moved the papal residency there. This remained the official residency of the popes until 1564, when the palace was given to the Republic of Venice for its ambassadors and the popes went back to the Vatican Palace, which in the meantime had been modernised and enlarged. The Vatican area was, however, flat land and particularly hot during the summer months. Consequently, in 1574 Pope Gregory XIII began the construction of a palace on the Quirinale hill, which became the papal summer residence.

Basilica of Santa Maria Maggiore

The last of the four basilicas that the pilgrim will visit in his mystical tour of Rome is Santa Maria Maggiore, the first Roman church dedicated to the Virgin Mary. Built by Pope Sixtus III in 432, it stands at the top of a small hill formerly called Mons Cispius. A magnificent square opens in front of it. At the centre there is the Corinthian column, 14.3 metres high, from the basilica of Maxentius. On top of the column is the bronze statue of the Virgin by Carlo Maderno, commissioned in 1614 by Pope Paul V. This was a magical place to be on Christmas Eve. Every year, on that night, from the end of the sixth century onwards, the pope officiated at mass outside the basilica in a grotto that simulated the stable in Bethlehem where Christ was born. On this special night, and during Holy Years, pilgrims could glimpse the holy relics brought back from the Holy Land: five wooden strips from Baby Jesus' crib (kept in a gold and silver urn) and His swaddling-clothes.

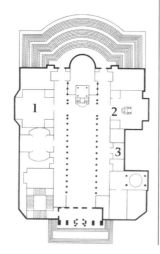

At the end of the thirteenth century, Pope Nicholas IV had the chapel of the Nativity modernised by the artist Arnolfo di Cambio, who created lifesize statues for it. According to tradition, whoever had mass celebrated in this chapel would escape the punishments of Purgatory.

At the end of the sixteenth century, Pope Sixtus V asked Domenico Fontana to move the Nativity into the Sistine Chapel, which had just been built inside the basilica. Unfortunately, the statues were damaged in the move.

In the Middle Ages, pilgrims flocked to the basilica to watch the famous procession held to commemorate the Annunciation, when the *acheropita* icon of Jesus, kept in the holy of holies, the Sancta Sanctorum, was brought to meet the one of the Madonna *Salus Populi Romani*, kept in the basilica of Santa Maria Maggiore. This was a magnificent procession, with a ritual that included the vesting of the pope along the way.

Outside the church:
☞ The Holy Door, on the left of the main entrance

Inside the church:
☞ **Scenes from the Old Testament,** above the columns of the central nave, mosaics, fifth century
Commissioned by Pope Sixtus III, these are 36 mosaics with stories of Moses and Joseph, on the right, and stories of Abraham, Isaac and Jacob, on the left.

Chapel of the Relics
fourth chapel in the right (south) nave (3)
☞ Holy relics
This chapel contains relics of various saints, kept in urns behind gilded grilles.

☞ **The Nativity statues,** in the Oratorio del Presepe,
Next to the Sistine Chapel, a staircase leads to the oratory of the Presepe, the ancient chapel modernised in the thirteeth century by Arnolfo di Cambio and brought here in 1590 by Domenico Fontana. The statues of the Three Wise Men, Saint Joseph and those of the ox and donkey are the original ones by di Cambio. The statue of the Madonna and Child is by Valsoldo.

A night to remember
On Christmas Eve 1075 Pope Saint Gregory VII, Hildebrand of Soana, was celebrating mass in the Chapel of the Nativity when a group of thugs burst in and dragged him off by the hair to the tower of their leader, Cencio Cenci, the prefect of Rome. The next morning, when the people of Rome learnt what had happened, they rushed to the tower and threw stones at it until the pope was released. Gregory emerged and calmed the people who wanted to kill Cencio, asking them to forgive him. He then walked back to the basilica of Santa Maria Maggiore and took up where he had left off saying mass, when he had been so rudely interrupted.

The dedication
The following is a dedication to the Virgin Mary on the portico of the basilica built by Pope Eugene III (1145-53). It can be seen on the right-hand side of the church:
Tertius Eugenius romanus Papa benignus, obtulit hoc munus Virgo sacra tibi, quae Mater christi fieri merito meruisti, salva perpetua virginitate tibi, es vita salus totius gloria mundi, da veniam culpis virginitatis honor.
(Eugene III, benevolent Roman Pope, offers this gift to you, Holy Virgin, who have deserved to become the Mother of Christ, maintaining your virginity intact. You are life, salvation and glory to all the world, honour to your virginity, forgive our sins.)

Brief history of the Basilica of Santa Croce in Gerusalemme

The basilica was built in the fourth century from a section of Saint Helena's palace, the old Palazzo Sessoriano, the imperial residence. Emperor Aurelian (AD 270-75) built a new city wall, which cut across the Sessorian buildings (the Aurelian wall is still visible today at the back of the church). The basilica is believed to have been built in the atrium of the imperial palace. Restored in 716 by Pope Gregory II, it was renewed in 1144 by Pope Lucius II. In 1744, during the papacy of Benedict XIV, Domenico Gregorini and Pietro Passalaqua added the bold convex rococo façade and the oval vestibule.

DEVOTIONAL PLACES

No visit to Rome would be complete without visiting the wealth of holy relics cherished inside the city's churches and monasteries. As early as the third and fourth centuries, pilgrims venerated them. Their cult grew from that of the martyrs. They included bones and bodily remains, as well as instruments of torture, which, it was believed, bore witness to the ultimate sacrifice of Christian martyrs.

Special saintly powers were attributed to relics. The first Christian reference to them speaks of handkerchiefs carried from the body of Saint Paul, in Rome, to heal the sick. As the struggle against paganism reached its final phase, the cult of the relics blossomed, and, with it, a lively trade. Among the first relics to be traded were the bones of Saint Polycarp, Bishop of Smyrna, martyred between 156 and 167, which were described as 'more precious than costly stones and more excellent than gold'.

Throughout the centuries, relics have played a crucial role in the history of Christianity. For the faithful they represented a link with saints and martyrs and, as such, they had to be made accessible during special rituals (for example when the fragments of the True Cross, which were kept in the Lateran, were taken in procession by the pope).

Relics were also used by popes to ask for divine intercession in moments of great crisis. In 1241, when the city was under threat from Frederick II, Pope Gregory IX carried the True Cross, with the relics of Saints Peter and Paul, to the Vatican, where he took refuge.

Basilica of Santa Croce in Gerusalemme

Legend relates that the True Cross was found by Saint Helena, mother of Constantine. During her pilgrimage to the Holy Land, about 326, she had a vision showing her where it was buried. The next day, she went to search for it and found three crosses. Not knowing which one was the True Cross, she asked a crippled man to lie on each of them. When she saw that his sick body had been cured by touching one,

The chapel was built in 1930 to house pieces of the True Cross and other relics. It was completed in 1952 by Florestano di Fausto.

Veneration of the Cross
The earliest historical reference to the veneration of the True Cross occurs in the mid-fourth century, after Saint Helena brought it back to Rome. By the eighth century the accounts were embellished by legendary details describing the history of the wood of the Cross before it was used for the Crucifixion. Roman Catholic theologians claimed that the blood of Christ lent the True Cross a kind of material indestructibility, so that it could be divided indefinitely without being diminished. Such beliefs resulted in the multiplication of relics of the True Cross wherever Christianity expanded in the medieval world, and fragments were deposited in most of the great cities and in a great many abbeys. Reliquaries designed to hold the fragments likewise multiplied, and some precious objects of this kind survive. The desire to win back or obtain possession of the True Cross was claimed as justification for military expeditions, such as that of the Byzantine Emperor Heraclius against the Persians (622-28) and the capture of Constantinople by the Crusaders in 1204.

she realised that this was the True Cross.

Saint Helena brought to Rome large sections of the True Cross along with many other relics, among them the staircase of Pontius Pilate's palace in Jerusalem. Inside her palace in Rome, later converted into the church of Santa Croce in Gerusalemme, she treasured several fragments of the True Cross.

☞ **Apparition of the Cross,** in the vault of the presbytery, painting, by Giaquinto, 1744
☞ **Saint Helena Finding the True Cross,** in the apse, fresco, probably by Antoniazzo Romano, end of the fourth century
The other frescoes are: Glory of the Cross *and* Christ in the Act of Blessing.

Chapel of the Cross
This chapel was built to facilitate pilgrims' visits to the relics contained in this church.
☞ **Cross of the Good Thief,** in the Way of the Cross, on the wall
Until 1930 the relic was kept in the transept of the church.

Rituals
The Feast of the Finding of the Cross was celebrated in the Roman Catholic Church on 3rd May until it was omitted from the Church calendar in 1960 by Pope John XXIII.

The chapel was built by Saint Helena in what used to be her bedroom. In 430 the Emperor Valentinian III, to fulfil a promise made to his mother, Galla Placida, and his sister, Honoria, decorated the vault of the chapel with a mosaic, which became very famous during the Middle Ages.

☞ **Three fragments of the True Cross,** inside a silver box

In 1492, they were found inside a box in a small window of the triumphal arch, where they had probably been placed in ancient times.

☞ **The finger that Saint Thomas stuck in the side of Christ,** in the reliquary

Chapel of Sant'Elena

steps lead down to the chapel from the right aisle

Many believe that the chapel rests upon a layer of soil brought back by Saint Helena from the Way of the Cross, in Jerusalem. An old Roman legend says that Pope Sylvester II, the pope of the transition from the first to the second millennium, a phenomenon feared by many as heralding the end of the world, was rumoured to be a wizard. He owned a prophetic bronze head (similar to the one used by the Templars three centuries later), which predicted events, among them his own death, which would take place in Jerusalem. And, indeed, in 1003, while he was celebrating mass inside the chapel of Sant'Elena, he dropped dead.

Feast day of the Triumph of the Cross: 14th September

☞ **Christ in the Act of Blessing,** in the vault, mosaic by Melozzo da Forlì, 1494

The other frescoes are: in the oval, the Evangelist; in the triangle, from the right: the Finding of the True Cross, Adoration and Division of the True Cross by Saint Helena, Procession of Heraclius towards Jerusalem.

Scala Santa and Sancta Sanctorum

The Scala Santa is the legendary staircase of Pontius Pilate's palace in Jerusalem. Called 'Scala di Pilato' in the Middle Ages, this was the staircase of 28 steps that Christ descended after His final judgement and which was washed by His blood during the Passion. In memory of, and out of respect for, this sacrifice pilgrims kneel while ascending the staircase. Brought to Rome by Saint Helena, the staircase was reassembled and used as the main staircase to the holy of holies, the chapel of San Lorenzo. In the

Prayer for the Feast Day
We should glory in the Cross of our Lord Jesus Christ, for He is our salvation, our life and our resurrection; through Him we are saved and made free.

eighteenth century, Pope Innocent XIII had them covered in wood.

The Scala Santa is flanked by two staircases on each side covered with frescoes of scenes from the Old and the New Testaments.

Chapel of San Lorenzo

At the top of the stairs is the holiest place on earth, the private chapel of the pope. This is where, through the centuries, popes have stored the most important relics. Pope Leo III (795-816) had a special wooden box built to house them, perhaps with reference to the biblical Ark of the Covenant. This was kept in the holy temple of Jerusalem, called the Sancta Sanctorum (holy of holies), and was accessible once a year, only by the highest religious authority.

In the three altars, safely stored behind bronze doors, and in the niches, protected by grilles, were placed the heads of Saint Peter and Saint Paul, a relic of Saint Lawrence, one of the fragments of the True Cross (sunk in a balsamic ointment in a precious container, inside a silver box, which rested on a silk cushion), a small part of the skin of Jesus from His circumcision, a lock of hair from the Madonna, the head of Saint Agnes, kept inside a silver box donated by Pope Honorius III (1216-27) and the head of Saint Prassede. Today these relics have been moved to the major basilicas.

Although pilgrims did not have access to these relics, during the solemn processions they could glimpse the miraculous portrait of Christ, the *acheropita* icon believed to have been painted by angels. The icon, brought to Rome from Jerusalem, was venerated by pilgrims and Romans. People used to ask the miraculous image for special intervention and help. The holes, produced by the nails of the *ex votos* pinned to it by those who had been granted help, are still visible around the frame of the icon.

In the Middle Ages, it was taken in procession by the pope whenever special protection by God was needed. In the eighth century, for example, Pope Stephen II used it to ask for divine intervention against the threat of the Lombards.

The rebellion of Martin Luther
For centuries pilgrims have ascended the steps on their knees - the only way permitted since Martin Luther in 1510 crawled halfway up and, claiming to have heard a voice saying, 'The just shall live by faith, not by pilgrimage, not by penance', did the unthinkable: he stood up and walked back down.

Brief history of the Sancta Sanctorum
Pope Honorius III (1216-27) had the chapel modernised after an earthquake. He changed the position of the altars and commissioned some of the frescoes. In the sixteenth century Pope Sixtus V asked Domenico Fontana to redesign the building, which today houses the holy of holies. Originally the chapel of San Lorenzo was part of the papal residence in the Lateran, and it maintains the structure of a building of the thirteenth or fourteenth century. However, in the basement there are ruins of much older construction, which probably used to be the library and archive of the Lateran. Here Leo III (795-816) built the *Triclinio Leoniano* (a dining room), embellished by beautiful mosaics, one of which contains the story of the creation of the Holy Roman Empire and of the coronation of Charlemagne.

☞ **The three doors,** inside the chapel,

Pope Nicholas III (1277-80) had these three doors brought to Rome from the Praetorium of Jerusalem and placed in the chapel.

☞ **The icon of the Saviour,** image *acheropita*, fifth century

The image is covered by a silk reproduction, probably painted in the twelfth century. The cult of the icon is documented in the Liber Pontificalis *of the eighth century. In 752, Pope Stephen II led the entire city in a procession to ask for God's help against the threat of invasion by the Lombards. He himself carried on his shoulders the image of the Saviour. This was probably the origin of the procession of the Saviour, which was celebrated each 15th August, the Assumption Day of the Virgin Mary, a ritual suppressed by Pope Pius V (1566-72) because of problems of public order.*

☞ **Scenes from the Lives of the Martyrs,** on the wall of the holy of holies, frescoes, attributed to Pietro Cavallini, 13th century

☞ **Christ in the Act of Blessing,** in the vault, mosaic, perhaps by Cosmati or Rosuti, end of 13th century

☞ **Ruins of the tower of Pope Zacharias,** in the Convent of the Padri Passionisti, accessible from the basement of the Sancta Sanctorum

Basilica of San Giovanni in Laterano

This was a very important church to visit, especially at Easter, when its relics were displayed to pilgrims during the religious ceremonies.

In the Middle Ages, pilgrims approached the basilica from Porta Asinara, along a path covered by a portico. Built by Pope Zacharias (741-52), it was decorated with frescoes and led to a tower, Pope Zacharias's Tower, embellished with paintings and frescoes from all over the world. The tower was destroyed during the earthquake of 904.

Once inside the basilica, from the right nave of the church, up a big staircase, it was possible to reach the Hall of Councils. On the opposite side, Pope Boniface VIII (1294-1303) built his loggia.

☞ **Silver reliquaries with the heads of Saint Peter and Saint Paul,** two boxes, below the papal altar

Only popes can celebrate mass from this altar. The original boxes for the relics were produced by Giovanni di Bartoli in 1370 but were destroyed in 1797 to obtain silver to pay the heavy duty payable under the terms of the Peace of Tolentino.

☞ **Half of Saint Peter's communion table,** at the end of the left transept, behind the altar of the Holy Sacrament

This is believed to be the altar where Peter said mass. It comes from the church of Santa Pudenziana.

Basilica of Santa Prassede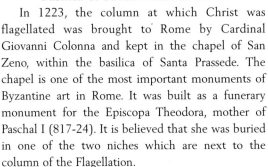

In 1223, the column at which Christ was flagellated was brought to Rome by Cardinal Giovanni Colonna and kept in the chapel of San Zeno, within the basilica of Santa Prassede. The chapel is one of the most important monuments of Byzantine art in Rome. It was built as a funerary monument for the Episcopa Theodora, mother of Paschal I (817-24). It is believed that she was buried in one of the two niches which are next to the column of the Flagellation.

☞ **Column of the Flagellation of Christ,** in the chapel of San Zeno (1), in a small nook to the right of the entrance

This is believed to be the column where Christ was tied up and flagellated by the soldiers of Pontius Pilate. The lunette outside the shrine showing the Flagellation of Christ is by Francesco Gaj.

☞ **Three thorns from Christ's crown of thorns,** kept inside a precious reliquary, in the sacristy

☞ **The Flagellation,** in the sacristy, painting by G. Romano, 16th century

Santa Maria dell'Aracoeli
Stairway of the Aracoeli

During the plague, the people of Rome promised the Madonna of the Aracoeli that they would build a beautiful stairway to the church if the city were

Ritual
On 29th June, on the feast day of Saints Peter and Paul, the relics of their heads are exposed to viewers inside the basilica. On the same day a celebration is held at the Mamertine Prison, which includes a visit to the cell where Peter and Paul were kept prisoners.

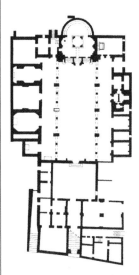

Stairway of the Aracoeli
The foot of the stairway is a fatal spot in Rome's history. Here in 212 BC a gang of senators and their clients murdered Tiberius Gracchus, known as the Tribunus Plebi, the representative of the people in the Roman senate. In 1354 in the same place, Cola di Rienzo, trying to escape Rome in disguise, was recognised by the rings on his fingers and torn to pieces by a mob of citizens for his treachery.

Brief history of the Chapel of the Santo Bambino
In 1888 the chapel of the Santo Bambino was demolished and rebuilt to house the miraculous statue of the Holy Baby.

Ritual
Every year, around Christmas time, groups of children visit the statue and pay their respects, reciting poems and songs they have composed in its honour.

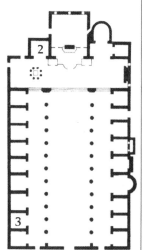

spared from the epidemic. Rome was saved and, in 1348, the Senate ordered Lorenzo di Simeone Andreozio to build the stairway. The steps were taken from the Temple of Quirinus on the Quirinale hill. Cola di Rienzo inaugurated the staircase, becoming the first to climb the 124 steps.

Chapel of the Santo Bambino
second chapel on the left of the main altar (2)

Towards the end of the fifteenth century, a Franciscan monk began carving the image of Baby Jesus in Jerusalem, using wood taken from the orchard of Gethsemane. While on its way to Rome, the sculpture was completed by angels. During a terrible tempest, it fell into the sea and reached the shore near Rome by itself, where a crowd of people and priests was waiting for it to arrive. Since the beginning of the sixteenth century, the sacred image, which is believed to have miraculous powers, has been kept in this church. Every day from all over the world messages arrive for it, especially from children, asking for protection and blessing. The statue of Baby Jesus is often taken out, as a last resort, to the sickbeds of the desperately ill.

☞ **The miraculous statue of Baby Jesus,** on the main altar, reproduction

Believed to have been carved by angels, the statue in olive wood is completely covered in gold and precious stones. In 1997 it was stolen and replaced with a copy.

Chapel of the Nativity
second chapel on the left (3)

Every Christmas the *Santo Bambino*, the Holy Child, is brought to this chapel to be part of the Nativity.

☞ **Nativity,** wooden statues, Madonna and Saint Joseph by Giacomo Colombo, 1731, and Luigi Cecconi, circa 1858-61.

The statues are lifesize.

Church of the Santissimo Nome del Gesù

✝ 🕮 🕮

Chapel of the Madonna della Strada
left of the tribune (2)

On the feast days dedicated to the Virgin Mary, pilgrims gather in this church to participate in the festivities and to witness the ritual of the relic of the Madonna. On these occasions, the miraculous image of the Madonna della Strada is removed from the niche on the main altar, where it is kept, revealing behind it a precious silver box. Inside the box is kept a sacred relic, a piece of cloth that is believed to have belonged to the Virgin Mary.

On the day of the Immaculate Conception, 8th December, and of the Assumption, 15th August, all the paintings of Mary kept in the chapel are removed from their niches, revealing other precious boxes containing the relics of martyrs and saints.

Church of San Marcello al Corso

According to tradition, Pope Saint Marcello (307-09) was sentenced by Emperor Maxentius to work as a cleaner in the big stables of the *Cantabulum*, the centre for the Roman postal service built by Emperor Hadrian (AD 117-38). In his memory, a church was built on the site. In AD 418 Boniface I (418-22) was consecrated pope here. At the end of the eighth century, Pope Marcello's relics were brought to the church.

In 1519 the church burnt down, but a wooden crucifix was found in the ashes, miraculously saved from the flames. Since then the relic has been venerated in the church.

☞ **The miraculous crucifix,** fourth chapel, wooden cross of the 15th century

☞ **The baptistery,** below the church, eighth century
One of the few full-immersion baptisteries left in Rome.

Brief history of the Church of San Marcello al Corso
Built between the end of the fourth century and the beginning of the fifth, the church was rebuilt in the eleventh century and in 1368 it was given to the Order of Servi di Maria. After the fire of 1519 the church was rebuilt by Sansovino, who altered the plan, modifying the apse area. The original church was much lower, at the same level as the baptistery near by. The façade is by Carlo Fontana, who worked here from 1682 to 1685.

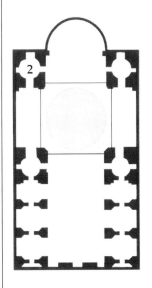

The body of Cola di Rienzo
In 1354, the body of Cola di Rienzo was hung for three days behind the apse of the Church of San Marcello, before being burnt in front of the Mausoleum of Augustus. His ashes were thrown into the Tiber.

Brief history of the Church
of San Vincenzo
e Anastasio de Trivio
The church was already known in
the twelfth century. In 1650, in
honour of the Jubilee, the church
was rebuilt by a man from the
neighbourhood, the famous
Cardinal Mazarin who became
chief minister of France in 1642.
The façade is by Martino Longhi.

Church of San Vincenzo e Anastasio de Trivio

During the summer months, when popes resided in the Quirinale Palace on the Quirinale hill, the church of San Vincenzo e Anastasio was their parish church.

A unique treasure is kept inside. For about three centuries, from the papacy of Sixtus V in 1590 to that of Leo XIII in 1903, all popes donated their hearts and entrails to this church.

☞ **Popes' hearts,** in the crypt, inside marble urns

Church of San Giuseppe a Capo le Case
Chapel of the Scala Santa

This chapel has been inaccessible to pilgrims for three centuries. Only the cloistered nuns of the convent of Barefoot Carmelites are permitted to climb up and visit it. In 1598 Francesco Soto, a friend of Saint Filippo Neri, with the help of a pious Roman noblewoman, Fulvia Conti, founded the convent. Like Filippo Neri, Soto was a fervent admirer of Saint Teresa of Àvila, the founder of the Order of Barefoot Carmelites. The idea was to help poor girls of the city to enter the order. The convent was consecrated by Pope Clement VIII and, in 1628, it was rebuilt by Cardinal Marcello Lante.

In 1717, the mother superior of the convent, Serafina, had a dream about a holy staircase. She immediately called in Tommaso Mattei, a disciple of the well-known architect Carlo Fontana, and asked him to build the staircase. The following year, Pope Clement IX consecrated it.

The nuns of the convent were promised indulgences if they would climb the staircase on their knees.

☞ **The Scala Santa,** behind the altar of the chapel

The staircase leads to a small altar drenched in candlelight and decorated with frescoes of angels telling the story of the Passion of Christ.

Church of Santa Susanna †

During the Middle Ages this was an important church, visited by a steady flow of pilgrims. People came to see the relics of martyrs and saints kept in the church, for example the relics of the Roman martyr Felicita and of his son Siliano, brought here from the catacomb in Via Salaria, as well as the bodies of Saint Susanna and her father.

According to the old pilgrims' guides, the church also housed relics of the True Cross, of the Holy Sepulchre, fragments of the dress of the Madonna and a lock of her hair.

Basilica of Saint Peter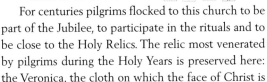

For centuries pilgrims flocked to this church to be part of the Jubilee, to participate in the rituals and to be close to the Holy Relics. The relic most venerated by pilgrims during the Holy Years is preserved here: the Veronica, the cloth on which the face of Christ is imprinted.

Surrounding the altar, the four massive piers supporting the dome are graced by enormous statues of saints associated with Saint Peter's most treasured relics. During Holy Week the relics used to be displayed to the faithful from the pier's upper balconies.

☞ **The lance,** incorporated in the statue of Saint Longinus, by Bernini, 17th century

Longinus was the Roman soldier who pierced the side of Christ on the Cross with the lance. He immediately repented and understood that it was the Son of God on the Cross. He is also said to have collected drops from the blood of Christ that he took to the city of Mantua. Longinus is the patron saint of this Italian city.

☞ **A piece of the True Cross,** incorporated in the statue of Saint Helena

☞ **The Veronica,** incorporated in the statue of Saint Veronica

This handkerchief preserves the imprint of Christ's features. In 1208 Pope Innocent III instituted the ritual of

Veronica
The name derives from *vera icon*, meaning 'true image'.

The head of Saint Andrew
This relic was kept here, incorporated in the statue of Saint Andrew. It has recently been returned to Patras in Greece, from where it had been stolen by the Despotate of Morea in the fifteenth century.

Ritual
On the Thursday before Easter, after vespers, the cloths in which the bodies of martyrs were wrapped, when they were transferred from the catacombs to the churches dedicated to their memory, are displayed inside the basilica.
Inside the basilica the cardinal, archpriests and canons wash the altar with wine and vinegar and then dry it with *aspergilli*, special dusters originally made of plants and nowadays made of wood shavings. They then expose the most important relics in the basilica, such as the fragment of the True Cross.

the procession of the Veronica. On the first Sunday after Epiphany the precious relic was taken from Saint Peter's to the nearby church of Santo Spirito in Sassia, where the pope had built a hospital for the sick, the poor and the pilgrims. Here it was displayed to the people through a window, known as Finestra Serliana. At the end of the sermon of the service, at which the pope officiated, pilgrims were asked for a contribution to the cost of the hospital, in exchange for one year of indulgences.

Saint Peter's Treasury
in the left aisle

Those relics that were not taken by the Saracens are housed here.

☞ **The Holy Column,** near the entrance to Saint Peter's Treasury, in the first room

The beautiful twisted column of Parian marble is believed to be the one on which Christ leant while disputing in the temple. In the Middle Ages exorcists used it to chase the devil out of their patients.

☞ **The golden cockerel,** near the entrance to Saint Peter's Treasury, in the first room, ninth century

Pope Leo IV set it on top of the campanile of the old basilica. According to tradition, its crowing will announce the end of the world.

☞ **The Vatican cross,** Saint Peter's Treasury, second room

In 578 this cross was donated to the basilica by Emperor Justin II. The relic includes portraits of the emperor and his wife.

☞ **Madonna della Febbre,** in the chapel of Chierici Beneficiati, painting by Lippo Memmi, 14th century

This portrait of the 'Madonna of the Fever' is venerated by pilgrims and is believed to have the power to cure malaria.

Church of San Michele e Magno
Scala Santa

People used to visit the burial ground of the martyred Frisians, killed while defending Rome from the Saracens. A staircase was built to facilitate access to

the cave where the bodies had been buried. There were 33 steps, the same number as the years of Christ's life. People began to climb them on their knees as a sign of respect. Soon indulgences and privileges were attached to this religious practice. In 603 when the church was restored, the staircase was modernised.

🖙 **Scala Santa,** at the end of the left nave, through a door

This used to be the old entrance of the church. The portal built in 1628 can still be seen between numbers 14 and 15 on Borgo Santo Spirito.

Brief history of the Chapel of the Crocifisso
The chapel was built to house the wooden cross venerated in the old church of Santa Maria in Traspontina. It was decorated by Francesco Bido and consecrated in 1649.

Church of Santa Maria in Traspontina ✝
Chapel of the Crocifisso
fourth chapel on the right
The two columns where Saint Peter and Saint Paul were believed to have been flagellated, before being martyred by order of Emperor Nero, were kept in the old church of Santa Maria in Traspontina, on the bank of the river Tiber, adjacent to Castel Sant'Angelo. They were placed near the main altar where pilgrims could venerate them. In the sixteenth century, when the church was demolished and moved away from the river bank, the columns were placed in the chapel of the Crocifisso, next to the miraculous sculpture of Christ on the Cross.

🖙 **Flagellation columns,** on the sides of the altar
These are believed to be the columns where the two Apostles were flagellated before being martyred.

Brief history of the Church of San Crisogono

In 1123-24 the church was built over a third-century basilica by Cardinal Giovanni da Crema. Of the older church only the baptistery is left. It is believed that this was the workshop of a dyer where the Christian community used to meet. The baptismal bath was originally a *fullonica*, or dyeing tank. The church was modernised in 1623 and again in 1866.

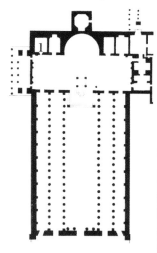

Church of San Crisogono

Pilgrims used to flock to this church to admire the many relics kept in the *confessio*.

These were later moved to the new church built by Cardinal de Crema in the twelfth century. The relics were placed inside the seven altars, as in the most important basilicas of the city. On the feast day of San Crisogono, pilgrims and other faithful worshippers who visited and prayed inside the church were granted plenary indulgence.

Basilica of San Paolo fuori le Mura
Chapel of Santissimo Sacramento
on the left-hand side of the transept (1)

In this chapel in the basilica of San Paolo fuori le Mura, the precious relic of a medieval crucifix is treasured. According to a legend, Christ spoke to Saint Bridget from this cross during her pilgrimage to Rome for the Jubilee of 1350.

☞ **The crucifix,** on the altar, polychrome wood, Sienese circle, beginning of 14th century

☞ **Saint Bridget,** on the left-hand side, in a niche, statue, attributed to Stefano Maderno, 16th to 17th century

Brief history of the Chapel of Santissimo Sacramento

The chapel was designed by Carlo Maderno in the seventeenth century. It was rebuilt in 1725 on the occasion of the Jubilee to house the wooden crucifix.

252

☞ **Saint Paul,** on the right-hand side, in a niche, wooden statue, by unknown artist, 13th century

This wooden statue, which miraculously survived the fire of 1823, has since been damaged by pilgrims who have taken pieces of it away with them as relics.

Tre Fontane Area

It is said that after leaving Saint Peter, Saint Paul was taken to a valley infested by malaria, to be decapitated. Here there were a few hot springs, hence the name *Aquae Salviae* ('Healthy Waters'). When the head of the saint was cut off, it bounced on the soil three times and each time it touched the earth, a spring of water appeared. Since then the area has been known as the Tre Fontane ('Three Fountains').

Early Christians built a chapel on the site of each of the fountains: one dedicated to Saint Paul, one named Scala Coeli, from the miraculous vision of Saint Bernard, and one in honour of the Saints Vincent and Anastasius.

During the Middle Ages the area was rife with malaria and was eventually abandoned by the Franciscan monks, who lived in the monastery near by. In 1868 Pope Pius IX gave the area to the Trappist monks. The monks decided to plant hundreds of eucalyptus trees as a prophylactic measure against malaria. The forest of eucalyptus still stands.

Church of San Vincenzo e Anastasio

The three churches and the monastery are within an enclosure, on land believed to have been donated by Charlemagne in 805. Fragments of frescoes, still visible on the entrance arch, known as Arco di Carlo Magno, show episodes from the life of the emperor. Entering the walled garden, the pilgrim first sees the church of Saint Vincenzo and Anastasio.

The church was originally dedicated to the Persian martyr Saint Anastasius, when his head and a miraculous image were brought here in 640. The cult of the martyr grew quickly, partly because it was linked to the cult of the True Cross. Anastasius converted to Christianity when he saw people venerating the True Cross, which had been secretly brought to Jerusalem by King Khosrow II. According to legend it was the Byzantine Emperor Heraclius who donated the head of the martyr to the monastery; he is also believed to have returned the True Cross to the Holy City. Anastasius was strangled and subsequently beheaded for having refused to abjure the Christian faith.

From the thirteenth century onwards the cult

of Saint Anastasius was linked with that of Saint Vincent. The Spanish martyr is well known to have survived the most atrocious tortures, only to die when his torturers put him on a bed, in an attempt to find a different way to make him renounce his religion.

Church of Santa Maria Scala Coeli

This is said to have been the place where Saint Paul was imprisoned while awaiting execution. A medieval tradition also identified the place with the site where, during the persecutions ordered by Emperor Diocletian, Saint Zeno, a general of the Roman army, was martyred along with fellow soldiers.

The octagonal church takes its singular name 'Stairway to Heaven' from the vision of Saint Bernard. While he was praying inside the church for the soul of a friend who had died, he had a vision in which he saw his friend's soul ascending from Purgatory to Paradise.

☞ The altar, in the crypt, Cosmati work
Dedicated to Saint Zeno, this is the altar where Saint Bernard had his vision.

Church of San Paolo

In about the fifth century this chapel was built on the site where Saint Paul suffered his martyrdom. It was a well-known stop on the pilgrims' itinerary of Rome, as the *De Locis* reports.

☞ The miraculous three fountains, inside three *aedicolae*, designed by Giacomo della Porta,
Water used to spring from these three fountains, which have, however, been closed for several years.

☞ The column where Saint Paul was tied up, behind a grille, between the two altars

☞ The Execution of Saint Peter and Saint Paul, on two lateral altars, paintings
The first is a copy of the original by Guido Reni, kept in the Vatican Pinacoteca, the second is by Passerotto Passerotti.

Brief history of the Church of Santa Maria Scala Coeli
In the seventh century there was already a church here dedicated to Mary. The crypt that commemorates the vision of Saint Bernard is dated 1138.

Brief history of the Church of San Paolo
Built in the fifth century, the church was modernised in 1599 by Giacomo della Porta, at the suggestion of Cardinal Aldobrandini, nephew of Pope Clement VIII.

Arch of Constantine
Piazza del Colosseo

Basilicas:
Maxentius
Via di San Gregorio
tel. 066990110
Mon-Sat 9.00-16.00
Sun. 9.00-13.00

Sant'Agnese fuori le Mura
Via Nomentana, 349 (00162)
tel. 068610840
Mon. and Wed.-Sat.
9.00-12.00, 16.00-18.00
Sat. and holidays 16.00-18.00

Santa Cecilia
Piazza di S. Cecilia, 22 (00153)
tel. 065899289
10.00-12.00, 16.00-18.00

San Clemente
Via di San Giovanni in Laterano (00184)
tel. 068106721
Mon.-Sat. 9.00-12.30, 15.30-18.30
Sun. 10.00-12.30, 15.30- 18.30

Santa Croce in Gerusalemme
P.za S. Croce in Gerusalemme, 12
(00185)
tel. 067014769
6.00-19.00

San Giovanni in Laterano
Piazza S. Giovanni in Laterano (00184)
tel. 0669886452
7.00-19.00

San Lorenzo fuori le Mura
Piazzale del Verano, 3 (00185)
tel. 06491511
7.00-12.00, 16.00-17.30

San Marco dei Veneziani
Piazza di San Marco, 48 (00186)
tel. 066795205
8.00-12.30, 16.00-19.00

Santa Maria Maggiore
Piazza di Santa Maria Maggiore
(00189)
tel. 06483195
7.00-19.00

Santa Maria in Trastevere
Piazza S. Maria in Trastevere (00153)
tel. 065814802
7.30-13.00, 16.00-19.00

San Paolo fuori le Mura
Via Ostiense, 186 (00154)
tel. 065410341
7.30-19.00

Saint Peter
Piazza San Pietro, Vatican City
tel. 0669884466-066984866
7.00-19.00

San Pietro in Vincoli
Piazza S. Pietro in Vincoli, 4/A (00184)
tel. 064882865
7.00-12.30, 15.30-19.00

Santa Prassede
Via di S. Prassede, 9 A (00184)
tel. 064882456
7.30-12.00, 16.00-18.30

Santa Sabina
Piazza Pietro d'Illiria, 1 (00153)
tel. 065743573
7.00-12.45, 15.30-18.00

San Sebastiano fuori le Mura
Via Appia Antica, 136 (00179)
tel. 067808847
8.30-12.00, 14.30-17.30

Castel Sant'Angelo
Lungotevere Castello (00193)
tel. 066875036
9.00-19.00

Catacomb of San Callisto
Via Appia Antica, 110 (00179)
tel. 065136725
Tue.-Thu. 8.30-12.00, 14.30-17.00

Catacomb of Santa Domitilla
Via delle Sette Chiese, 282 (00147)
tel. 065110342
Mon.-Wed. 8.30-12.00, 14.30-17.30

Catacomb of Priscilla
Via Salaria, 430 (00199)
tel. 0686206272
Mon.-Wed. 8.30-12.00, 14.30-17.00

Catacomb of Via Latina
Via Dino Compagni

Chapel of the Madonna dell'Archetto
Via di S.Marcello, 24

Churches:
Sant'Agostino
Piazza Sant'Agostino (00186)
tel. 0668801962
Thu.-Su. 7.45-12.00, 16.00-20.00
Fri.-Sat. 7.45-12.00, 13.30-20.00

Santi Ambrogio e Carlo al Corso
Via del Corso, 437 (00186)
tel. 066878335
7.30-12.30, 17.00-19.00

Sant'Andrea al Quirinale
Via del Quirinale, 29 (00186)
tel. 064744801
10.00-12.00, 16.00-19.00

Sant'Andrea delle Fratte
Via Sant'Andrea delle Fratte, 1 (00187)
tel. 066793191
6.30-12.30, 16.00-19.00

Santissimi Apostoli
Piazza SS. Apostoli, 51 (00187)
tel. 066794085
6.30-12.00, 16.00-19.15

Santa Balbina
Piazza di S. Balbina, 8 (00153)
tel. 065780207
8.00-18.00

San Bartolomeo all'Isola
Isola Tiberina, 22 (00186)
tel. 066877973
9.00-12.00, 16.00-18.30

San Biagio della Pagnotta
Via Giulia, 64 (00186)
tel. 0668804891
16.30-19.00

San Biagio Carlo ai Catinari
Piazza B. Cairoli, 117 (00186)
tel. 066893874
Mon.-Sat.. 7.30-12.00, 16.30-19.00
Sun. 8.30-12.30, 16.30-19.30

Santa Bibiana
Via G.Giolitti, 154 (00185)
tel. 064461021
7.00-10.00, 16.30-19.30

Santi Bonifacio e Alessio
Piazza S. Alessio, 23 (00153)
tel. 065743446
8.30-12.00, 15.30-18.30

San Carlo alle Quattro Fontane
Via del Quirinale, 23 (00187)
tel. 064883261
9.30-12.30, 16.00-18.00

Santa Costanza
Via Nomentana, 349 (00162)
tel. 068610840
Mon. and Wed.-Sat. 9.00-12.00, 16.00-18.00
Sun. and holidays 16.00-18.00

San Crisogono
Piazza Sonnino, 44 (00153)
tel. 065818225
7.00-11.00, 16.00-19.00

Domine Quo Vadis?
Via Appia Antica, 51 (00179)
tel. 065120441

8.30-12.00, 14.30-17.30

Santa Dorotea
Via di S.Dorotea, 23 (00153)
tel. 065806205
7.00-9.00, 17.30-19.00

Santa Francesca Romana
Piazza di Santa Francesca Romana (00186)
tel. 066795528
9.30-12.30, 15.30-19.00

San Francesco a Ripa
Piazza S. Francesco d'Assisi, 88 (00153)
tel. 065819020
7.00-11.30, 16.00-19.00

Santissimo Nome del Gesù
Piazza del Gesù (00186)
tel. 066786341
7.00-12.30, 16.00-19.15

San Giorgio in Velabro
Via del Velabro, 19 (00186)
tel. 066832930
9.00-12.30, 16.00-19.00

San Giovanni Decollato
Via di S. Giovanni Decollato, 22 (00186)
tel. 066990728

San Giovanni dei Fiorentini
Via Giulia (00186)
tel. 0668135120
7.00-12.00, 17.00-19.30

Santi Giovanni e Paolo
Piazza di SS.Giovanni e Paolo, 13 (00184)
tel. 067005745
8.30-12.00, 15.30-19.00

San Giovanni in Oleo
Via di Porta Latina, 17 (00178)
tel. 0670491777

San Girolamo della Carità
Via di Monserrato, 62 A (00186)
tel. 066879786
Mon.-Sat. 7.40-12.00
Sun. 10.45-12.00

San Giuseppe a Capo le Case
Via Francesco Crispi, (00187)
tel. 06483423

Sant'Ignazio de Loyola
Piazza Sant'Ignazio (00186)
tel. 066794560
7.30-12.30, 16.00-19.30

San Lorenzo in Fonte
Via Urbana, 50 (00184)
tel. 064825361
7.30-11.30, 16.30-19.00

San Lorenzo in Lucina
Via in Lucina, 16 A (00186)
tel. 066871494
8.30-12.00, 16.30-19.30

Santa Lucia in Selci
Via in Selci, 82 (00184)
tel. 064827623
17.00-18.00

San Luigi dei Francesi
Piazza S. Luigi dei Francesi, 5
(00186)
tel. 06688271
8.00-12.30, 15.30-19.30

San Marcello al Corso
Piazza S. Marcello, 5 (00187)
tel. 06699301
7.00-12.00, 16.00-19.00

Santa Maria dell'Anima
Via della Pace, 20 (00186)
tel. 066833729
Mon.-Sat. 7.30-19.00
Sun. 8.00-13.00, 15.00-19.00

Santa Maria Annunziata
Lungotevere Vaticano, 1 (00193)

Santa Maria Antiqua
Via di San Gregorio
tel. 066990110

Santa Maria in Aracoeli
Piazza d'Aracoeli (00186)
tel. 066798155
7.00-12.00, 16.00-17.30
(Jun.-Sep.. 18.30)

Santa Maria in Campitelli
Piazza Campitelli, 9 (00186)
tel. 0668803978
7.00-12.00, 16.00-19.00

Santa Maria in Campo Marzio
Piazza in Campo Marzio, 45 (00186)
tel. 066787021
7.00-12.00, 16.00-18.30

Santa Maria della Concezione
Via Veneto, 27 (00187)
tel. 064871185
7.00-12.00, 15.45-19.30

Santa Maria Maddalena
Piazza della Maddalena, 53 (00186)
tel. 066797796
7.30-19.00

Santa Maria ad Martyres
(Pantheon)
Piazza della Rotonda (00186)
tel. 0668300230
Mon.-Sat. 9.00-18.30
Sun. and holidays 9.00-13.00

Santa Maria Sopra Minerva
Piazza della Minerva, 42 (00186)
tel. 06679280

7.00-12.00, 16.00-19.00

Santa Maria dei Miracoli
Piazza del Popolo (00187)
tel. 063610250
6.00-13.00, 17.00-19.00

Santa Maria dei Monti
Via Madonna dei Monti, 41 (00184)
tel. 06485531
7.00-12.00, 17.00-19.30

Santa Maria dell'Orazione e Morte
Via Giulia (00186)
tel. 0668802715
dom. 16.00-18.00

Santa Maria dell'Orto
Via Anicia, 10 (00153)
tel. 065883250

Santa Maria della Pace
Vicolo dell'Arco della Pace, 5 (00186)
tel. 066861156
7.00-12.00, 16.00-19.00

Santa Maria del Pianto
Via di S. Maria de' Calderari, 29
(00186)
tel. 066861796
6.30-12.00, 16.00-18.30

Santa Maria del Popolo
Piazza del Popolo, 12 (00187)
tel. 063610836
Mo.-Sat. 7.00-12.00, 16.00-19.00
Sun. 7.30-13.30, 16.30-19.30

Santa Maria della Quercia
Piazza della Quercia, 27 (00186)
tel. 066865196
Sun. 10.30-11.30

Santa Maria della Scala
Piazza della Scala, 23 (00153)
tel. 0658062330
7.45-12.30; 16.30-18.30

Santa Maria in Traspontina
Via della Conciliazione, 14 (00193)
tel. 0668300063
6.30-12.00, 16.00-19.30

Santa Maria in Vallicella
Piazza della Chiesa Nuova (00186)
tel. 066875289
6.30-12.00, 16.30-19.00

Santa Maria in Via
Via del Mortaro, 24 (00187)
tel. 066793841
7.00-13.00, 15.30-20.00

Santa Maria in Via Lata
Via del Corso, 306 (00186)
tel. 066796190
7.00-13.00, 15.30-20.00

Santa Maria della Vittoria
Via XX Settembre, 17 (00187)
tel. 064826190

6.30-12.00, 16.30-19.00

San Martino ai Monti
Viale del Monte Oppio, 28 (00184)
tel. 064873166
7.00-12.00, 16.30-19.00

San Michele e Magno
Via Paolo VI, (00167)
9.00-12.00, 17.00-18.00

Santi Nereo e Achilleo
Via di Porta San Sebastiano, 4 (00179)
tel. 065757996
Wed.-Sat. 10.00-12.00, 16.00-18.00

Sant'Onofrio
Piazza S. Onofrio, 2 (00165)
tel. 066864498
10.00-13.30

San Pietro in Montorio
Piazza S. Pietro in Montorio, 2 (00153)
tel. 065813940
9.00-12.00, 16.00-18.00

San Pietro in Vincoli
Piazza S. Pietro in Vincoli, 4/A (00184)
tel. 064882865
7.00-12.30, 15.30-19.00

Santa Prisca
Via di S. Prisca, 11 (00153)
tel. 065743798
8.00-12.00, 16.30-19.00

Santa Pudenziana
Via Urbana, 160 (00184)
tel. 064814622
8.00-12.00, 15.00-18.00

Santi Quattro Coronati
Via SS. Quattro Coronati, 20 (00184)
tel. 0670475427
9.30-12.00, 15.30-18.00

San Rocco
Largo S. Rocco, 1 (00186)
tel. 066894416
Mon.-Sat. 7.30-9.00, 17.00-19.45
Sun. 9.00-13.00, 17.00-19.45

San Saba
Piazza G.L. Bernini, 20 (00153)
tel. 065743352
7.00-12.00, 16.00-18.30

Santo Stefano Rotondo
Via di S. Stefano Rotondo, 7 (00184)
tel. 0670493717
9.00-13.00, 15.30-18.00

Santa Susanna
Piazza San Bernardo, (00187)
tel. 064827510
Mon.-Sat. 9.30-12.00, 16.00-19.00
Sun 10.00-12.00

San Vincenzo e Anastasio de Trivio
Piazza di Trevi (00187)
tel. 066783098
7.00-12.00, 16.00-19.00

San Vito e Modesto
Via Carlo Alberto, 47 (00185)
tel. 064465836
9.00-12.30, 15.30-18.00

Collegio of Piazza del Gesù
Piazza del Gesù, 45 (00186)
tel. 066786341
7.00-12.30, 16.00-19.15

Colosseum
Piazza del Colosseo (00184)
tel. 0670040261
9.00-19.00

Column of the Immaculate Conception
Piazza Mignanelli

Mamertine Prison
Clivio Argentario, 1 (00186)
tel. 066792902
Apr.-Set. 9.00-12.00, 14.30-18.00
Oct.-Mar. 9.00-12.00, 14.00-17.00

Monastery of Tor de' Specchi
Via del Teatro di Marcello, 32 (00186)
tel. 066795281
9th March and Sun. in March
10.00-12.00, 15.00-17.00

Scala Santa and Sancta Sanctorum
Piazza di S. Giovanni in Laterano, 14
(00184)
tel. 0670494489
Apr.-Sep. 6.00-12.00, 14.30-18.30
Oct.-Mar. 6.00-12.30, 15.00-19.00

Tempietto di Bramante
Piazza S. Pietro in Montorio, 2 (00153)
tel. 056813940
9.00-12.00, 16.00-18.00

Tomb of Saint Peter
Piazza San Pietro, Città del Vaticano
tel. 0669884466-066984866
7.00-18.00 (ott.-mar. 17.00)

Tre Fontane Area
Via di Acque Salvie, 1 (00142)
tel. 065401655

Church of San Vincenzo e Anastasio
daily 8.30-12.30, 15-17

Church of Santa Maria Scala Coeli e San Paolo
Daily 8.00-18.00

CHRONOLOGICAL LIST OF POPES

The letter M. indicates a martyr; the antipopes are in brackets.

1. ST PETER, M. 42-67
2. ST LINUS, M. 67-78
3. ST ANACLETUS I, M. 78-88
4. ST CLEMENT I, M. 88-97
5. ST EVARISTUS, M. 97-109
6. ST ALEXANDER I, M 109-116
7. ST SIXTUS I, M.115-125
8. ST TELESPHORUS, M.125-136
9. ST IGINUS, M. 136-140
10. ST PIUS I, M. 140-155
11. ST ANICETUS, M. 155-166
12. ST SOTER, M. 166-175
13. ST ELEUTHERUS, M.; 175-189
14. ST VICTOR I, M. 189-199
15. ST ZEPHYRINUS, M. 199-217
16. ST CALIXTUS I, M.; 217-222
    [HIPPOLYTUS, 217-235]
17. ST URBAN I, M. 222-230
18. ST PONTIANUS, M. 230-235
19. ST ANTERUS, M. 235-236
20. ST FABIAN, M. 236-250.
21. ST CORNELIUS, M. 251-253
    [NOVATIAN, 251-258]
22. ST LUCIUS I, M. 253-254
23. ST STEPHEN I, M. 254-257
24. ST SIXTUS II, M. 257-258
25. ST DIONYSIUS, M. 259-268
26. ST FELIX I, M.269-274
27. ST EUTYCHIANUS, M. 275-283
28. ST GAIUS, M.283-296
29. ST MARCELLINUS, M. 296-304
30. ST MARCELLUS I, M. 307-309
31. ST EUSEBIUS, M.309-310
32. ST MELCHIADES, M. 311-314
33. ST SYLVESTER I, 314-335
34. ST MARK, 336
35. ST JULIUS I, 337-352
36. LIBERIUS, 352-366
    [ST FELIX II, 355-365.]
37. ST DAMASUS I, 366-384
    [URSINUS, 366-367]
38. ST SIRICIUS, 384-399
39. ST ANASTASIUS I, 399-401
40. ST INNOCENT I, 401-417
41. ST ZOSIMUS, 417-418
42. ST BONIFACE I, 418-422
    [EULALIUS, 418-419]
43. ST CAELESTINUS I, 422-432
44. ST SIXTUS III, 432-440
45. ST LEO I, 440- 461
46. ST HILARIUS, 461-468
47. ST SIMPLICIUS, 468- 483
48. ST FELIX III, 483-492
49. ST GELASIUS I, 492-496
50. ST ANASTASIUS II, 496- 498
51. ST SYMMACHUS, 498-514
    [LAURENTIUS, Nov. 498-505]
52. ST HORMISDAS, 514-523
53. ST JOHN I, 523-526
54. ST FELIX IV, 526-530
55. BONIFACE II, 530-532
    [DIOSCURUS,
    22 Sept. 530-14 Oct. 530]
56. JOHN II,533-535
57. ST AGAPITUS I, 535-536
58. ST SILVERIUS, M. 536-537
59. VIGILIUS, 538-555
60. PELAGIUS I, 556-561
61. JOHN III,   561-574
62. BENEDICT I, 575-579
63. PELAGIUS II, 579-590
64. ST GREGORY I, 590-604
65. SABINIANUS, 604-606
66. BONIFACE III, 607-607
67. ST BONIFACE IV, 608-615
68. ST DEUSDEDIT I, 615-618
69. BONIFACE V, 619-625
70. HONORIUS I, 625-638
71. SEVERINUS, 640
72. JOHN IV, 640-642
73. THEODORE I, 642-649
74. ST MARTIN I, 649-655
75. ST EUGENIUS I, 655-657
76. ST VITALIAN, 657-672
77. DEUSDEDIT II, 672-676
78. DONUS, 676-678
79. ST AGATHO, 678-681
80. ST LEO II, 682-683
81. ST BENEDICT II, 684-685
82. JOHN V, 685-686
83. CONON, 686-687
    [THEODORE, 687]
    [PASCHAL, 687]
84. ST SERGIUS I, 687-701
85. JOHN VI, 701-705
86. JOHN VII, 705-707
87. SISINNIUS, 708-708
88. CONSTANTINE, 708-715
89. ST GREGORY II, 715-731
90. ST GREGORY III, 731-741
91. ST ZACHARIAS, 741-752
92. STEPHEN II, 752
93. ST STEPHEN III, 752-757
94. ST PAUL I, 757-767
    [CONSTANTINE II, 767-769]
    [PHILIP, 768]
95. STEPHEN IV, 768-772
96. ADRIAN I, 772-795
97. ST LEO III, 795-816
98. ST STEPHEN V, 816-817

99. ST PASCHAL I, 817-824
100. EUGENIUS II, 824-827.
101. VALENTINE, 827-827
102 GREGORY IV, 827-844
103. SERGIUS II, 844-847
[JOHN, 844]
104. ST LEO IV, 847-855
105. ST BENEDICT III, 855-858
[ANASTASIUS, 855]
106. ST NICHOLAS I, 858-867
107. HADRIAN II, 867-872
108. JOHN VIII, 872-882
109. MARINUS I, 882-884
110. ST HADRIAN III, 884-885
111. STEPHEN VI, 885-891
112. FORMOSUS, 891-896
113. BONIFACE VI, 896
114. STEPHEN VII, 896-897
114. ROMANUS, 897
115. THEODORE II, 897
117. JOHN IX, 898-900
118. BENEDICT IV, 900-903
119. LEO V, 903
[CHRISTOPHER, 903-904]
120. SERGIUS III, 904-911
121. ANASTASIUS III, 911-913
122. LANDO, 913-914
123. JOHN X, 914-928
124. LEO VI, 928-928
125. STEPHEN VIII, 929-931
126. JOHN XI, 931-935
127. LEO VII, 936-939
128. STEPHEN IX, 939-942
129. MARINUS II, 942-946
130. AGAPITUS II, 946-955
131. JOHN XII, 955-964
132. LEO VIII, 963-965
133. BENEDICT V, 964-966
134. JOHN XIII, 965-972
135. BENEDICT VI, 973-974
[BONIFACE VII, 974
for the first time]
136. BENEDICT VII, 974-983
137. JOHN XIV, 983-984
[BONIFACE VII, 984 –985]
138. JOHN XV, 985-996
139. GREGORY V, 996-999
[JOHN XVI, 997-998]
140. SYLVESTER II, 999-1003
141. JOHN XVII, 1003
142. JOHN XVIII, 1004-1009
143. SERGIUS IV, 1009–1012
144. BENEDICT VIII, 1012-1024
[Gregory, 1012]
145. JOHN XIX, 1024-1032
146. BENEDICT IX, 1032- 1044
147. SYLVESTER III, 1045
148. GREGORY VI, 1045-1046

149. CLEMENT II, 1046 – 1047
150. DAMASUS II, 1048 – 1048
151. ST LEO IX, 1049-1054
152. VICTOR II, 1055-1057
153. STEPHEN X, 1057-1058
[Benedict X, 1058-1059]
154. NICHOLAS II, 1059-1061
155. ALEXANDER II, 1061-1073
[Honorius II, 1061-1072]
156. ST GREGORY VII, 1073-1085
[Clement III,1080-1100]
157. B. VICTOR III, 1086-1087
158. B. URBAN II, 1088-1099
159. PASCHAL II, 1099-1118
[THEODORIC, 1100]
[ALBERT, 1102]
[SYLVESTER IV, 1105-1111]
160. GELASIUS II, 1118-1119
[GREGORY VIII, 1118- 1121]
161. CALIXTUS II, 1119-1124
162. HONORIUS II,1124-1130
163. INNOCENT II, 1130-
164. [ANACLETUS II, 1130-1138]
[VICTOR IV, 1138-1138]
164. CELESTINE II, 1143-1144
165. LUCIUS II, 1144-1145
166. B. EUGENIUS III, 1145-1153
167. ANASTASIUS IV, 1153-1154
168. HADRIAN IV,. 1154-1159
169. ALEXANDER III, 1159-1181
[VICTOR IV, 1159-1164]
[PASCHAL III, 1164-1168]
[CALIXTUS III, 1168-1178]
[INNOCENT III, 1179-1180]
170. LUCIUS III, 1181-1185
171. URBAN III, 1185-1187
172. GREGORY VIII, 1187
173. CLEMENT III, 1187-1191
174. CELESTINE III, 1191-1198
175. INNOCENT III, 1198-1216
176. HONORIUS III, 1216-1227
177. GREGORY IX, 1227-1241
178. CELESTINE IV, 1241-1241
179. INNOCENT IV, 1243 – 1254
180. ALEXANDER IV, 1254-1261
181. URBAN IV, 1261-1264
182. CLEMENT IV, 1265-1268
183. GREGORY X, 1271-1276
184. INNOCENT V, 1276-1276
185. HADRIAN V, 1276
186. JOHN XXI, 1276-1277
187. NICHOLAS III, 1277-1280
188. MARTIN IV, 1281-1285
189. HONORIVS IV, 1285-1287
190. NICHOLAS IV, 1288-1292
191. ST CELESTINE V, 1294
192. BONIFACE VIII, 1294-1303
193. B. BENEDICT XI, 1303-1304

194. CLEMENT V, 1305-1314
195. JOHN XXII, 1316-1334
    [NICHOLAS V, 1328-1330]
196. BENEDICT XII, 1334-1342
197. CLEMENT VI, 1342-1352
198. INNOCENT VI, 1352-1362
199. URBAN V, 1362-1370
200. GREGORY XI, 1370-1378
201. URBAN VI, 1378-1389
202. BONIFACE IX, 1389-1404
203. INNOCENT VII, 1404-1406
204. GREGORY XII, 1406-1415
    Popes at Avignon:
    [CLEMENT VII, 1378-1394]
    [BENEDICT XII, 1394-1423]
    Antipopes at Avignon:
    [CLEMENT VIII, 1423-1429]
    [BENEDICT XIV, 1425-1430]
    Popes at Pisa:
    [ALEXANDER V, 1409-1410]
    [JOHN XXIII, 1410-1415]
205. MARTIN V, 1417-1431
206. EUGENIUS IV, 1431-1447
    [FELIX V, 1439-1449]
207. NICHOLAS V, 1447-1455
208. CALIXTUS III, 1455-1455
209. PIUS II, 1458-1464
210. PAUL II, 1464-1471
211. SIXTUS IV, 1471-1484
212. INNOCENT VIII, 1484-1492
213. ALEXANDER VI, 1492-1503
214. PIUS III, 1503-1503
215. JULIUS II, 1503-1513
216. LEO X, 1513-1521
217. ADRIAN VI, 1522-1523
218. CLEMENT VII, 1523-1534
219. PAUL III, 1534-1549
220. JULIUS III, 1550-1555
221. MARCELLUS II, 1555
222. PAUL IV, 1555-1559
223. PIUS IV, 1559-1565
224. ST PIUS V, 1566-1572.
225. GREGORY XIII, 1572-1585
226. SIXTUS V, 1585-1590
227. URBAN VII, 1590-1590
228. GREGORY XIV, 1590-1591
229. INNOCENT IX, 1591-1591
230. CLEMENT VIII, 1592-1605
231. LEO XI, 1605-1605
232. PAUL V, 1605-1621
233. GREGORY XV, 1621-1623
234. URBAN VIII, 1623-1644
235. INNOCENT X, 1644-1655
236. ALEXANDER VII, 1655-1667
237. CLEMENT IX, 1667-1669
238. CLEMENT X, 1670-1676
239. INNOCENT XI, 1676-1689
240. ALEXANDER VIII, 1689-1691

241. INNOCENT XII, 1691-1700
242. CLEMENT XI, 1700-1721
243. INNOCENT XIII, 1721-1724
244. BENEDICT XIII, 1724-1730
245. CLEMENT XII, 1730-1740
246. BENEDICT XIV, 1740-1758
247. CLEMENT XIII, 1758-1769
248. CLEMENT XIV, 1769-1774
249. PIUS VI, 1775-1799
250. PIUS VII, 1799-1823
251. LEO XII, 1823-1829
252. PIUS VIII, 1829-1830
253. GREGORY XVI, 1831-1846
254. PIUS IX, 1846-1878
255. LEO XIII, 1878-1903
256. ST PIUS X, 1903-1914
257. BENEDICT XV, 1914-1922
258. PIUS XI, 1922-1939
259. PIUS XII, 1939-1958
260. JOHN XXIII, 1958-1963
261. PAUL VI, 1963-1978
262. JOHN PAUL I, 1978
263. JOHN PAUL II, 1978-

List of Roman Emperors

27 BC-AD 14	AUGUSTUS		268-70	CLAUDIUS II
14-37	TIBERIUS		270	QUINTILLUS
37-41	CALIGULA		270-75	AURELIAN
41-54	CLAUDIUS		275-76	TACITUS
54-68	NERO		276	FLORIAN
68-69	GALBA		276-82	PROBUS
69	OTHO		282-83	CARUS
69	VITELLIUS		282-85	CARINUS
FLAVIANS			283-84	NUMERIAN
69-39	VESPASIAN		285-305	DIOCLETIAN
79-81	TITUS		286-305	MAXIMIAN
81-96	DOMITIAN		305-06	CONSTANTIUS CHLORUS
96-98	NERVA		305-10	GALERIUS
98-117	TRAJAN		308-24	LICINIUS
ANTONINES			306-07	FLAVIUS SEVERUS
117-38	HADRIAN		306-12	MAXENTIUS
138-61	ANTONINUS PIUS		308-14	MAXIMINUS
161-80	MARCUS AURELIUS		306-37	CONSTANTINE THE GREAT
161-69	LUCIUS VERUS		337-40	CONSTANTINE II
180-92	COMMODUS		337-50	CONSTANS
193	PERTINAX		337-61	CONSTANTINUS II
193	DIDIUS JULIANUS		361-63	JULIAN
SEVERIANS			363-64	JOVIAN
193-211	SEPTIMIUS SEVERUS		364-75	VALENTINIAN I
211-13	CARACALLA		364-78	VALENS
211-12	GETA		367-83	GRATIAN
217-18	MACRINUS		375-92	VALENTINIAN II
218-22	HELIOGABALUS		378-95	THEODOSIUS I
222-35	ALEXANDER SEVERUS			
235-38	MAXIMINUS			
238	GORDIAN I		**WESTERN EMPIRE**	
	GORDIAN II		395-423	HONORIUS
238	PUPIENUS		425-55	VALENTINIAN III
	BALBINUS		455	PETRONIUS MAXIMUS
238-44	GORDIAN III		455-56	AVITUS
244-49	PHILIP I		457-61	MAJORIAN
247-49	PHILIP II		461-65	LIBIUS SEVERUS
249-51	DECIUS		467-72	ANTHEMIUS
251-53	TREBONIANUS GALLUS		472	OLYBRIUS
253	AEMILIAN		473	GLYCERIUS
253-60	VALERIAN		474-75	JULIUS NEPOS
253-68	GALLIENUS		475-76	ROMULUS AUGUSTULUS

753 - Rome is founded by Romulus and Remus

578-534 - The city is divided into four regions and encircled inside the Servian Walls

509 - Inauguration of the *Capitolium*, of the Republic and Temple of *Zeus Capitolinus*

456 - *Lex Icilia* grants the Aventino Hill to the plebeians

390 - sack of Rome by the northern population of Gallia leaded by Brenno

312 - Opening of the Appian Way

49 - The invasion of Great Britain begins

40- Mecenate encourages the development of literature and arts in Rome

31 - Ottavianus defeats Anthony in Anzio

27- Ottavianus is declared Emperor

7 - The construction of the *Ara Pacis* begins

ANNO DOMINI

64 - Great fire of Rome

80 - Inauguration of the Colosseum by Emperor Titus

118 - Construction of Pantheon begins under Emperor Hadrian

123 - Emperor Hadrian begins construction of his mausoleum

212 - The *Constituio Antoniana* grants the Roman citizenship to the people of the provinces

271- Aurelius rebuilds the wall of Rome

285 - Partition of the Roman Empire into western and eastern empires

306 - Constantine succeeded his father 3 and reuniting the Empire

312 - Battle of the Milvian bridge, Constantine defeats Maxentius

313 - Seat of Roman Empire moved to Constantinople

340 - Rome again splits into two empires: West and East

383 - Roman legions begin to evacuate Britain

402 - Emperor Honorius moves the seat of the Western Roman Empire to Ravenna

410 - Sack of Rome by the Visigoths of Alaric

476 - End of the Western Roman Empire

552 - Rome is occupied by Byzantine troops and falls under the jurisdiction of the Eastern Roman Empire

663 - Emperor Constante II visits Rome

756 - With the donation of King Pipin III of France, later on confirmed by Charlemagne, the first nucleus of the Papal State is formed

800 - Charlemagne is crowned first Holy Roman Emperor by Pope Leo III

846 - Saracens invade Rome

852 - Leonine Wall is completed

1083 - Emperor Henry IV occupies Rome

1084 - The Norman King, Robert the Guiscard, frees Pope Gregory VII, imprisoned by Henry IV inside Castel Sant'Angelo

1111 - Henry V is crowned emperor in Rome

1144 - Republican regime is established in Rome under Arnold of Brescia

1145 - Pope Eugene III proclaims the Second Crusade

1147 - Crusaders perish in Asia Minor: failure of the Second Crusade

1155 - Arnold of Brescia is hanged

1188 - Pope Clement III and the City hall of Rome reach an agreement on the management of the city

1189 - Third Crusade begins

1202 - Fourth Crusade starts under Boniface of Montferrat

1204 - Crusaders take Constantinople and establish Latin Empire

1212 - Children's Crusade

1220 - Frederick II is crowned emperor in Rome by Pope Honorius III

1228 - Sixth Crusade led by Emperor Frederick II

1248 - Seventh Crusade, led by Louis IX

1347 - Cola di Rienzo, tribune of the people, rules Rome

1309 - Pope Clement V moves the papal residency to Avignon

1354 - Cola di Rienzo is murdered after another attempt to establish tyranny

1420 - Pope Martin V enters Rome, re-establishing papal authority

1434 - Pope Eugenius IV is driven into exile by the Romans

1443 - Pope Eugenius IV returns to Rome from exile in Florence
1453 - Fall of Constantinople to the Turks. Plot of Stefano Porcari and a band of Roman nobles to assassinate Pope Nicholas V is discovered
1455- the Lega Italiana is established by Pope Nicolas V
1475 - Pope Sixtus IV founds the Vatican Library
1491 - Turks are driven from Granada
1402 - Columbus discovers America
1494 - King Charles VIII of France invades Italy
1506 - Pope Julius II defeats Bentivogli and enters Bologna in Triumph
1507 - Pope Julius II's triumphal entry into Rome
1522 - Fall of Rhodes to the Turks
1525 - Battle of Pavia
1527 - Sack of Rome by Imperial Troops
1530 - Pope Clement VII crowns King Charles V emperor in Bologna
1531 - Formation of the Protestant Schmalkaldic League
1535 - Turks in Tunisia defeated by King Charles V
1536 - King Charles V's triumphal entry into Rome
1538 - Treaty of Nice between King Charles V and King Francis I brokered by Pope Paul III as a first step towards a Crusade
1546 - Imperial and papal forces defeat the Schmalkaldic league
1551-52 - War of Parma: the Farnese allied with France defeat the papacy allied with King Charles V
1559 - Treaty of Cateau-Cambresis: ends the wars in Italy and confirms imperial (Habsburg) hegemony over Italy
1571 - Battle of Lepanto: the Holy League (Spain, Venice and the Papacy) defeats the Turks
1572 - Saint Bartholomew's Day Massacre of French Huguenots, Paris
1582 - Gregorian Calendar is adopted in Papal State, Spain and Portugal (Oct.); France, the Netherlands and Scandinavia (Dec.); England 1752
1587 - Mary, Queen of Scots, is executed at

Fotheringay. Pope Sixtus V proclaims Catholic crusade for invasion of England
1620 - Battle of the White Mountain near Prague: Catholic League under Count Tilly defeats army of King Frederick of Bohemia
1798 - French troops capture Rome and proclaim Roman Republic. Pope Pius VI leaves the city for Valence
1809 - Napoleon annexes Papal States
1815 - After the fall of Napoleon, Pope Pius VII comes back to Rome. Congress of Vienna.
1832 - Giuseppe Mazzini founds the 'Giovine Italia' with the aim of achieving national independence
1848 - Revolt in Rome, Count Rossi, the papal premier, is assassinated. Pope Pius IX flees to Gaeta
1849 - Rome proclaimed a republic under Giuseppe Mazzini. French enter Rome and restore Pope Pius IX
1864 - Italy renounces its claims to Rome; Florence is made the capital (1870)
1867 - Garibaldi begins the 'March on Rome' and is defeated by French and papal troops at Mentana and taken prisoner
1870 - Italians enter Rome and name it their capital city
1914 - 1918 - World War I
1922 - After the 'March on Rome', Vittorio Emanuele III gives Mussolini the task to form the Government
1929 - Signature of Patti Lateranensi between the papacy and the Kingdom of Italy
1939-1945 - Second World War

GLOSSARY

AEDICULA: similar to a tabernacle or a small temple.

ALABASTER: a semitransparent type of gypsum. It is said to be from Alabastron, a town in Egypt.

ALTARPIECE: a devotional work of art placed on an altar. It usually represents episodes relevant to the Sacred literature.

APSE: a vaulted space of semi-circular or polygonal shape at the eastern end of a church.

ARCHITRAVE: the architectural surround of a window or a door. In classical architecture the lowest division of the entablature, which is the horizontal part that surmounts the columns.

ATTIC: the top storey of a building

ATRIUM: the forecourt of an Early Christian church.

BALDACCHINO: a canopy supported by columns.

BAPTISTERY: a circular or octagonal building where the sacrament of Baptism is performed. It always has a font with water for the ritual of the Baptism.

BAROQUE: a term created by art historians in the 19th century to define a style that spread throughout Western Europe in the 16th and early 17th centuries. The style involves the use of all the arts in combination, including architecture, painting and sculpture, in order to create a flamboyant and exuberant style with an accent on dramatic swirling movements and saturated colours.

BARREL DOME: constructed as a semi-circular arch, like a tunnel.

BORGO: a borough of a town.

BYZANTINE: the art of the East Roman Empire from the 5th century AD to the fall of Constantinople in 1453. The style in art is characterised by a hieratic and frontal representation of the figures.

CANVAS: a piece of cloth made out of cotton or any other material which is used as a support for a painting.

CHANCEL: the eastern part of the church reserved for the clergy. It is sometimes divided from the rest of the church by a screen and it contains the choir.

CHOIR: part of the church reserved for singing the divine service.

CRYPT: a chamber or vault beneath the main floor of a church.

CRYPTOPORTICUS: a vaulted subterranean corridor.

DIACONIA: an Early Christian welfare centre.

DOME: a curved vault on a circular, polygonal or elliptical base.

EX VOTO: an object, tablet, or painting dedicated in fulfilment of an obtained grace.

FAÇADE: the central vertical face of a building.

FRESCO: a technique of painting on wet plaster.

FRISIANS: people from the Dutch province of Freisland.

GRANITE: a crystalline rock composed of quartz, feldspar and mica.

JASPER: a precious opaque stone. It can be red, yellow, green or brown in colour.

LAPIS-LAZULI: a deep blue stone that comes from Afganistan.

LOGGIA: an arcade or colonnade in the open air, usually preceding a larger building

LOW RELIEF (OR BAS RELIEF): a composition in which figures and objects carved on a flat surface project a little from their background.

LUNETTE: a semi-circular space in a vault or ceiling.

NAVE: the main space in a church.

PAPAL BULL: an edict or order proclaimed by papal authority.

PARIAN MARBLE: a white marble from the island of Paros in the Aegean Sea.

PIERS: in architecture, the solid mass of masonry between doors or windows. Also, in Romanesque or Gothic architecture, a name given to large-scale supporting pillars.

PIETRA MAIOLICATA: a type of tin-glazed pottery fired at a low temperature.

PIETÀ: a representation of the dead Christ lying in the lap of the mourning Virgin.

PORPHYRY: a stone, green or red in colour. The red type is considered the imperial stone *par excellence.*

PORTICO: a roof supported by columns attached to a building.

PREDELLA: the lower subdivision of a devotional painting. It functions as a narrative plinth of an altarpiece and it is generally of long and narrow shape. It tells religious stories of saints or sacred people found in the main painting above it.

PRESBYTERY: part of the church reserved for the clergy.

PRESEPE: a group of statues which represent the scene of the Nativity of Christ in a manger.

PROTIRO: the architectural part which is supported by two columns above the entrance of a Romanesque church and functions as a vestibule.

ROCOCÒ: from the French word *rocaille*; it denotes a style in the art and decoration of the 18th century which is characterised by the use of S- shaped curves and C- scrolls inspired by natural motifs taken from rocks, shells, and plants.

SACRISTY: the room at the back of the church used for storage of vestments and liturgical vessels.

SCHOLA CANTORUM: from the Latin, it means school of singers. It denotes the part of the church where the choir stays during the service.

STUCCO: a material used for both internal and external decoration. It is malleable and quick to set. In its mixture it may contain ground marble, but it is mainly made of sand, gypsum and water.

STYLOBATE: the basement of a columnar temple.

TABERNACLE: a niche where a holy image is housed or the place where the consecrated host is kept.

TERRACOTTA: fired clay without any vitreous coating.

THOLOS: a round building or dome.

TONDO: a round painting or relief.

TRANSEPT: the part of the church that crosses its main axis.

TRAVERTINE: a hard white limestone found in the area near Tivoli and Rome. It is a good substitute for marble.

TRIBUNA: a gallery in a church.

TYMPANUM: in a building or a temple, it is the triangular space between the mouldings of a pediment or the space between the lintel of a doorway and the arch above it.

VAULT: a curved roof.

Index of Places and Churches

Bibliography

Assessorato alla Cultura, *Guide Rionali di Roma,* Roma, Fratelli Palombi Editori, 1973-1998

Bernstein C. Politi M., *Sua Santità,* Milano, Rizzoli, 1996

Blunt, A, *Baroque and Rococo Architecture and Decoration,* London, Granada, 1978.

Cardilli Alloisi, *La Via degli Angeli,* De Luca, 1988

Caselli G., *La Via Romea, Cammino di Dio,* Firenze, Giunti, 1990

Cattabiani A., *Calendario,* Rusconi, 1993

Chadwick, O, *A History of Christianity,* London, Weidenfeld and Nicolson, 1995

Chapman, G., *Catechism of the Catholic Church,* Libreria Editrice Vaticana, 1994

Chiovaro F. and Bessière G. *Urbi et Orbi, i Papi nella Storia,* Electa, Gallimard, 1996

Claridge A. and Cunliffe Barry, *Rome: An Oxford Archaeological Guide,* 1998

Clément O., *The Roots of Christian Mysticism,* London, New City, 1997

Comitati Mirabilia, *Guida del Rione Borgo,* Roma,

Connel J., *Meetings with Mary,* New York, Ballantine Books, 1995

Cuomo F., *Le Grandi Profezie,* Roma, Newton, 1997

Davidson, G, *A Dictionary of Angels,* New York, The Free Press, 1967

Dunn-Mascetti M., *Faints the Chosen Few,* London, Boxtree Ltd.

Foster J., *The First Advance,* London, University Press, 1994

Giovanni Paolo II, *1000 Giorni al Duemila,* Milano, San Paolo, 1997

Giovetti, P, *Angels,* Maine, Samuel Weisnre, Inc. , 1993.

Gligora F. and B.Catanzaro, *Anni Santi,* Libreria Editrice Vaticana, 1996

Grimal, P. and Rose, C, *Churches of Rome,* London, Tauris Parke Books, 1997.

Hale, J.R., *Encyclopedia of the Italian Renaissance,* London, Thames and Hudson, 1981

Hall J., *Dictionary of Subjects and Symbols in Art,* John Murray, 1974

Hamarneh B. and Manacorda S., *Pellegrini a Roma,* Edizioni San Paolo, 1997

Harvey Andrew, *The Return of the Mather,*

Berkeley, Frog, 1995

Hibbert C., *Rome, The Biography of a city,* Viking, 1985

Laurentin R., *Lourdes,* Milano, Mondadori,1996

Laurentin R. Rupcic L., *La Vergine Appare a Medjugorie?,* Brescia, Queriniana, 1984

Lozzi Bonaventura M.A., *A piedi per riscoprire Roma,* Quaderni Turistici, Edizioni Iter, 1996

Magnuson, T, *Rome in the Age of Bernini,* Humanities Press, 1982.

Marder, T, *Bernini'Scala Reggia,* Cambridge University Press, 1997

Masson Georgina, *The Companion Guide to Rome,* The Society of Authors, 1998

Murray, P and L, *The Oxford Companion to Christian Art and Architecture,* Oxford University Press, 1996.

Nagel, A, *Cherubs,* London, Thames and Hudson, 1994

Paoletti J. and Radke G., *Art in Rennaissance Italy,* Laurence King, 1997

Papafava F., *The Vatican,* Firenze, Scala, 1984

Partridge Loren, *The Rennaissance in Rome,* The Everyman Art Library, 1996

Rendina, *I Papi, Storia e Segreti,* Roma, Newton, 1983

Rev. Butler Alban, *Lives of the Saints,* London, Studio Editions, 1990

Sacra Bibbia, Roma, Paoline, 1964

Sainte Thérèse de l'Enfant Jesus, *Manuscripts Autobiographiques,* Lisieux, Office Central de Lisieux

Squadrilli T., *Roma, Storia e Monumenti,* Rusconi,

Stumpo, E. *Il Viaggio del Perdono,* ATS Italia Editrice, 1997

TCI, *Roma, Guida d'Italia,* Milano, 1993

Warner, M, *Alone of All Her Sex,* New York, First Vintage Books, 1976

Wilson, A.N., *Paul, the Mind of the Apostle,* Pimlico, 1997

Wittkower, R, *Bernini,* Electa, 1990

Zeppegno L. and Mattonelli R., *Le Chiese di Roma,* Roma, Newton Compton Editori, 1996

Zizzola G., *Il Successore,* Bari, La Terza, 1997

Zizzola G., *Il Conclave,* Roma, Newton, 1993

To our readers

This book is not exclusively a guide for the faithful, for Catholic pilgrims, but a book for whoever is willing to listen to the voices of this unique city. At the gate of the third millennium, we have tried to give space to the memories of the past, to record the tales of a city which is not only Christian but universal. The common denominator that we have found in each story is the message of peace, the very core of the teaching of Christ. This is our wish to all our readers for the new millennium.

Acknowledgements

The idea to write a guide to Rome that relates the story of Christianity through the monuments and churches of the city was given to us by Alberto Napoleoni, a passionate art lover. Alberto, together with his wife, Ornella Napoleoni, are volunteers in the Roman community charity for the homeless run by Father Sebastian of the Missionary of Charity. We want to thank him and his wife for all their help and Father Sebastian for the enlightening preface.

We also want to thank Siobhan Breen, Patrizia Collesi, Sandra den Hertog, Peter Higgins, Paola Mora and Sue Winter for their support and help.

Finished printing January 2000
Printed by Porziuncola
Assisi - Italy